THIS MARQUEZ THING

a memoir

Luis Carlos Márquez

This is a nonfiction story. The events here described are all true and have been faithfully described by the author as much as recollection and retrospective allow. Some names, identities and circumstances have been changed to protect the identity of various persons involved.

To my father, who chose to place his family ahead of him; to my mother, to whom I never gave enough recognition; and to my sister, who lovingly took care of her until her last day; while I was running away.

To my daughters: Carla and Beatriz, who faithfully followed their mother and me on a rough journey.

CONTENTS

FOREWORD

This is a story about forgiveness and understanding that life must continue, regardless.

"This Márquez Thing" is in my blood. I inherited it from my father, who passed it unaltered to me, and he in turn learned it from his father. I am, as he was, insecure. All my life I have been trying to destroy myself. The mighty forces of nature must have been on my side because, so far, I have not been successful. My father and my grandfather were. They didn't have anyone to help them in their time of need as I did. They dealt with it themselves the best way they knew how. Constantly, they seemed to enjoy battling armoured soldiers, totally unprotected and pretending to heal their wounds as they fought; but that's impossible. So did I, and when my warranties expired, I reinvented myself into a different instrument. I had to! I refused to be thrown away like a worn-out toaster. With time, I have become very resilient and, I have to admit, also very fortunate. That is why I am still here.

I

NOBODY'S FAULT

(Memories 1941 – 1958)

And we decide to stay in a Caribbean island
Whose language we don't even understand
Seeking peace
As if we could decide to own our own life
No one can…

Now they carry our empty coffins
Piggy-backing on the shoulders of their minds
There are no corpses inside, because they never let us die
They love us

And we decide to stay in a Caribbean island
Whose language we don't even understand
Because we have no choice

And we decide to take what does not belong to us
Our own life
Because we have no choice

Chapter 1

~

The greatest masterpiece of all is a life well lived. Life rewards those who dare.

~

Barbados 1958. Every morning around six o'clock he plunged into the Caribbean green-blue waters, the same ones that have cleansed the beach for millions of years, trying to wash away his tribulations, hoping that piercing the waves head-on would provide a clear future when emerging on the other side, as if entering a new fresh life. He tried it over and over, every day, for two gruelling months. It did not work.

"Have you seen the gentleman from Venezuela?" the maid asked Mr. Dugan.

"No, I haven't. Since he arrived, he comes down every day, takes a stroll and a swim, before coming up for breakfast. Never misses a day, but not today, very strange," Mr. Dugan replied.

"Well, I'll go clean his room."

The maid knocked on Room 206. Since no one answered, she opened the door and wheeled the cleaning cart in, changed the bed linen, arranged a few scattered things, picked up the Windex bottle and her scrubbing cloth from the cart and walked towards the washroom. She opened the washroom door and exploded into a screaming frenzy, running out of the room.

"There is a man hanging from the shower in Room 206!" she said, sobbing to Mr. Dugan, the manager.

Both rushed to the room and found the body of a man, dressed in grey trousers and white shirt, suspended by a belt around his neck. A fallen chair lay on the floor beneath him and his arms were tied by a shoelace behind his back. Mr. Dugan called the police.

After the mandatory questions, examination of the identification card found in his wallet, the passport found in his suitcase, and the hotel record, the body was identified as that of Manuel María Márquez. It was taken away with his belongings to the morgue, where the coroner would conduct an autopsy to comply with the legal procedures.

It was a beautiful day outside. It should not happen, but it does; the combination of extreme beauty and extreme sadness kills people.

On the way, the coroner mentioned to the driver, "He was supposed to be a high official in the recently deposed Venezuelan government."

The man hanging in that washroom was my father. When you love too much nothing is enough. You have regrets about everything: what you have done, the way you have done it, or what you didn't do. My father died of regrets because he loved us too much.

No one knew what he was doing in the island, but everyone was sad about the wife and two children he left behind, still unaware of the tragedy. I was seventeen, miles away in a boarding school in America and oblivious of everything, when the thunder of this lightning struck. Then, I could not accept the reality. Fifty-one years have passed and I still can't.

* * *

In 1941, Caracas was still a small town and gossip flew fast. Small towns like these cease to exist without it. Following politics was not a pastime, more of a necessity. Every change affected one's life: the way we breathed, ate, and even died.

It took my family one hundred and fifty slow years and a few generations to come down from the Andean mountains to the Caracas Valley. Andean people are slow movers. Venezuela, my country of birth, was in the midst of change from a small, rural agricultural country to an oil-producing and exporting power. The explosive growth initiated an enormous exodus towards the capitol, which carried *Manuel* and *Teresa*, like two margaritas flowing on the riverbed towards the inevitable.

***

Manuel would become my father. The hazel-eyed law student at the *Universidad de Mérida* met my future mother on her way to teach school. Manuel was not tall, more on the thinner side, with a longish neck, aquiline nose, and gorgeous almond-shaped hazel eyes that give him an incisive, inquiring look like an eagle. He had a distinctive mole on the left cheek, which he sometimes used to nick when shaving. When that happened, he placed a speck of tissue to stop the bleeding, sometimes forgetting and going around with the piece still on.

He was also an avid reader, often reading two or three books at a time, before bed, in the washroom, on the bus, during lunch, everywhere! He read the cheaper paperback editions, the only ones he could afford. Often, these books came with the pages uncut. He unfolded them by cutting the edges with a feather-thin razor blade, which he left in the book as a marker. He was so good at handling the razor blade that he even used it to trim his fingernails and toenails, by grasping the razor with his thumb and index finger and shaping a perfect curve, with the precision of a surgeon.

As a self-made intellectual, he had the power of an analytical mind combined with openness of criteria. He was always willing to listen and admit his mistakes and prepared to rectify. He used an "h" at the end of his signature to distinguish his from his father's identical rubric. This showed his personality, the very one he passed to me. I am, as he was, insecure. The attribute I admire most about him, is the contrast between his brilliant mind and his simple personal taste, simple but elegant, and also his dedication to our family and generosity to others. He needed very little to feel happy; he understood the art of living in its simplest form.

Teresa, the first grade teacher in Mérida, who would become my mother, was the youngest of twelve siblings and had fair skin, great-sized brown eyes, brown hair, fine red lips, and a real mole on her left cheek. Every time I see Betty Davis movies she reminds me of her. She had calligraphic, perfect handwriting and made people feel at ease when she talked. She was sincere. One was able to feel the warmth of her soul through her eyes, and if one still had any doubts, her smile would make them disappear. Her eyes made even a wicked soul feel tender.

Her body had curves that refused to be hidden. Her white terse skin gave her the appearance of an angel. That is why my father often referred to her as "wholesome." She was proud of having been born in the Andes, high in the mountains.

* * *

The tropical rains of March were pouring hard in 1941. The world was in commotion and my mother, in a clinic converted from an old mansion right in the center of Caracas, was having her first child. I was born in a large Spanish colonial house with tall imposing windows, an ornate entrance, and an exuberant central garden, planted with tropical exotic specimens. My subconscious mind recalls there being in a corner an Amazonian Toucan swinging on a ring, looking everywhere and seemingly asking, "What am I doing here? Shouldn't I be flying high, deep in the jungle?" Likewise, I kept looking, also unconsciously, asking much the same question.

I have hazel eyes, dark brows, and, like my father, an inquisitive expression. I have my father's eyes, my mother's lips, and a mixture of their two souls. They named me Luis Carlos. The other alternative would have been Manuel María, like my father and my grandfather, but then the other kids would have called me simply "María." When my father remembered how many times he had to fight to save his honour, he quickly rejected the idea.

At first, Caracas was not what Mother expected. Father kept moving us, from rented room to rented room, like fugitives from justice, trying to find a stable home. And Mother kept asking, "Why?" For Father this was a hard question, because he had to deal with his constant mood changes, sometimes optimistic and bright as a lark, other times gloomy and dark as a crow. He used to explain, almost apologizing, that the Márquez family had this characteristic for generations, most noticeably when they turned fifteen and began questioning life.

He interpreted this as being intellectual, intelligent, and creative and called it "This Márquez Thing." Other people might have read between the lines as us being plain crazy. The truth is that if we ignore the word 'why,' everything becomes explicable. "Why are we here?" becomes simply "We are here."

* * *

At first we lived in La Florida, in a refurbished mansion converted into a rooming house, located in what once was an affluent neighbourhood. Father rented the best room, the one up front, facing the "once upon a time" beautiful garden. It was his way of providing the best he could. There was a terrace from where I was able to see a flower shop, bursting with gorgeous red and yellow roses, terse white callas and violet pink orchids. The colors fascinated me. Often I looked at the front garden, and imagined it just as beautiful as it would have once been. I developed early this ability to look at life as the illusion I wanted it to be, without any relation to what it really was. This ability would come in handy throughout my life because, after all, life is of little consequence deprived of interpretation and meaning. Meaning is what elevates simple consciousness into superior existence.

I felt so happy. I used to spin with my arms wide open and pretend the whole world revolved around me, like a merry-go-round with me in the center. The kitchen, which we shared with other tenants, was just a simple faucet and a sink, a kerosene stove, a cupboard, and a small dining table with four chairs. When the table was not being used for dining, it became an ironing board covered by an old burned blanket with patches here and there.

To make life a little more pleasant and the house more amenable, the tenants often organized get-togethers. One of those nights, I found myself standing in my crib holding the railings and looking out a tall window, while Mother and Father celebrated New Year's downstairs in the company of the other tenants.

I was three years old. Beyond, in the dark blue sky, dazzling fireworks exploded in a multicolour array at midnight. Beams pierced the window glass like lances, illuminating the room and casting silhouettes upon the wall, like an epic in motion. I was so enchanted with the vision that I watched it for a long time until I fell asleep hanging on the rail of my crib, the very way my mother found me. This is the earliest memory I have.

In those days Mother took me everywhere and had me always in sight. This allowed her to do her housework and, at the same time, keep me safe. But it was ill fate when, on one occasion while ironing, she sat me on a corner of the small table and turned around to get a glass of water. As if guided by the devil, at that very instant I grabbed the piping hot iron and planted it on my thighs.

A horrific cry was heard, followed by Mother's, and the iron fell to the ground. Mother turned around, picked me up, and discovering that I'd been badly burned, cried: "Oh my baby, my dear love!" She wrapped me in a sheet and ran downstairs. "Please call a taxi. My baby is hurt!" she cried.

Nobody answered. She ran outside, hailed a passing taxi and rushed us to the emergency room downtown. Along the way, all I heard was the deafening taxi horn announcing my emergency and Mother clutching me and sobbing, "My baby, my baby!"

When we arrived, the nurses placed me on a stretcher and the doctor examined my wounds: two "V" shapes etched into the raw flesh of my tights. "These are third-degree burns. He is lucky the iron did not fall between his legs."

The doctor cleaned my burns with boric acid, spread a white powder on them, wrapped my legs with gauze, and told Mother it would take three to four weeks for the burns to dry. He gave her some pills to avoid infection and sent us home.

Strangely, my mind disallowed my consciousness. All this I know because the allusions Mother provided, little by little through the years. I have no recollection whatsoever of the real event, except for the two "V's" visible for years on my thighs. This was the first time of many I would be chased to the edge of death. I have no scientific proof, but I know well this incident had an effect on my personality. Since then, I became fragile and vulnerable.

When Father came home that night, he found me wrapped like a mummy and instinctively blamed Mother. "How could you?" And when she explained he simply argued, "Why did you have to set him on the table? I can't depend on you to take care of my boy! What kind of mother are you? How could you be so careless?" And on, and on, and on… as if life was that simple and blaming somebody would fix everything. She'd already asked herself those questions a million times and kept silent, blaming herself, again and again. Father didn't speak to her for weeks and she cried herself thin through this incident. The world knows she didn't mean to hurt me. Nevertheless, Father never forgave her.

I healed, but the two "V's" remained visible. For years I looked like a branded steer. The memory remained, and even though we can't see the original ones, I still have two "V's" branded somewhere in my soul, which I like to think are the "V's" of victory that convinced me early on that nothing gets resolved by finding a scapegoat.

* * *

It was 1944. I went to daycare for the first time. On the first day, it was painful to see Mother walk away and leave me, but I didn't cry. I wanted to, but I didn't. Now Mother walked me to school around ten every morning.

The regular school was a large building, but our daycare was only an open shed in the middle of a dusty patio. To me, it was just a place to paint, look out the window, and wait for Mother to pick me up. Of all things, a slowpoke sloth lived on a mango tree in the middle of the patio. It was interesting to watch him take such a long time to move from branch to branch. If I had to move like that, I couldn't go anywhere and would be in constant desperation!

At home, Father complained constantly about not getting the recognition he deserved. I think he regretted studying so much and not getting enough in return. I heard Mother tell him to be patient, because good things happen in their own time to those who persevere. Mother had a sixth sense, because the opportunity arrived this year. Mother was thrilled to hear the Minister of Finance offered Father a post in recognition of his excellent performance as a mercantile judge. Father was to direct the drafting of a new law to tax the oil companies and also to open a new service for the general public once Congress approved the law, an opportunity that could change our lives. We were excited but sceptical, because high profile government jobs, in this country, were considered political, even if they were only of a technical nature.

In this country, Mother said, politicians were labelled and as soon as the regime fell, which incidentally happened often, they were persecuted without mercy and generally found guilty of something. Father argued that these were risks we must take if we wanted to be somebody in this land. I wished with all my heart Father would get the job so he could get to be somebody. As he said: "No risk, no loss and no gain."

At the end of the week my father was invited to a meeting at the Ministry and the following day appointed Income Tax General Director of the newly created Tax Administration. Father was assigned an armed guard, government chauffeured car, and offices in an exclusive central complex. He didn't really fancy all this, but it came with the job.

Eventually, Father and I went to see his new office. We moved from office to office saying "hello" and I could see he was proud to tell everyone I was his son. All the women ruffled my hair as we passed by. Why would they do that? I hated them messing up my hair.

"What a handsome boy. He looks just like his father!"

"What gorgeous eyes he has!"

When we arrived at the office near the end of the corridor, Father said, "This is my office," and pointed to a sign painted on the door: 'Director General.' He looked at me and winked. When he opened the door a lady sitting in front of a typewriter smiled.

"Luis Carlos, this is Miss Carmen, my secretary--well, my assistant."

"Carmen, this is my son."

She touched my hair like the other women and whispered, "He looks just like you," looking at my father. "I am Carmen Villasmil, your father's assistant," she said, looking at my Father, again. "I am not married, but if I was I would like to have a son just like you!" she said, looking at Father, once more.

* * *

It had been a year already since Father took office. During dinner he told us he was putting the final touches on the law, to be presented to the Finance Minister and the President this coming March for their signatures, then to Congress for their final approval. Most people were in favour of the new law, because it made the oil companies pay income tax and increase government revenue. As soon as the law was approved, Father would be well known and become a public personality.

In preparation for the event, Father was having his picture taken, to be placed beside the newspaper article he wrote about the new law. I ended up wearing an embroidered cream short pantsuit, because Father was taking me with him to have my photo also taken.

"Is my boy ready? Let's go; otherwise we are going to be late. The appointment is at four."

The photographer's studio was located in the most exclusive area of town. As soon as we arrived he fixed Father's tie and took his picture, then combed my hair, placed me on top of a stool, and shot a full-length pose and a portrait.

Father's article about the new law appeared on the front page of all the newspapers that Sunday, right beside his picture. Mine ended up on top of our living room coffee table. That year Father was also appointed to the Board of Directors of the Central Bank. He was 29 and at his prime.

Not long after, I discovered life was not entirely perfect, when I heard Father arguing and Mother crying. Father was waving his hands in the air, saying in desperation, "I have nothing to do with her. Carmencita is just my secretary."

"Don't call her 'Carmencita.' Her name is Carmen!" Mother said.

They saw me and stopped. I spooked and ran to my room.

"I think Father's secretary wants to steal him away from us. She wants Mother's place, but I will not let her. Mother will always be with Father. She's been with him since he was a university student in Mérida. She cooked for him, washed his shirts, lived in rental rooms and always cared for us. Now that everything is good, this woman wants to steal my Father. I hate her! She is not going to have a boy like me, ever!"

That night before I fell asleep, Father walked into my room tucked me in and told me, "Tomorrow I am going to take you to your Aunt Alicia. Your mother and I have things to resolve, and it's best you be with your aunt for a while."

"What things, Father?"

"Things, Luis Carlos, things!"

I knew what things, but how can a boy tell his father that he knows the secretary who messed up his hair is the cause of all this trouble?

"Why can't you just get along and not fight?" I asked.

Father looked at me, through the sad part of his hazel eyes, and just mumbled, "It's not that easy, Son. It's not that easy. Tomorrow I will take you there."

I couldn't sleep that night, thinking about Mother and Father. I wanted them to get along and I didn't want to go to my Aunt Alicia. I could not figure out how come I did all the things I was supposed to do: took my vitamins, brushed my teeth, and showered every day and still had to be punished by going to my Aunt Alicia.

Somehow I felt guilty about what was happening. Later, Mother packed my toys, my vitamins, my pillow, and the white rosary Grandma gave me on my first communion. While Father was getting the car, Mother embraced me and began reciting out loud my night prayer "Precious Guardian Angel, my dear sweet companion, please do not forsake me during the night or during the day…"

It scared me. Why was she saying my night prayer in the morning? Father sat me beside my suitcase in the back seat, and the three of us drove away. As the car turned the corner, I began to bite my lower lip like Mother did when she was nervous. There was not a lot of talking on the way. In fact, there was none. The thick forest along the road looked so wonderful that day that I couldn't help but admire it sweeping past by my side, and I forgot I was being taken away. Instead of feeling sad, I felt as if I was going on a most marvellous trip.

The road skirted the edge of the mountain, at times cutting right through the middle of the forest. Father began to tell us about this region being similar to the Black Forest in Germany.

Aunt Alicia was married to an Air Force officer, my Uncle Humberto. They lived in the same town, Maracay, where my Grandma María settled with her children many years ago. Their house was small and had a little garden up front and a patio in the back, where I was supposed to play with my cousin Humber, who had a pedal Jeep I liked. The problem was that every time I wanted it, he also wanted it and yanked it away from me. If I happened not to want it, he didn't want it either. I was quickly fed up with him!

Every day Aunt Alicia took Humber and me across the street to the nun's school. It was really boring. We had to bring our own blackboards and chalk and spend all day drawing and singing songs to learn to count:

Dos y dos son cuatro

Cuatro y dos son seis

Seis y dos son ocho

Y ocho dieciséis....

She told me Father and Mother were separated and Mother was being treated, because she got sick of sadness. In the meantime, I must stay with her while Mother recuperated. She knew I wanted to see my Mother but I couldn't for now. Neither of us could do anything about it.

We were just placed here to do what we were supposed to do: she to carry me over and I to try earnestly not to cry, but I really missed my Mother. One day without notice, Father and Mother came to pick me up. She hugged me so hard I thought she was going to break me. That day we went home as if nothing happened. I was so happy I didn't want to ask, afraid to find out it was a mistake.

* * *

March 1944. Congress finally approved Father's new law. His hazel eyes twinkled with a brighter color and his thin lips turned into a permanent smile. Our life changed. Father said everything was going so well it was time for us to move to a new house all to ourselves. So we moved to San Bernardino, which at the time was a nice upper middleclass Jewish neighbourhood, even though we were not Jewish. Most neighbours were business owners: jewellers, furriers, gift shop owners, and such.

On Sunday we were going to see a beautiful house at the foot of the mountain. Lots of trees and a cool breeze flowed from the sea over the mountain. Father described this setting to us with enthusiasm. Mother looked at me and smiled. It had been a long time since I had seen her smile.

Father continued to explain, "The house has two floors and plenty of washrooms so we don't have to wait for one another anymore. We are going to be very happy there, you wait and see." He said this with total certainty, as if he really knew, and added, "The house already has a dog house, in case we want a puppy to keep us company."

At that precise moment, I looked at Mother and she was smiling again. We didn't say anything but decided right then to get one.

That night, I dreamed about my own puppy and my own bicycle. Our life was turning out better and better, thanks to the government and the Minister of Finance. I could not wait for Sunday to come!

There was so much beauty in San Bernardino. When we arrived at the house, we first came up to an impressive entrance, tall windows, large social areas, four good-sized bedrooms, each with an in-suite washroom and walk-in closet, a large kitchen, maid quarters, and a two-car garage. The windows had stained glass folding doors and were guarded by steel bars. A breathtaking garden included green lawns, mangos, and flowers everywhere: daisies, alpines, begonias, and blue jacarandas. It was the first real house we lived in and it also became the best, setting a new standard, never to be matched again. The house was so big, Father decided to bring my cousin Rafael to live with us.

My cousin Rafael always needed a place to live, because he was an orphan. His mother died when he was still a kid and his father didn't want anything to do with him and his sisters anymore. They were always jumping from house to house within our family.

I liked Rafael living with us, because he could roll his nose and his mouth to look like a mouse. When he did, it made me laugh so much I could pee. He went to school in the morning and helped Mother with the house and the garden in the afternoon.

Now, Father's government car took him to the office every day and Mother afterwards went everywhere she wanted. She said life was easier when you have money and power and we had both now. Life was good these days. To top it all, that same year Sis was born and everything began to revolve around her.

One day after my evening bath Mother sat me between the steel bars and the screen in one of the front windows, closed the latch, and left me playing bus driver. I pushed the steel bars (the bus brakes) so hard with my legs that the window screen snapped. I fell backwards and my collarbone cracked. While still sprawled on the floor, Mother blamed me, as usual. This time the doctor wrapped a cast around my chest and shoulder to hold a double fracture!

Six slow weeks passed and then came the day we were going to the doctor to take my cast off. I was skinny as a bone and my left shoulder was thinner than my right shoulder. My own mother squealed to the doctor that I refused to eat, had a nasty cough and fever, and the doctor recommended 'temperance' for fifteen days.

"The iodine of the ocean will clean his system."

The following week, Father sent my Grandma María and me to a small hotel in La Guaira, the Caracas waterfront. "I wonder how kids that have no grandmas or fathers to pay for 'temperance' could get better at all. I guess they just break down and die."

My Father was made of gold and my Grandma María and I were very close. She was a full-blooded Andean Indian and the illegitimate child of a prominent man. I can still see the shame in her eyes and feel the tenderness of her embrace.

So Father left us at the Hotel La Francia, a two-storey building with hallways around a central garden, swarming with beautiful green ferns. The hotel was old but clean, reflecting its white silhouette like a mirage on the blue Caribbean waters. On the ground floor there was an enormous dining room. Fronting the building under a long canopy, a hallway was lined with white lounge chairs, where old folks sat at five o'clock to soak in the warm draft from the ocean and drink British tea until the sun went down.

Every morning, my Grandma María and I crossed to the beach and found the lifeguard. His name was Longa. Of pure muscle, he was a tall, slender black guy, with pearls instead of teeth. He wore no hat and no shoes, just a flimsy whistle tied around his neck on a black string and a pair of faded black trunks. He walked tall on the sand, as if he owned the waterfront.

"Buenos días, Doña María. Cómo está usted hoy?"

"Muy bien, gracias," Grandma responded.

"Vamos, Luis Carlos!"

Longa swept me off my feet with one hand and placed me around his neck, ran towards the ocean, splashed, and plunged in to swim with me on his back. When we reached deeper water, he just submerged and left me flapping. Longa always rescued me at the right time, one split second before I was about to drown. That's how I learned to swim. I wonder how many kids Longa made ocean swimmers. I learned much later from the newspapers that it was hundreds. He was the lifeguard on that waterfront for fifty years. I guess he did own that waterfront after all!

Now, I was very serious about being a kid. My Father said it was the way we Márquez were. I was four years old. My temper was troublesome, I had difficulties eating, and I thought noisy kids were silly.

To make things worse, I had a cowlick. Mother tried to control it, placing a nylon stocking on my head. She put it on me at night and sometimes during the day, if we were not going out. It made me look very stupid, and not enough blood flowed to my head so I couldn't think clearly. It was no use; as soon as she took the stocking off the cowlick sprang back. But she told me if I didn't get rid of it, "You will live a rebellious life and never stay put," because cowlicks like mine were a sign of revelry. I just shrank my shoulders and let her think whatever she wanted. She ended up being right anyway.

* * *

It was 1945 and Caracas was still a small city of about two hundred and fifty thousand people. A gusty wind swept through the city all year round, and on nice days my grandma took me for a ride on the streetcar to run her errands. I liked to sit close by the window, watch the city go by, hear the conductor call the stops and be yanked around every time he stopped.

Those days Mother complained about not having anything to wear when required to attend the functions related to Father's job. She could not understand how a woman was able to remember the dress worn by another three years before, as well as the time and date of the function. She thought it was amazing anyone was able to remember such a thing.

"Luis Carlos, get ready. We are going to Mrs. María de Lugo to take a look at the dresses she brought from New York. I want to set one aside. I have to accompany your father to the Ministry's reception this year and I don't have a thing to wear. I want you to come with me and tell me which one you like best."

"Yes, Mother."

Mrs. María de Lugo ran a ladies' boutique from her house, a large colonial house in the old part of Caracas.

She knew everybody and everybody knew her, especially the ladies that had to go to receptions with their husbands and didn't have a thing to wear. She sold dresses, purses, and fashion jewellery on instalments, charging three times their value. No one complained. If you didn't pay on time she told everyone and your life was ruined forever. Everybody paid on time!

Mrs. María had big eyeballs like an owl and a deep voice like a man. Mother said she suffered from thyroid, whatever that was. She wore silk dresses and lots of fashion jewellery and when she got tired of them, she returned the pieces to the store as 'new arrivals.' I remember her wearing some and then seeing them hanging on the rack again.

We took a taxi at the corner and Mother told the driver, "Cruz Verde a Zamuro." That's where Mrs. María de Lugo lived. There was no conversation during the ride, because Mother didn't like to speak in front of strangers; she said it was a bad habit.

"Right here, please."

We stopped in front of an impressive colonial house with many windows, passed down through three generations of de Lugos. Mother rang the bell and Mrs. María appeared, clad in one of her silk dresses. She was always dressed as if she was going to a function.

"I am expecting you, Teresa. Come in, come in ... And this must be Luis Carlos, the man of the house. How grown up he is! He must be seven now."

"No, four," I say.

"My goodness, you are very tall for your age. For sure you are going to be taller than your father!"

She knew my father was not very tall and she knew of course I would be taller than he. Anybody was taller than my father!

Mother tried several dresses, while I browsed the fashion magazines that lay on top of a round marble-top table. I couldn't see well, because the lights were dim, but enough to see the shadows of dresses and shawls hanging on the rails and a purple, feathered hat resting on the shelves. Mother chose two dresses, one linen suit, and a chiffon cocktail dress, and asked me if I liked them too.

"Yes, I do, Mother." (What else could I say?)

She charged them to her account and swore to pay them by signing a small green invoice pad that contained the signatures of half of the penniless bourgeois ladies of Caracas.

Mrs. María was very pleased and kissed Mother on the cheek as we left, which my mother wiped with her hanky as soon as we walked away from the door, saying, "That woman should not show her appreciation this way."

Chapter 2

Shortly after we arrived home Mother received a phone call, when she was just about to call Father to tell him about her new dresses. She began to cry as she listened, nodding her head right and left and up and down. **It was October 18, 1945.**

"Oh, God, it can't be!" She paused to listen to the other end of the line.

"What are we going to do now?" Another pause.

"Where do you want me to go?" Pause.

"All right, I'll meet you at Graciela Márquez' house in El Conde. Please take care; you are our *life!*"

"What is the matter, Mother?" I asked.
"People are shooting far and wide. There is a revolution going on."

She told me, shaking her hand, to be quiet. Drying her tears with the sleeve of her blouse, she said, "We have to go right now to Graciela Márquez' house. Go get your sister and help me pack some clothes. Hurry, hurry, please hurry!"

We grabbed the suitcase and Sis' ragdoll, because she didn't go anywhere without it, walked to the corner, and at that precise moment a taxi rolled up. Mother stopped it and said to the driver, "To El Conde, please! When we get there, I will tell you where to turn."

"Madam, we shall see if we get there. There is a lot of shooting going on."

The taxi's radio was on and the announcer said, "A group of young military men, in combination with the Venezuela Democratic Party, have taken over the government."

"Turn right," Mother said. "Right here, the yellow house on the corner, with the broad staircase."

Mother paid the driver in a hurry. Some coins dropped to the floor, but she didn't dare to pick them up. We climbed the stairs, rang the bell, and Graciela opened the door. "Hurry, come, come on in," she whispered in a low voice, as if it was a secret, patting us on the back and hugging my Mother. She took us into one of the rooms and called Jesús Francisco and Carmen Josefina to take care of my sis and me. Legally they were my uncle and aunt, because they were the offspring of my grandpa's second marriage, despite the fact they were not much older than we were. Jesús was my age and Carmen three years older.

Mother said, "Your father will be coming soon."

I wanted to ask more questions, but Mother signalled me to go with Jesús Francisco and Sis with Carmen Josefina. Mother and Graciela continued to listen to the radio, handkerchiefs clutched in their hands. Jesús Francisco took me around the house, across the central patio to the basement and up the spiral staircase to the terrace. Once there, we walked, keeping our heads low, as though on the prowl, to avoid the stray bullets. We stayed for a while, hearing the shots sniping overhead and enjoying the excitement of the revolution, but not quite understanding it.

Maybe this was no different to me than a Saturday afternoon cowboy movie, but this was the real thing. That day three hundred people died and one thousand were wounded.

* * *

In the afternoon Father arrived with his cousin Arturo Luis, who was the closest thing he had to a brother. Father's beige linen suit was all soiled with grease, and ripped at the knees and elbows. What followed was an account of how they crept under parked cars and crawled for blocks to avoid the bullets and be able to reach the house. They drank fresh water, washed a little, and changed into the clothes Mother brought. Father had a gun sticking out of his pocket in a brown leather holster. I didn't know Father owned a gun. Everyone gathered around the radio to hear the news, while Graciela and Mother prepared chicken soup for dinner.

28

Later that night we - Jesús Francisco, Carmen Josefina, Sis and I - told each other scary stories and shivered and laughed every time we got scared. Around ten, the four of us went to bed, I in Jesús' room and Sis in Carmen's. The grownups stayed up, listening to the news, drinking hot chocolate, and eating bits of pound cake.

At dawn the radio announced, "Betancourt, the leader of the Democratic Party, is now President of Venezuela."

Difficult to understand, how the leader of the "democratic" party could seize power by force. I turned it all over in my mind. "This is all I have known. What is going to happen to us now? How is Father going to take care of us?" I wanted to help, but I was four.

How can I explain? My father was not a real politician, only a civil servant who just wanted to contribute with his expertise, had no desire for power or richness, and was happy with no more than recognition. I can testify to that because I am his son.

The 1945 civic-military coup ended 46 years of Andean supremacy, despite being considered not too bright because of the Andean's slow manner of speaking. The electoral promise, which hadn't changed since colonial times, still remained to be fulfilled. When ignorance takes over and everyone is at fault, justice can't be served.

* * *

After the October revolution, Father resumed private practice, with the help of many friends who considered him a fair man and kept him safe from the new political regime. He was given a space in Casa Paris, one of the oldest commercial enterprises in Venezuela.

Servicing The Conglomerate became a full-time job. Father's position in the Central Bank's Board of Directors was also ratified. We lived four years in San Bernardino and now were forced to move to more modest quarters, but we preferred to stay in the neighbourhood if at all possible. San Bernardino was an upper middle class, predominantly Jewish neighbourhood, in which it was almost impossible to find a modest rental space, and that was what the family needed at this time. But life smiles sometimes, and Father found a nice flat in the lower part of San Bernardino, not as high on the mountain as before, but still within the boundaries of the subdivision.

The house was the residence of the Berlin family, who was, of course, Jewish. We rented the upper floor. It became a nice arrangement for both families: they needed the extra money and having a lawyer like Father as a tenant was not a bad idea either, just in case. The Berlins owned a jewellery store right across the Capitolio, the building of Congress. Their clientele was politicians and socialites who had money to spare.

Once again we were living in a refurbished flat like in the past, similar to La Florida. When we moved in, all of us felt like we were going backwards in time but were grateful to have it. By enormous coincidence, the name of the house was Villa Teresa, Mother's name. I told everyone we named our new house in Mother's honour. That made me happy. A white lie, now and then, never hurt anyone.

Our new street name was La Estrella (translated as "star"), which I took as a sign of good luck, representing the many good things in store for us. On this street I met my first real friends, a close group of six, drawing nearer to what was to be one of the happiest days of my life.

Eduardo, my best friend, was my age. He had black hair, thick eyebrows and front teeth like ears of corn. At first, we were the same height and competed on all fronts. As time passed, he grew taller than I, because his father was a giant and my father was short. At that time we stopped competing at the physical level and started competing at smarts and cleverness.

We were a tight bunch, 'The Pack,' and only school separated us for a few hours; the rest we spent like family. Differences we settled peacefully, with no fighting between us. At five, after school, a hurried wash-up, and a quick snack, our day began. Whenever he was home, Eduardo's father, a traveling salesman, allowed us to play in his car, taking turns at the wheel, pretending to go on long trips like he took. Sometimes we hung out well past dinnertime and, when that happened, asked for permission to stay and enjoy delicious tastiness different from home. No better, just different.

We couldn't go through a day without seeing each other, except when we were sick. Whoever was free from school first whistled a special tune we had, something like *fuiii ... fu ... fui ...* until one of us answered. If no response, one moved to the next house, until three of us were rounded up. Three was the magic number.

One day, I determined it was too conventional to enter my house by the front door. A tall mango tree grew beside the house and I decided to climb the tree to reach the terrace. The trick was to climb the tree to the edge of the terrace, extend one leg, set foot on the edge, and jump. There was no room for error. I used to appear right on our terrace as if nothing happened. I told no one about my daring entry, not even my friends.

I turned six in 1947, and it was time to attend a proper school. I had twice before: the school with the sloth in La Florida and the nun's school in Maracay when I was exiled. I didn't learn anything there, except not to be afraid when left alone. Mother was the one who taught me to count, read, and write. But I had no credentials and had to start from the beginning.

The school was a large grey square building with a central patio, surrounded by classrooms. Each classroom had a long blackboard, a large desk and rows of small desks. No more open sheds. The washrooms were in the back of the building: girls to the right, boys to the left. Mother walked me in the mornings but allowed me to come back by myself in the afternoons. I didn't understand the difference, but I knew she knew better.

* * *

Around this time Aunt Braulia called an emergency family meeting, which gave me the opportunity to meet some of Father's relatives. She was not my aunt or Father's aunt, but everyone in the family called her "Aunt," a small chubby little woman, almost a midget, her hair tucked in a bun, lavish red lipstick and a heavily rouged and powdered face. She was the matriarch of Father's clan who reigned over distinguished Andean families now living in Caracas: Gabaldón, Berti, Briceño, Carrillo, Nuñez, Iragorry, Carrasquero, Matheus, and, of course, Márquez. Everyone was her subject in this far-reaching domain.

She had power over life and death, just like a queen. She picked candidates to represent the family at elections and decided who filled what post. To get her protégés in, she manipulated presidents, ministers, governors, and congressmen, as well as anybody with financial power. No matter what political party was in power, Aunt Braulia managed to include the family, the powerful formula that assured the continuation of her reign. My father's family had been into "politics as an art" for hundreds of years.

The rendezvous was arranged as an innocent game of checkers, complete with home-baked butter cookies and rich hot chocolate. This time in 1948, the occasion was about the coup that brought President Gallegos down at only eight months past his inauguration. Today my father's family was in full action, coming together as one. It took a special occasion, another revolt, coup, or revolution to bring them together as one. The current events were followed on the radio and from time to time someone made a phone call to confirm the details.

The efforts paid, and a family member, Delgado Chalbaud, was nominated head of the new military junta. Three additional high positions were secured.

Out of nowhere, a gunshot was heard and everyone in the house ran towards the door. Out on the street, Guido (Arturo Luis' brother, Father's cousin) lay inside his car, splashed with blood from the neck down: he had shot himself. Arturo Luis moved his brother to the passenger seat and Father wrapped his head with a sheet and rushed away to the emergency ward. It seemed Guido was disillusioned about nothing in particular, just about life in general.

By Fates' will, he survived this misfortune and lived to an advanced age. Was this another consequence of "This Márquez Thing"?

This feeling of emptiness was common, one time or another, within Father's family. I often heard the words 'fracasado' (failed) and 'birote' (opinion-less), as part of the daily expressions of judgement. Demanding intellectual excellence, recognition, and respect, was part of being Márquez.

Chapter 3

One day while wrestling, Alfonsito, my next-door neighbor, choked me to the ground. Somehow I managed to free myself and ran towards the rose garden, with such bad luck that a thorn brushed my face, slitting a deep cut right under my right eye.

"Holy shit!" Alfonsito yelled, when he saw my face soaked in blood.

Scared, I covered it with my forearm and ran home. As soon as Mother saw me, she began to scream about how careless I was. Mother had to blame someone before taking any action when a misfortune came along.

I hollered in desperation, "Mother, cut it out! Please take me to the hospital!"

She pressed a towel around my face and to the emergency post we went, the same painful route we had made twice before: the day I branded my thighs and the day I broke my collarbone. More traffic this time, because the city had grown. Stitches were not needed and the doctor cleaned it, covered it, taped it, and gave me a tetanus shot.

"The cut will close better this way. He is lucky; five millimetres higher and he would have slit his eye open." Once more, a few millimetres saved me from a bigger tragedy.

"How is my little pirate doing? Can I see the black patch on his eye?" That night Father came to my room and asked in his ironic way to add humour to the tragedy!

In my version, a revelation occurred. I was kneeling on my bed saying my night prayer. "Precious Guardian Angel, my dear sweet companion, please do not forsake me during the night or during the day." I looked through the corner of my good eye and saw the profile of a boy kneeling beside me, saying his prayers too. His face looked familiar, but I hadn't seen him before. I said a little more of my prayer and he did too.

I turned my head towards him and asked, "Who are you? Where did you come from?"

He smiled, looked at me, and asked, "Don't you recognize me? I am your brother Alvaro, the one that didn't make it. I am the reason you are here. I have been watching over you since you were a baby. I am your guardian angel, but I am also your brother."

I was shocked, but continued the conversation as normal. "Why have I not met you before?"

"I waited until you were seven, so you could understand. Before, you couldn't, and once grown up, you wouldn't. Haven't you noticed every time your life is threatened, the end never comes? An unexpected solution appears and your life continues. I make it happen! I am your guardian angel. On occasions we shall meet and talk. Don't tell anybody, not even Mother and Father. They would never believe you. I must keep you safe. We depend on each other, and when needed, I will be there." Alvaro disappeared with a smile and I kept my secret, wondering when I would see him again.

* * *

After rounding up everyone, we used to sit in front of the corner store to figure out what to do. We laid our pennies and nickels on the ground, counted them and, depending on how much we had, made a decision. Sometimes we ate the money, one bag of potato chips at a time, for six. If there was enough, we went to the corner restaurant after their delicious cheese custard. Other times, we bought a tennis ball and played handball on the street, and the passing drivers shouted, "Crazy kids!"

My game of choice was "car brand challenge." While sitting on the front fence, we called the brand and model as the cars approached. Whoever guessed the most won. To this day I continue to silently play "car brand challenge" everywhere I go and claim to know every brand and model.

At times we exchanged information about girls. To be precise, about what girls were supposed to be, because no girls lived on our street, except Alfonso's sister whom we seldom saw. Our knowledge was limited to our prolific imagination and spurred by a soap opera, *The Right to be Born*, that was broadcast on the radio. It was a story about a lady who had an illegitimate son and her struggle raising the boy while trying to keep the secret. Much of our conception came from that broadcast and was of course distorted, as illustrated by the following incident.

A Czechoslovakian housekeeper and her daughter came to work for the Berlins at that time. The girl was about my age, seven. I daydreamed how it would feel to kiss her. One day she was playing around the garden and I worked up enough courage, pinned her against the wall, and kissed her. Quickly, she pushed me away and ran like a rabbit.

From that day on, she made sure to be far away from me. When I told the guys, none of us could understand why she ran. We all thought girls liked kissing. Wasn't she supposed to like it too?

* * *

We never owned a car before, not counting the Chevrolet assigned to Father while he worked for the government in 1947. Without warning, Father bought a brand new green Renault. The car was not impressive but it was ours. It was small and not designed for hilly country, which was hard to believe because France is alpine. Often we had to get out and push the car uphill; it was exhausting! Mr. Berlin used to park his green Pontiac on the street and Father, in order not to upset things, chose to park the same way.

One morning, Father found his Renault smashed. Somebody wrecked Father's car during the night! Almost crying and cursing whoever did it, he showed us what was left of the car. It was a total loss and was towed the same day to the salvage yard. To make things worse, we didn't have insurance.

Hard to believe, that same day Father purchased a brand spanking new yellow Packard, only on his signature, at a client's distributorship. The car was as big as an ocean cruiser. When we arrived home, Father said with a smirk of a smile, "I'd like to see anybody wreck this one!" and parked the new car on the very same spot where the Renault was smashed.

All and all, Father had simple tastes, came from simple origins, and kept himself that way. He admired nice things, but had great difficulty being comfortable around them, because he just felt unworthy, disregarding what a marvellous human being he was and how much he deserved everything.

* * *

Life continued as usual, except one day Sis got sick. Mother gave her hot lemonade, aspirin, and hot poultices to try to control her high fever but to no avail, blaming the weather for it. Father was at the office. Fearing the worst, I declared an emergency and decided without any consultation to get Doctor Cardenas, the family doctor who delivered Sis and me.

His clinic was twelve blocks from home. I ran all the way. When I arrived, the doctor was in the middle of his consultation. I must have been panting like a mad dog, because when his secretary heard my half-choking story, she immediately asked the doctor to come home with me. As soon as we arrived home, he examined Sis and was relieved to find out the situation was not as bad as we thought. He handed Mother a prescription for antibiotics to take care of the diagnosed bronchitis.

Before he left, he told Mother, "You should be very proud. Luis Carlos is a very resourceful young man." It felt so good to hear that about me that I still remember it with joy. I completed my mission by rushing to get Mother the antibiotics.

When Father came home and found out about my story, I could see he was swollen with pride, even though he only smiled. From then on, Mother would often tell Sis the story and remind her she was very lucky to have a brother like me. We would protect each other always, she used to say.

Mother was right; when the time came, Sis pulled through in my time of need. Time proved that I was the one who was very lucky to have a sister like Sis.

By the middle of the rainy season, Mother took up interest in mail order catalogues. Mother justified her purchases by saying, "Better than buying imported dresses from Mrs. María de Lugo." She claimed the easy instalments were the only reason she had bought from Mrs. de Lugo. Otherwise, she wouldn't have bought even a pin from her. Now she bought her dresses at half price through the Sears and Montgomery Ward mail order catalogues. I spent hours browsing in the men's and hardware sections. I'd never seen so much merchandise in one place before.

Now, Mother ordered dresses to sell and a couple for herself every time. She was a home business lady! When the merchandise arrived, we went to Caño Amarillo (where the customs office was), paid the import duties and picked up the brown packages. As soon as we got home, she opened them in front of Sis and me, for us to share the excitement.

The item I liked most in the catalogue was the Bowie knife. I could already see myself cutting brush, skinning game and fending against wild beasts.
"What in the world are you going to do with a knife like that? Well, you may even cut a finger or a tendon and end up 'hook-handed' like your grandfather Manuel!" Mother said.

"Mother, soon I am going to be a Boy Scout at school and the knife will come in handy. It will probably be the best knife any Boy Scout ever had."

"Yes, but you are not in the bush yet. You must wait until you become a Boy Scout."

Father was more understanding, being a man himself. When I told him about the knife, he decided in favour and the knife was ordered, period.

* * *

It was 1949. I turned eight in March. I was now in second grade and Mother let me walk both ways to school. She called me her "little man."

Miss Julia, my teacher this year, was pretty and wore flowery cotton dresses, like Mother used to wear when she was a teacher herself in Mérida. She popped questions about arithmetic and spelling. If you didn't know the answer, she made a monkey out of you in front of everybody and then asked Prince, who, to make things worse, knew every answer. She had a preference for this Prince and thought he was smart and cute. I hated this Prince and his rosy cheeks. I didn't know what I hated most: him or not being like him!

Those days Mother was always busy. Every morning she picked up the bread and milk left by the milkman downstairs. One day she was climbing the stairs carrying the bottle of milk and the bread, when she slipped and fell. The bottle exploded under her right hand and made a nasty twisted cut, as broken bottles do. The doctor stitched her hand, but this incident left a scar for life, a sign of her devotion to our family.

Mother loved us beyond description. Her life was devoted to Sis and me. She expressed her dedication the best with the wholesome soups and tortuous vegetable juices she made for us. I still shiver at the thought of them!

* * *

Around that time, Father added the Sugar Cane Association to his client list, in addition to Casa Paris. The association, among other things, made sure there was never enough sugar so the prices remained high. They were good to Father, recognized his talents, and their plantations were simply 'picture perfect' beautiful. At that time, anybody who recognized Father's talents got the very best of him, and they did. Recognition was the key that opened Father's heart; it completely disarmed him.

One important benefit they provided was free housing for our family, which doubled as the association's office. In addition, they paid Father a good salary. Altogether, it became a good opportunity to save for the down payment of our own house. Before long, we said goodbye to San Bernardino. The new house was Spanish colonial and all Spanish colonial houses look alike, very predictable. This old house was similar to the one where we once lived in La Florida, except bigger and all to ourselves.

Fronting the street there were three enormous windows and a tall entrance. A long foyer took us to a large waiting room, leading to the main living room used as the association office. A central patio with a small fountain was in the middle, surrounded by four rooms. I am sure the fountain was once filled with crystalline water. Beyond the patio, a multi-colored stained glass partition enclosed the dining room. Towards the back, a door opened to a second patio, the kitchen, maid quarters, an extra room, and a bathroom. A spiral stair climbed to the second floor, where there were an additional room, laundry facilities, and a terrace.

The old colonial towns are also almost identical: a center square that usually has a statue of someone important in the middle, a cathedral on one side, the government palace on the other, then the houses of the rich, and, far away, the houses of the poor.

Because the house was huge, Mother placed an ad in the paper to hire a housekeeper, and soon a lady appeared. Her name was Teresa Gutiérrez. A strong woman, about 27, younger than Mother, with long black hair she wore down to her waist, Teresa had a large bust, narrow waist, wide hips, thick thighs, and always wore sandals. Mother didn't like her because she looked like a gypsy, but out of need she hired her anyway. Teresa brushed her hair after taking cold showers and always complained about the heat.

While doing housework she smoked black tobacco cigarettes, with the burning tip inside her mouth and looking as if hiding a mysterious past, like in the scary movies. As time went on, she became more secretive. No one knew where she came from or if she had a family.

Ideal for my curious personality, the house had plenty of rooms to explore, tall, stark, and old. Despite the simple layout, the place was filled with an aura of mystery, and I began to imagine being different people.

The office was my favourite room. Father's desk sat high on a stage, like a judge, across a long meeting table surrounded by twelve chairs and lots of files and magazines about sugar cane scattered everywhere. After business hours, the office became mine. I was the boss, opened the windows, and set up shop. I arranged the magazines on the windowsill, pretending to be a magazine stand owner and my customers the people who passed by. Other times, I placed the files in front of the twelve seats and conducted a great meeting. I directed these meetings with rigueur. Everyone had to follow my strict rules. If anyone dared to speak out of order, he - there were not 'she's on the boards at that time - was thrown out, without any chance of ever returning. Not even if he begged.

Sis was also in need of playmates and she had no other choice but me, so I got invited to more of her tea parties than I cared to attend. Not to mention, her play song-singing sessions,

"Tengo una muñeca vestida de tul
Con zapatos blancos y vestido azul
Esa muñequita también sabe hablar
Sabe decir Papá y también Mamá..."
Y no se cuando vendrá..."

* * *

Around this time, Mother began to take typing and leather embossing lessons. Peculiar, because Mother never tackled anything other than housekeeping before, except the time she ran the catalogue business that didn't last long. I wondered if she wanted to become independent or she had problems with Father again, like the time with Carmencita.

"What are you doing, Mother?"

"Learning, my love."

"Why, Mother?"

"Because of you, my love. This could come in handy someday."

Then she looked down and, caressing my cheeks, her eyes became glossy, her cheeks rosier, and she began to bite her lower lip, like when she was nervous. My Mother had the ability to sniff trouble way ahead of time and suffer before and after it became reality. This was the first time I saw our dining table being used for anything other than eating.

I spent hours watching Mother practice her typing on the grey Underwood and shape flowers on the wet hide. Instead of delivering the feeling of safety she was trying to create, she used to frighten me, and I became more and more insecure. I felt something was about to happen, but I could not tell what.

* * *

When I needed it most, a black Chihuahua appeared. I don't recall how, but she became very special to me. I named her Lilita like the small flowers. At that time, I was missing my friends from San Bernardino very much. This old, narrow street had no green lawns, no mango trees, and no excitement. Lilita took their place, tiny but able to jump high. After school I would whistle the same tune we used in San Bernardino to round up the pack. She would run, jump high on my chest, and give me a smack of a lick on my face.

Sometimes, I would place shoeboxes like hurdles. She would wait motionless on the other side with her ears upright, until I gave her the signal to jump, which she did with the grace of the most elegant horse. The patio, in my eyes, became the most beautiful competitive track, with greens and sand patches, white and red hurdles, thousands of people clapping, and the megaphone announcing, "Lilita to the arena." At times, Sis played the audience and clapped. Lilita and I became inseparable. To keep us more company, I created other imaginary friends, doing three voices at a time. And later on Sis also changed her play song to "Mambrú,"

42

"Mambrú se fue a la guerra,
Qué dolor, qué dolor, qué pena...
Mambrú se fue a la guerra
Y no sé cuándo vendrá...
Tra la la...
Tra la la...

* * *

Then, Christmas arrived. As every year, Mother was doing her best to make our Holidays happy. Christmas and New Year's were the merriest days of the year. Good things happened on those days. Somehow, an optimistic disposition had the power to turn wishes into reality. Later on, I discovered one has to plan, act, fail, persist, work hard, and, if one is very lucky, sometimes, some things, somehow, do come true.

On these two days we wore new clothes and shoes, needed anyway but nice to buy them at Christmas to give Father breathing time to save up the money. We chose with enthusiasm. I recall, "This year I am getting a white shirt, blue pants, black shoes, and, for the first time, a tie."

Food was important during these days and that was Mother's department. With our help, she prepared the most delicious 'hallacas,' like Mexican tamales but larger.

It was a pleasure to be alive during this time of the year.

We were not a very religious family, so midnight mass and communion were not for us. Instead, we carried love in our hearts, and not harming people was our best religion. Given a choice, we much preferred to see more good being done than prayers being said.

The older boys went roller skating at three in the morning on Christmas. They enjoyed the freedom of roaming around in the wee hours, eating hot patties, drinking black coffee and behaving like grownups. I was eight, so I just had to wait until I was ten.

43

* * *

I saw people coming and going, carrying gifts and food, and Mother giving the final touches to our dinner. On Christmas we stayed up late and got up first thing. Sis and I, still in pyjamas, ran to find what baby Jesus brought us.

We were not supposed to know, but knew already little Jesus was not real, because we peeked behind Mother's dresser and found the gifts stashed. We pretended not to know; we didn't want to disillusion Mother and Father. That year our gifts were left in the room beside Father's office, and, the same as every year, they anxiously asked, "Is this what you wanted?"

And we said, "Yes. Exactly!"

Of course it was "exactly," because they asked us beforehand when we went to the toy store and made sure that "Baby Jesus" could afford them. That year again we received the toys we saw at the toy store: I got the 'Lionel' electric train, and Sis the doll with real hair and winking eyes, the exact toys we dreamed about. That is why I loved my family!

* * *

In July I was invited to Chuchu's and Carola's sugar cane plantation. I spent the night dreaming about riding wild horses, cattle rustling, and good guys chasing bad guys. No Indians in my dreams. We convened to join Jesús María and Humberto, my hosts for the week, at seven. Before we left, I embraced Father and he reminded me to be careful. We headed east.

"How long is the trip?" I asked Jesús María.

"Two hours. The asphalt road goes to Guarenas, then we go over a dirt road until we reach the plantation."

Before long Chuchu drove past the main gate, taking a narrow trail toward a green sea of sugarcane, down a stiff cobblestone lane, and finally arrived at the main house atop a majestic hill. We carried our luggage into the house.

Carola showed us the room we were to share and said, "You boys show Luis Carlos the stables and the horses. When you are done, take a shower and be ready by dinner."

"Yes, Mom," Jesús María said.

The house was built to please, stately as a castle but simple as a country house. From the large terrace we could see the whole plantation in various shades of green. The main door resembled the entrance to an ancient city, bigger than any house needed. Past the entrance were white walls, red floor tiles, carved hardwood sculptures, and rawhide mats. The rooms were bigger and taller than normal and were connected with grand doors to enable a larger area if desired. The hallways were magnificent and the inner garden was planted with the most exquisite varieties of ferns, roses, and orchids.

When we got to the stables, the most beautiful palomino horse I have ever seen stuck his head out of one of the stalls and nodded as we passed.

"He is my father's horse," Jesús María pointed out.

A nice rusty mare and another horse were in the following stalls and a donkey in the adjacent corral. Belandia, a black, older, white-haired man wearing wicker sandals, greeted us and asked Jesús María when we would be riding the horses.

"Tomorrow after breakfast," Jesús María answered.

After a quick wash-up we had a delicious dinner. The rest of the evening was spent chatting about our riding schedule. That night I couldn't sleep.

At the break of day we had a delicious country breakfast. Later, while Belandia saddled the horses, I paid close attention. I'd never ridden a horse before, but I have seen so many cowboy movies that I thought I knew.

Before long we were riding along the dirt road, downhill, and the horses slumped in jumpy jerks. I had no choice but to trust their instincts. Once on level ground, I became more confident.

45

We stopped at a stall where there was this gigantic black and white bull with balls like bowling pins. I have never seen anything like that before, and I think he noticed by the way he looked at me.

The Holstein cows were being milked. The boys told me they were the most milk-producing cattle in the world; that's why they had enormous teats and had to be milked by automatic machines. There was a mixed smell of pee, wet hay, and musk, but not offensive at all. It smelled like nature's forest.

We continued on the trail west, heading towards the sugar mill, at times galloping and trotting so as not to tire the horses. The boys were very eager to show me how much they owned. When we arrived at the mill, I didn't think it was a big deal. Maybe I didn't want to admit I didn't own anything.

Afterwards we went to the plantation store to buy pops, and then continued along the trail until we found a creek and a pond, watered the horses, and allowed them to nibble the fresh grass. The air was cool and fresh, so we settled under a mango tree to cool off and rest for a while. When it was almost six, the mosquitoes gathered around the pond like a grey cloud and began to bite. We rushed back to the house. When we arrived at the straightaway approaching the house, Jesús María yelled, "Let's see who gets to the house first!"

We healed the horses and raced all the way up the hill. If a horse had tripped, we could have had a catastrophe. In my version, my brother Alvaro was riding a white stallion and protecting us.

The following day, the worst happened. It rained all day. We didn't have any choice but to spend the day indoors, in a room filled with toys collected when the boys were younger. So we turned back the hands of time to age three and in full contentment spent the whole day galloping and wrestling imaginary cattle.

Nature sometimes has mercy on little boys and the next day was sunny again. Chuchu joined us on his palomino that shone like a gold ingot. That day I ended up riding the donkey, like Sancho Panza in *Don Quijote de la Mancha*!

The following day we crossed the road to a neighbouring farm that belonged to a gentleman named Beaumester. When we reached his house, without warning, Jesús María rushed his horse and began to shout, "Beaumester is a sonafabitch!"

Humberto and I yelled as well, not even knowing why. I guess it was an old grudge between the two families.

A little ahead, as we followed a river, Humberto and I decided to speed up the pace and left Jesús María behind.

After a little while Jesús María cried like a baby, "Please don't leave me behind. Please!"

I was so tickled to hear a boy my own age, who was supposed to be so macho, crying like a baby.

The last day we didn't go riding because Jesús María caught the flu. What a softy, getting sick on our last day of vacation! He was just a pussy after all!

Anyway, I was happy to come home. That summer I felt I had grown a notch.

Chapter 4

La Salle was, and still is, one of the two best schools in Caracas. Of course it's a Catholic school. They are the masters of the art of lifting one's self-esteem, to the point that one feels destined.

Father said, "The boys that go to the best schools have an advantage in life, not because they get the best education, but because they grow among the rich and powerful who become the future leaders. It allows early relationships that last a lifetime. That's why they charge such high fees to let one be part of the group. Now that you are nine and in third grade, it's the right time to be transferred and be part of the group."

An entrance examination was required, and Father made the appointment for that coming Monday at eleven. I entered the mahogany-paneled room holding my father's hand. As soon as we walked in, a passing member told us, "Brother Luis is coming in a few minutes." How did he know we were expected? Catholic schools weren't an inexpensive gift, but they were good. It was a privilege to be accepted.

A very thin man with a very long neck, wearing the traditional La Salle brotherhood black robe and the white linen split-neck cravat, time-honoured since Fifteenth Century France, appeared and said, "I am Brother Luis, Mr. Márquez. How are you, Luis Carlos? This questionnaire contains twenty arithmetic concepts we expect you to know before entering third grade. Please write your solutions and final answers in this booklet. When you are finished, just pull that rope in the corner and a bell will ring in my office. It should take you about forty-five minutes to solve the twenty problems. That is, if you are well prepared!"

This last comment was enough to set me into a panic. Their interest was in arithmetic. I was suspicious at the time, but it came true that life is greatly about numbers.

I tried to pull the deviant thoughts out of my head, looked at the clock on the wall, and started to work on the problems. No calculators were allowed, only paper and pencil. A small eraser on the

"Mongol" 2B pencil reassured me I could correct a few mistakes. Nevertheless, the pencil felt cold clutched between my thumb, pointer, and middle finger of my shaking right hand. My biggest fear was about what would happen if I ran out of lead or eraser before finishing the test. The thought of it weighed like a ton of lead in my neck, on top of the tension I had because of those damned numbers to start with!

Father left the room and went for a stroll around the school. I finished the test on time and pulled the cord as I was told. Brother Luis came to collect my notebook and said, "I will notify your father about the results in a couple of days," and disappeared.

I looked for my father and found him sitting on one of the benches on the upper patio, looking at the school. I wonder what my father might have been thinking that day, perhaps about his own youth.

When Father saw me, he began to praise the school, "Look, Luis Carlos, what a wonderful building! Look, three levels surrounding the central patio." He pointed in that direction with excitement, and continued, "The patio is laid out for all kinds of sports: soccer, volleyball, basketball, baseball, and tennis. Isn't it wonderful? "

I could feel his excitement about making it possible for me to attend the school. The greatest satisfaction parents have is to give their children what they, for one reason or another, didn't have when they were young themselves.

This is their way of getting even with the circumstances of life.

* * *

I started at La Salle in September 1950. Getting ready for school that year was more exciting than ever. Mother and I went to the school bookstore to buy the long list of textbooks, supplies, and uniforms required: books, notebooks, pencils, crayons, eraser, glue, pencil sharpener, green binding paper, and a new briefcase big enough to hold everything. The thing I liked most was my soccer uniform and my white gymnastics tee shirt, embossed with the school crest. The school also required a navy blue wool suit, as dress uniform for special occasions, which we had to wear with a white shirt, black shoes, and a school crest lapel pin. For daily wear, Mother bought khakis and new buck boots. I have never gone through so much preparation before, just to go to school. Father said, "All worth it."

On my first day of class my third grade teacher introduced himself as Brother Benito and moved on to roll call. He called everyone by family name and took a hard look over his rimless glasses at each one of us, as he went down the list. He wrote on the blackboard the subjects to be covered during the school year and handed us a detailed schedule.

He reminded me of Pinocchio's father, from the Disney movie. A soft spoken, gentle, older gentleman, wearing rimless glasses, his grey hair parted on one side and folded over his head in an attempt to disguise his baldness. The first time I engaged in close conversation with him, I noticed he had bad breath and yellowish small teeth, like grains of corn. He had been teaching third grade for 40 years: arithmetic, geography, history, drawing, religion, and Castilian (traditional Spanish). He was by far the most conscientious teacher I ever had. He was capable of handling us like a docile flock of sheep, which we weren't.

I called my friends at school by their family name, which was the custom: Marrero, Avellaneda, and Poleo. Marrero was a spectacled, freckle faced, reddish-haired kid with an incredibly creative imagination, who kept telling Avellaneda and me the most extraordinary stories. At recess, we used to sit on the far benches of the patio to listen to Marrero's accounts of an ancient civilization and a young prince called Samir, who lived in the island of Sumatra and defended his reign against invaders. I vividly recall his fantastic description of the island, an exotic place full of incense fumes, the prince fending off attackers with his scimitar, wearing a shiny blue silk turban, and riding a white Arabian stallion.

Other times, Marrero delivered exhaustive tales about the battles he made his lead toy soldiers fight. He described to us in detail how he constructed fortresses out of glued cardboard to shelter his regiments and how the conqueror looted, killed the men, abducted the women, rounded up the elders and the children, set them on fire, and destroyed the fortress of the losing army. By the time recess was over, we walked back to class, still trembling about Marrero's fantastic and bizarre scenarios!

Another rage was racing small matchbox cars. Poleo and I modified the little cars, shortening the spring of the winding mechanism and cutting off fenders, to give them a faster run. Marrero and Avellaneda raced them. The prize was the loser's car and an equivalent sum. We always won.

A guy named Julio was the best student in the class and got the honour medals. I admired him because he earned his recognitions, not like that Prince in first grade who was just a pretty teacher's pet.

* * *

Delgado Chalbaud, the President of the transitional military junta was assassinated on November 13, 1950. His motorcade riddled, his slaughtered body lay blood-splashed on the pavement, still clad in military uniform beside his black Cadillac limousine, in what seemed a failed kidnapping attempt, a dreadful site. Simón Urbina, a fanatic extremist, appeared as the alleged killer, but many people still think he was just a scapegoat.

Chalbaud's colleague, Army Colonel Pérez Jiménez, second-in-command and coauthor of the 1945 and 1948 coups, placed an interim puppet as President and, in 1952, was elected President of Venezuela. People say the election was rigged and held him responsible for Chalbaud's assassination, but nothing was ever proved. Another dictatorship!

New rules and trends began to appear: taxis painted with checkerboard patterns, drivers prohibited to honk their horns, radio transmitters on police vehicles, jet fighters added to the Air Force, tanks and soldiers on the streets, staged air raid war games, and the creation of an intelligence secret service called Seguridad Nacional. A mandatory parade was instated on Labour Day, renamed Día de la Patria. People began to feel like they were living in Nazi Germany and history was repeating itself.

Around this time, Father gave us the surprise of our lives: a house in San Bernardino! At first, I could not believe it. I was going back to the neighbourhood that had provided me with so many happy days. I was overwhelmed, ran to tell Sis the good news, and came back to embrace Father and kiss Mother. I kept saying, "Thank you, thank you!" and I meant it.

"But how did it happen?" I asked Father.

"Well, you know, one of the principals of the National Sugar Cane Association has two unmarried sisters and one of them inherited the house. I do legal work for them, and they asked me if I would be interested in purchasing the house, and if I wanted to use my outstanding fees as a down payment. I know how much we enjoyed living in San Bernardino and, besides, we need a house of our own, so I bought it! Of course we have to give up the house that the association gives us free of rent, but we shouldn't give up this opportunity."

I was not able to say anything more. I just sat on a corner, smiling and dreaming about being back with my friends. Within days, we moved to our new house. I was so happy to leave the old colonial house, even if free of rent! There, at times, I felt as if I was buried. If it wasn't for Lilita and Grandma, I don't know how much longer I could have pretended to talk in three voices and sell magazines. At last, real live playmates again!

Our old furniture was the only permanent thing in our lives: the blue leatherette living room with the glass-top table in the middle, our old Art Deco mahogany dining room, our matching bedroom sets, and later, in 1951, our cream vertical Sylvania television set, where I witnessed the birth of *Televisa* and *El Show de las Doce*.

* * *

In March 1951, I turned ten and passed into fourth grade at La Salle. I joined the gym, learned to perform on 'el potro,' the pommel horse, and because of my insatiable need for attention, dared the boys that I could fly over the spiked fence at Mauro's house. Twenty kids took the bet and I made a lot of money. They thought I was crazy.

Brother Ramón was now my teacher, not as good as Brother Benito, but no one can be lucky all the time. Our Spanish literature teacher was a victimized politician protected by La Salle. He told stories about how our land was conquered by the Spaniards, who raped, killed, and robbed the natives during 314 years of sad history, and how, since 1811, our land was governed by 'Caudillos' who tortured, killed, and robbed the citizens. He said they were vultures that traded influence, misappropriated public funds, exercised terror, and capitalized on ignorance. "No wonder," he said, "our liberator Simón Bolívar concluded his life disillusioned and convinced that these lands were ungovernable."

My teacher wanted to do something about it, but every time he tried he was thrown in jail. He knew his life was in danger, but he didn't care. Once in a while, he talked about literature and referred to the *Scarlet Letter* as a tale about a common prostitute.

* * *

Mass delivered in Latin, which we didn't even understand, was the crowning event of the week. Every Sunday the families attended nine o'clock mass. The chapel was swarmed right to the entrance, and most people didn't know why they were there, aside from the fact they were required. Many of them believed the Church and the State were the most important things in their lives, which was hard to understand, since both constantly failed them.

The Church, instead of providing hope, made them feel guilty; and the State, instead of providing the security of work, made them feel threatened. Nevertheless, they were the foundation upon which the lives of the people rested. In glaring contrast, the insecurity and lack of substance of the Church were exemplified by gruesome displays of ostentation.

Inside the church sanctuary it was hot, and the sun pierced the stained glass windows like lancets stabbing the bodies of the saints as punishment for sins they never committed. Light beams crisscrossed the incense fumes, hit the highest beams, and bounced against the murals, creating voluptuous forms like celestial battles between the forces of good and evil.

Women with their white, cream, grey, or black veils draping their heads sat in the front rows. They had their hands entwined and their heads inclined a little toward the floor as a sign of shame about something they did not know; their eyes were raised a little towards the atrium as a sign of hope. The women's gaze seemed to speak their thoughts: "Forgive me, Lord, for being so banal. Help me, Mother of God, to raise my family. San Judas Thaddeus, protect my husband; you know he is all I have."

A colossal sculpture of a crucified Christ was located high above the altar. The Madonna was in a lower niche to his right, and San Judas Thaddeus on an even smaller one to his left. Father José was delivering mass in Latin and, as usual, no one understood what was being said. That Sunday, the sermon, which at least was delivered in Spanish, was about being faithful to one's beliefs. Father José said it in plain words, "If you believe in God's word, he will protect you against all evil."

I wanted to believe, but it was impossible to accept as true something I couldn't understand. Was this my weakness? Because I wasn't sure, I prayed and asked for forgiveness. Behind the front rows, some estranged women prayed for all of us, and some families sat together to profess their deep love and devotion. Among them were the elder women and men, who had given their lives to their family and now depended on them, not the Church or the State. In the last rows sat those who came purposely late to be near the door for the occasional smoke or the frequent flirtation with their sweethearts.

My family sat in the middle. Not too close, not too far. That was how they looked at God and lived their lives. Father José continued his prayers, turned around, offered two chalices and said in

Latin, "This is the chalice of salvation. This is my body. This is my blood. Consume it, do this in my memory."

The families rushed to communion, kneeled in front of the altar to receive their waffle and, as soon as they took it, turned around and walked back with their hands knotted and a solemn expression on their faces, as if their lives had changed. The collection ladies passed through the aisle, extending their baskets, almost touching the congregants' faces, not to embarrass anyone but with the clear intention to force everyone to give. Most people in that community needed the money but, afraid of seeming impious, gave it to the church.

Then, since I didn't understand anything, I was tempted to think that men created the concept of God out of need to have questions answered...

So convinced was I about this, that I wrote these lines,

> *And in desperation we invented our latest God*
> *An eternal Father who would give us life, purpose and*
> *answers*
> *Securing our past and future*
> *And we believed and we trusted and we hoped*
> *And we lied...*
> *And we placed the essentials aside*
> *Clean water, food and shelter*
> *And became greedy*
> *And we fought*
> *And in desperation we invented our latest God*
> *And we lied...*

At the end I was as sad as when I found out "Baby Jesus" was not real.

* * *

That Christmas I was allowed to go roller skating for the first time. I was already ten. The boys would wake me up at 2:00AM. I tied a string to my toe and dropped it down the window so they could pull it. The night before, I oiled my skates and went to bed with three layers of clothes on, ready to go. The string worked perfectly, and out I went to my first roller skating adventure.

As soon as we reached the top of Parque Los Caobos, I started skating down the steep hill and, on the way down a cyclist ran over me, slitting my head. The guys wrapped a sweater around my bleeding head and rushed to the emergency post. This time I required ten stitches. Mother blamed me as usual and, when Father arrived, he didn't say much. But Father woke me around 3:00AM, asking, "Aren't you going to go roller skating again today?" My Father couldn't miss an opportunity like this to be sarcastic!

* * *

Now my room faced north and had its own balcony. The mountain breeze wafted through a tall pine, bathing my room. The tranquil Sunday afternoon siestas could not possibly be replicated. Avila was now the name of my street, like the mountain that shields Caracas from the Caribbean, and Avileña the name of our house. The boys were older. Sis turned seven and she was now in first grade at the same school I was when I was her age, Colegio America. Mother walked her two blocks to and from school as she did with me at seven.

The 'Pack' met now at the corner convenience store, no whistling from house to house this time. The storeowner was delighted because we constantly purchased pop and sweets. There was always a lot of discussion and sometimes small brawls.

At that time in Caracas many conveniences were brought directly to our door. On Saturdays fresh vegetables and fruits were delivered by El Frutero, an old Portuguese man who rode a red and green cart pulled by a small grey donkey. His fresh vegetables and fruits looked like a rolling, colourful, massive garden salad. Fresh baked bread and cinnamon buns were also brought twice a day by El

Panadero, a mild-spoken Italian man, who drove a Harley Davidson connected to an insulated buggy.

Our favourite playground, La Quinta Anauco, was an historic landmark. Once home to El Marqués del Toro, a Spanish nobleman, and later to María Teresa Rodriguez del Toro, the young wife of Simón Bolívar, El Libertador. She died of malaria at 22 in this very house, eight months after her arrival from Spain. As some people do out of devotion, Bolívar, the liberator of seven Latin American nations, never married again.

The historic house was atop a hill and the Anauco Creek, from which it took its name, ran by its side. To us, it was just a dilapidated old house with an illustrious past. Two brothers lived in the house with their mother, who was the caretaker. They allowed each one of us to have a small hiding place among the ruins where we kept our treasures: sling shots, marbles, penknives and other valuables. Mine was a hole covered with a rock in the west wall around the central patio. Only I knew where it was.

* * *

The 'Pack' was joined by invitation only and one had to go through an elaborate initiation ritual to be accepted. Mine took place on a particularly hot Sunday afternoon. I was taken to the entrance of a well-hidden drainage pipe running from a higher level on the hill to one corner of the lower grounds of the Quinta Anauco estate, about 50 meters long and a tight 50 x 50 centimetres wide. If sudden rain fell at the top of the mountain and a flash flood came, anyone inside would be drowned.

To get in I had to crawl. I knew as soon as I went in there was no way to turn back. I had to crawl to the end, where the culvert widened into a sewer, to be able to turn around. I couldn't see anything, only able to feel the dusty sides with my hands. I knew snakes, scorpions, rats, and all kinds of vermin could be in the tunnel, but I had to prove to the boys and to myself that I was worthy. This was extremely important. There was no other way, that's how we separated the ten-year-old boys from the ten-year-old pussies. The way back lasted forever and my heart was relieved when I saw daylight again. In my version, I saw my brother Alvaro standing on a high branch, thumbs up and smiling widely.

There was no life membership in the Pack. We had to constantly go through new challenges. Sometimes we played a spooky hide-and-seek at night on the grounds of La Quinta Anauco. When it was pitch dark, vermin galore roamed the bush. Some say even a butterfly tiger (Jaguar) came down the Avila on nights of the full moon.

Other times, we jumped over the foundation trenches of construction sites. If we fell, we wouldn't be able to come out anyway because the trenches were two-stories deep. The need for identity was so strong that I would have done almost anything to be accepted. The reason I didn't die when I was ten is because I was not destined. I discovered we expend a great deal of our lives trying to prove ourselves.

That same year, 1953, Father made a very strange decision, the first of a series that would eventually change our life. He began to study medicine, and anatomy books appeared everywhere during the following three years. When this happened, Father was already a well-known lawyer. Why did he have to study medicine?

Around this time, I also began to change. My voice turned deeper and fuzz began to appear. I was turning eleven. Sis was now nine years old and in third grade and got transferred to Colegio Las Nieves around the corner from La Salle, of course another Catholic school. Now I, instead of Mother, had the responsibility to take Sis to and from school. We got on a 'carrito por puesto,' a shared taxi, at the corner of our house every morning. Curiously, the drivers placed the coins in the ashtray (which cars used to have) and one even stacked the coins on a magnet on the dashboard!

To keep Sis entertained I talked all the way. She didn't believe many of my stories and thought I made them up just to please her. The fact was most of the stories were original.

We finished school at four, and often Sis and I agreed to spend the fare on ice cream and walk back. We shared half and half, but she complained I always got the bigger half. It took 30 minutes, slowly walking, to get home.

My stories were usually short, but sometimes I got carried away until I found the right ending. On the way, Sis sometimes asked silly questions. One day she asked me if we were rich and I said as if I knew, "No, we just pretend to be, because Father is an intellectual, and true intellectuals are never rich."

Chapter 5

1954. Now Father had a partner, related by way of the Carrillo family, who graduated from Central University in Caracas and Harvard Law School. Father often commented, "José is just credentials and no brains."

But, José ran his family's ranch and logging operation, which gave him enormous money and he didn't need to rely on his law practice as much as Father did. To him, law was a status hobby; for my Father it was his whole life. Among other things, José believed lawyers should take great care of their image. That is why he drove a black Cadillac. Father, on the other hand, believed a valuable person doesn't need those accessories. Nonetheless, José influenced Father a great deal, to the point that when Father was about to change his car, he ended up buying a luxurious Packard. But not a Cadillac!

My Father was always looking for new projects. That year he started a rice plantation in Acarigua and a ranch on a stretch of land along the banks of the river Guanarito.

He hired Mora as his second, a large man from Trujillo with rosy cheeks and a shiny gold tooth, visible when he smiled. He looked like a gigantic baby, and his temperament was also mild, except when he had to exercise authority. Then he became very direct and didn't accept anything other than completion of his orders. Mora went and did what Father told him and followed his instructions to the letter.

What Mother had difficulty understanding was why Father couldn't be content with his already successful law practice. Why did he have to study medicine, log, ranch, farm, and be a lawyer at the same time? He was straining himself. What my Mother didn't realize was that he was compelled by "This Márquez Thing."

As part of his new plan, on November 1954, Father obtained a permit to log 1,500 cubic meters of mahogany in the San Camilo Jungle and went on his first trip. Beforehand, Mora hired hands, sat up camp, combed the jungle, and marked the trees to be cut. On those scouting trips, Father wore high boots, took machetes and guns for protection, and came back tanned and well soiled from head to toe, like returning from a war, tired but happy to be back. During the following months he continued to travel more often, coming back only every three weeks and later once a month.

In August, at the end of the school year, he took me with him for the first time.

Mother was furious, because I was supposed to go to Chuchu's sugar plantation and I was not going. She thought the experience of the plantation was better for me, but Father considered this trip more educational. He was taking me with him!

I arranged my fatigue gear: boots, hat, knife, canteen, and khakis, and placed the luggage in the trunk of the Packard the night before. Sis was still sleeping when I was ready to go. I went up to her room and took a peek at her before leaving. I kissed Mother and looked straight ahead to avoid seeing her disappear, because I get sad when I see people go away.

Soon the sun was rising and I began to enjoy the music and the fresh air flowing through the open windows of the Packard. It gave us a sense of freedom. We passed Maracay, where my Aunt Alicia lived. We passed Valencia, the roads narrowed to gravel roads, and we had to keep a fair distance behind the other cars to avoid suffocating in the clouds of dust. We even had to cover our noses with a wet handkerchief, to keep from chocking. From time to time we crossed streams but no bridges this far away. During the rainy season, people had to wait for hours to be able to cross, until overflowed rivers came back to their riverbed. It took us twelve hours to arrive at Tunapuisito, Father's logging camp (a mere two hundred kilometers away), a dusty little town with no more than ten buildings.

We met Mora at the room Father rented, outfitted with hammocks and cots to sleep in. It rained all night, and in the morning we rode an old Jeep (Father had bought) through a muddy road towards the jungle. Two hours on the dirt road, and we arrived at the edge of the jungle, left the Jeep parked there, and walked a narrow trail.

At one point, Mora heard the groaning of wild hogs and stopped. Father quickly lifted me on top of a tree branch. We waited but nothing happened, and we continued our walk. It took a good two hours to get to where the men were logging.

I soaked up every bit of what was happening for my memory diary. How they marked, cut down, cleaned, logged, winched, loaded, and chained the mahogany logs to the flatbeds and how the national guards inspected the cargo to issue the Bill of Lading. The next day Father took me to the mill to see the sawing operation: square, saw, classify, and store the logs to dry. I became very knowledgeable on this subject. Still, every time I see a timber truck, I try to estimate how many cubic feet are on the flatbed and what kind of wood they are carrying, another one of my secret fun games!

That year also, during my school vacation, Father took me to the rice plantation. When we arrived, we approached the field just before sunrise and found a herd of wild goats nibbling on the rice. Father became furious, jumped out of the Jeep and started to chase the goats with a machete. When he realized he was getting nowhere, he came back, grabbed the 38 Smith & Wesson he kept in the glove compartment and gave Chicho and me two more guns. We killed ten goats that day. Father gave them to the local butcher, who promised to distribute half to people in need for free. I still have difficulty reconciling the thought that life had to be killed, even under extreme circumstances.

On that trip I joined Father, Chicho, and Chucho at the Rice Growers Association annual party. When the party was over, around three in the morning, we walked Father to the car. He had a little too much to drink that night, which was the rarest thing, because Father never took more than two drinks on account of his liver condition. That night he drank way too much. We arrived at Father's office, which he also used as sleeping quarters, laid Father on his hammock, and called it a night, but when Chicho and his brother were ready to leave, Chicho asked me, "Do you want to come?"

"Where?" I asked.

"It's a surprise," he said.

"What about Father?" I asked.

"He is out cold; he would not mind."

"Okay," I said.

We drove to the outskirts of town, to a regular house, except that it had a red light on the entrance. I had an idea where we were going, even though I had not been there before, but I played dumb. Chicho parked the car in front of the red light house, rang the bell, and a lady dressed in a tight satin red dress welcomed him, as if she knew him very well.

A dimly lit saloon appeared, scattered with tables and a bunch of scantily dressed women, who went freely about. Behind the bar there was a man polishing beer glasses against a light. The jukebox was playing Perez Prado's *Mambo Jambo*. As soon as we sat, one of the women who seemed to know Chicho well approached him, caressed his neck, and asked what we wanted to drink. Chicho ordered two whiskies and one beer for me. She asked me if I was Chicho's kid brother. She knew he was old enough to be my father. I settled by saying, "No, he is my uncle."

Some of the women were already giggling at us, and I overheard one say, "I wouldn't mind having the young chicken." She also was old enough to be my mother.

Chicho asked me which one I liked best and told me I could dance with anyone I wanted to. I could choose whichever girl I wanted and he would take care of the rest. After a second beer, I worked up enough nerve to say, "Can I ask that one with the pink blouse over there?"

The girl was smiling at me. She was as curious about me as I was about her. She looked no older than eighteen. Neither of us should have been there. I was because Father was stoned, out cold, and she? Who knows why?

I called the girl over. She sat on my lap and ordered a drink, I guess to comply with the house rules. Since I had no idea what to say, I asked her to dance. She said, "Of course, Honey," caressing my neck with the palm of her hand, like the other one did to Chicho.

This neck thing! I began to dance, not too close, not too far. Then she snuggled up and pressed herself against me. She felt really warm, like a fresh baked loaf of bread just out of the oven. I had dreamed about this kind of thing before, while curling up with my pillow. The jukebox was now playing one of those old fashioned Cuban boleros, which have gotten so many people in so much trouble for so many years.

Her privates were now pressing so hard against me that I felt it was about time to do something. Sensing my urge, she grabbed my hand and led me in the direction of one of the rooms. Once inside, it turned out I needed less coaching than I anticipated. I just did what it was natural to do. We finished soon and I was chuckling now out of pure satisfaction. While she was also falling apart laughing her head off, my next sight was her wide-open mouth, and I could see she was missing four of her upper front teeth! Somehow I hadn't noticed that before, because she had thin tight lips and managed not to show much. Paradoxically, I remember her as one of the most beautiful girls I have ever met. Beyond a doubt, she must have been!

The following morning Father was sick as a dog, because of his liver, and had to stay in his hammock for three days. He tolerated only crackers and chicken broth, which I fetched him from the hotel across the street. Nobody made comments about the night before. Everything seemed to be so beautifully well arranged!

* * *

Two years passed. Mother, Sis, and I continued living in Caracas. Mother began to tell Sis and me more and more stories about when she was young in Mérida. "We were poor but happy," she used to say, kind of staring blankly at the walls, wishing her life was somebody else's and implying more or less to our understanding that she was not happy now, in spite of having more, even her own house. I think she missed the fresh air of the Andes, the tender vegetables, and the Sunday outings to Los Chorros de Milla, a beautiful national park with many waterfalls, called "chorros," where the people of Mérida go to relax on the weekend.

But everyone misses something when one looks back, and I knew that she wouldn't be happy if she returned. I wanted to tell her, but I knew she wouldn't listen. In the meantime, Father relied more and more on his agricultural operations. It became obvious that one day we would be asked to move.

In effect, one day Father said it: "We are moving to Acarigua next week. I need to concentrate full-time on the rice plantation, which is doing very well, and step up the ranch."

Mother was shocked. I could see her eyes widen, but she dared not say anything. She knew that when Father said we were moving, we were moving!

* * *

It was 1954. Acarigua was a small town that attracted a fair share of adventurers. My father was one of them. The land was fertile and the government offered liberal financing programs. The conditions led to quick money, potentially 30,000 dollars every three months.

Acarigua was truly a colourful place, where farmers, ranchers, and loggers rode expensive Cadillacs, bumping along the rustic gravel roads. They cruised through clouds of dust during dry season and muddy patches during the rainy season and seldom washed their cars. Instead, they bought a brand new Cadillac every year.

They wore khakis, expensive alligator cowboy boots, and Stetson hats, and loved to show off their financial success to cover their insecurities. They were bold and daring, the dream of the town women, but they never stayed in one place long enough to be caught by them.

When my father revealed the news to my mother, she felt thrown back into the life she left behind 150 years and many generations ago. After all, she married a lawyer, not a farmer, but she'd overlooked his love for nature. Father and I loved living in the interior, he because of his farming and ranching and I because of my riding and driving freely. Someday I would drive Father's own Cadillac! Why not?

* * *

Very quickly we were approaching our destination. "Are we almost there?" I asked.

Father pointed to a sign that read 'Acarigua 30 kilometres.' Sis and Mother remained silent all the way. When we arrived, we dragged our tired selves out of the car, and each one of us had a different opinion about the house. Father had, as always, already rented for us.

Mother saw it as a sombre, dark grey, gloomy little stone house, with a little dry garden and a dusty patio. No trees and not worthy of us, it mirrored her attitude towards the life she was approaching.

I brightened things up with my soul, and to me it looked different, as bright as the future I wanted. Each of us placed the suitcases in the rooms Mother assigned. I ended up in an open deck, between Mother's and Sis,' happy to have no doors to open or close. The next morning after breakfast, I swept the rubbish out of our dusty backyard. I wanted everything tidy.

***

Acarigua's public high school was the first co-ed school I ever attended. Distracted by the girls, I couldn't concentrate and my grades fell. I didn't want to disappoint Father, because education was the most important thing in his book, but I couldn't cope with the distraction of so many girls in their short skirts everywhere!

The corner store's 'dulce de leche' was the best in Acarigua: sweet, moist, and crumbly. It was served in ashtrays. Perhaps they had a surplus and decided not to waste them. Father and I shared a sweet tooth and simply adored it. I still remember him devouring up to six ashtrays and then gobbling a liter of cool water, finishing with a smack of his lips.

Four families, who owned just about everything, ran the town: the movie house, the pharmacy, the hotel, and most of the land for miles around. The other important person in town was Doctor Potenzini, a tidy, mildly soft spoken, short man with a bald head framed by two patches of black hair. He practiced out of his impressively large family home (four colonial windows up front) and was married to a much younger woman, who people said married him in pursuit of a fortune. They had no children.

As it turned out, with Father being a lawyer, we were also in a sort of privileged position in this town. "Better head of a mouse, than tail of a lion," my father used to say.

My grades kept falling and one day Father warned me: "If you don't do better in school, I will have to send you away to the nearest La Salle. I will have to ask them to take you as a boarder as a special favour, because they are not a boarding school. You will have to sleep in a little room like the priest and go to mass every day."

I took note, but not too seriously.

Mother didn't like the house we lived in and told Father to find another house or she was going back to Caracas. She didn't like this town and argued she had her own house in Caracas. "Why should I be living in somebody else's house?"

I ended up in a tug of war. I didn't want Mother to leave and I didn't want to go to that boarding school. But Father was determined to keep the family together, no matter what, and at the same time to keep his dreams alive. Finally, he found a house with lots of windows and a beautiful garden in the middle. At least Mother had no valid grounds to veto this house, because it was brighter and larger.

What was the main living room was converted into Father's office, and the sequence of rooms along the garden in the middle became our sleeping quarters. The tropical rains came and the variety of ferns, roses, margaritas, and orchids exuded the most exotic blend of fragrances. I guess we had a chance at being happy now, at least for a while.

That weekend Father took me to the farm and I drove the tractor, pretending to be "inspecting the premises." It was easy but dangerous; just recently a tractor overturned crossing a ditch and ended up on top of the driver. The man died.

* * *

A guy named Mario was now my best friend. His father owned the hotel, the pharmacy, the movie house, and drove a Cadillac. Father did not own his Cadillac yet, but I knew it was a matter of time, because he was about to get his 30,000 dollars out of the rice crop in three months, and since I was fourteen, I now would get to drive it. Untimely, these pleasant thoughts were interrupted by Father calling me into his office.

"Sit down, Luis Carlos. You are failing in school. I talked to the La Salle director in Barquisimeto. He is prepared to take you in. They are not a boarding school, but as a special favour to me, in recognition of the issues I have solved for them through the years, they are prepared to take you. Get your things together, because I am driving you next Monday. The school is only two hours' drive from here, so you may come home every other weekend."

When I thought my life was getting better, it began to stink like a rotten egg. Now I was being sent to a monastery!

* * *

My room along a corridor on the third floor of La Salle was small and narrow. A single iron bed was against the right wall, a tiny window at one end, a table and chair against the left wall, a sink and mirror beside it, a tall dresser in one corner, and a single light bulb hanging from the ceiling. The common showers and toilets were at the end of the hallway. That was all.

From my room I could hear the record player of the house next to the building playing this simple and melancholy song day and night. My heart tightened every time I heard that song, and I will always remember it. Even now my heart aches every time I bring it to mind, because it reminds me how lonely, how very lonely I was!

Every morning at six, the brothers walked along the hall to attend mass at the chapel, which was at my end of the hall. They didn't force me to attend, because they recognised I was not one of them. It was their way of respecting my sorry condition. I know they felt for me, but there was nothing they or I could do for the time being.

Every day at seven-thirty I went down to a huge dining room and had breakfast alone. A helper brought my breakfast, said, "Good morning," and left. It was the same dining room where lunch was later served to the regular students. Those days I felt the sadness privileged people perhaps feel when they are isolated for being so very special. But I was not special. Why should I be in this fix?

The employees had their meals together in the kitchen. I wished I was one of them, so I could have my meals there and have somebody to talk with. I was not kitchen staff, nor a brother; I was nobody.

At least during lunch I had the company of the other students, and I cherished every moment. At four when they left, I became the loneliest boy on earth.

One day, an old man who was also staying in the school asked me, "Are you the young man who is staying with the brothers?" and continued before I could answer, "I am painting the life of John Baptist of La Salle. Do you know his story?"

"Yes, of course. I am a La Salle student. La Salle is a brotherhood and the members of the order are called 'Brothers.' They don't conduct mass or confession like regular priests do. Their mission is education, but they are still part of the Catholic Church," I said.

"Do you want to see the paintings I am working on?" he asked.

"Yes! Yes!"

"Come with me, let me show you."

He took me to a very long room in the west wing of the building and opened a door. I was astounded by the sight of the huge canvases hanging on the walls, showing a life-size John Baptist of La Salle lecturing some boys in the middle of a very nice garden. His right hand was pointing a finger at an invisible message. Everyone in the painting looked alive. Every figure was life-size and from whatever angle you watched, John Baptist seemed to be looking at you. I wonder where these paintings are hanging now, maybe at the central office of the congregation in Paris.

My grades were better now. I don't understand it because La Salle was, no doubt, a demanding school; yet, I make better grades here. I guess it was just easier for me to follow a system I already knew.

Suddenly, one of my schoolmates became sick and died. Our teacher guide selected five of us to represent the school at his funeral. He didn't tell us how the boy died. I guess it didn't matter. I had never seen a dead person before. He was lying in a coffin surrounded by white flowers. He looked pale, wearing our gala uniform, and smelled like flowers only stronger. His mother cried and embraced each one of us, as if embracing her own son. I didn't know what to say but felt very sad.

Some men closed the coffin, lifted it, and placed the edges on our shoulders. It felt heavy. One of them grabbed my hands, placing one underneath and one on the edge of the coffin. We walked to the funeral car, placed the coffin on the platform, and took him to the cemetery. It was very sad.

My life was strange in those days. I was the only boarder in school, felt very lonely; the house next door played this sad song day and night, and my schoolmate died. I stood it because I loved my father and didn't want to disappoint him.

To make things even worse, around this time my grandma passed away. Aunt Alicia told me once that she spent her last days praying on her knees for God to take her away. She was soon gone without saying goodbye and, believe it or not, soon after her, so was the Caracas streetcar.

Chapter 6

It was 1955. Perez Jimenez continued to be the dictator. That year, he conducted a general 'referendum' to confirm his presidency and won. Many people believed the confirmation was rigged. He was a very controversial figure; some people considered him the most progressive president Venezuela ever had, and to others he was a tyrant. Most were aware of him executing an ambitious national development plan while running a corruption ring.

Not too much later, Father was offered a very high position in this very controversial government: Director of the Development Corporation, the very organism that carried out the projects. If Father accepted, we must go back to Caracas to a normal life again. Normal? Mom and Sis were delighted, because they were city girls. I was too, tired of being away at the monastery. Father was undecided, because in Acarigua he had all the things he always wanted and was also recognised as an excellent lawyer who developed a nice rice plantation, acquired a patch of ranching land, and bought a home in Caracas. He once told me, caressing my head, "Someday you will remember me for all this."

Mother was excited but apprehensive. She hadn't forgotten the time Father had a government position in 1945 in the Income Tax Service, when the government was overthrown, how he had to drag himself under parked cars to save his life, and how the opposition persecuted members of the deposed administration.

Father accepted the job and, before we realized it, we were on our way to Caracas. This was the way things were done in my family; before anybody had a chance to think, we were there, not sure if this move was for good, bad, or worse. But in life, can we ever be sure of anything?

Thank goodness, I finished the school year before we moved. My grades were not great, but decent enough so I didn't have to apologise.

This time, we were traveling in a grey air-conditioned Buick limousine, driven by a moustached Andean man from Trujillo, not by coincidence. His name was Juan, like Grandpa on Mother's side. He wore a brown military uniform and talked slowly.

"If you ever need someone of total trust, you must choose an Andean man from Trujillo and a dog from Mucuchies. They are both loyal and fierce. They will give their life to protect you, if ever the need arises." That's what my father said.

We stopped to pump gas and took turns in the stale, filthy washrooms, the only ones available. While waiting, we watched all the variety of things they sold in this roadside convenience store: Band-aids, sandwiches, pop, hats, flashlights, batteries, toys, and anything you may think of. We bought Pepsis and continued the journey.

At one point I turned my head, looked back, and saw the same sign I saw two years ago 'Acarigua 30 kilometres,' only I was going in the opposite direction. It seemed like yesterday I was asking Father, "Are we almost there?" when driving towards what was supposed to be our final destination, Acarigua. The sign disappeared and I questioned if we were going in the right direction or in circles.

Nearing Caracas, Father told us about the house he rented on the hills of Santa Monica. As always, he made arrangements ahead of time. The house had a marvellous terrace with a view of the whole city, an annex office for Father and his books, and was flanked by a massive stone retaining wall. Our own house, Quinta Avileña, in San Bernardino, was rented at the time.

Mother was the first one to survey the house. My room was at the back. It had a large closet and two large windows, through which I could see a white granite patio. When Father had his first government job, we also lived in a luxurious house, but this one was better.

* * *

Mother hired a middle-aged Spanish lady. On her first day, she served hot soup on a flat salad tray. Mother went to her rescue, showed her the soup tureen, made a sympathetic comment and promised to teach her. On my first day on the terrace, I saw a boy playing with his dog in the house across the street. I decided to go down to talk to him.

"Hello. My name is Luis Carlos. We moved here yesterday. What is yours?"

"Gabriel," he said.

I noticed he had cavities and smoking stains on his front teeth and a package of Marlboros in his front pocket. He was wearing khakis, which were too big, and a khaki shirt, hanging out. His hair was curly and he was not tidy at all. He asked me what Father did. I told him he was the Director of the Venezuelan Development Corporation.

"Is that why you have a chauffeured car?"

I told him we also had our own car, a Pontiac, and Father let me drive it sometimes. "Do you drive?" I asked him.

He told me his father had a Ford, which he also drove sometimes, and was a retired colonel who owned a beef distribution company. That's why they always had a freezer full of meat.

"Do you smoke?"

"Sometimes," I said.

He offered me a Marlboro cigarette and took one for himself, lit his and mine with his Zippo lighter, in a fast move like a cowboy drawing a gun. He was trying to impress me. Next day, Gabriel introduced me to the boys on the block and to his family.

Gabriel's father was a chubby, middle-aged bald man with thick glasses. Marisol, his older sister, was overweight; and Elena, his very spoiled younger sister, we introduced that same day to Sis. They were both eleven.

As we became better acquainted, Gabriel told me about his mother, who died six years before. I kept silent because I could see how much he missed her. Thank goodness, I had both Mother and Father!

Next, I met Gabriel's girlfriend and her younger sister, who was twelve, two years younger than I. She was just right for me-- maybe a little skinny, but that could be remodelled.

Back at La Salle in Caracas, I found my friends Marrero and Avellaneda again. Christmas went by, happier than ever, and my birthday was approaching that March.

* * *

I was turning fourteen and Father was taking me to see the motorcycle he promised me last year.

"This is the best motorcycle we have," Don Stelling said to Father and me. "It's a little expensive because it's made in England. But it's the best: hand polished, chrome trim, superb suspension, and 175 cubic inches of roaring engine. Do you want to start it, Luis Carlos?" Don Stelling asked me.

I looked at Father in disbelief and he said, "Go ahead. Start the bike."

I jumped on the bike, pressed the gear pedal to neutral, kicked off the starting pedal, and pumped up the gas handle. The most beautiful purrr... came out of the exhaust. I fell in love with that bike. The bike was as if made for me: the right size, black color, nickel-plated trim, hooded suspension, red leather seat, the perfect weight, everything...

Father went to a corner to talk to Don Stelling. I could see both men smiling, while looking at me. Somehow, I got the impression I reminded them of when they were young.

Father came back and asked me, "Do you like it?"

"Yes!" I said, "It's great.

"Well it is yours, my friend."

How can a 14-year-old boy thank his father for such a moment of happiness? It's impossible! I was the happiest guy in the world. Don Stelling would have the fluids and tires checked and transfer the license plates to my name. The bike would be delivered on my birthday, the fifth of March.

In the meantime, I must get my biker's driving license. I already knew how to ride, because the convenience store delivery guy let me drive his around the block when he made a delivery. One time I didn't stop on time, hit a light post, and ended up with a deep cut exposed to the bone midway below my knee. I didn't tell, because Father would have never bought me a bike. I can still see the scar on my leg.

The bike was delivered on time, and Mother cut a cake which read, "Happy birthday to my little man."

* * *

On a warm April night, only eight months after we moved, Father was pacing back and forth along the terrace from end to end like a caged animal, turning around and pacing again. He did that when he was trapped in a problem he could not solve. I knew we were in trouble. I grew up watching Father worry and suffer. He had to understand why things happened. Life would have been simpler if he just accepted it, but I guess he would then have been somebody else.

Within two weeks, we moved to Maracay, the small city where Grandma María and Aunt Alicia once lived, well known for being the headquarters of the Venezuelan Air Force and for its suffocating hot temperatures. Not rural enough like Acarigua or enough of a city like Caracas. To ensure they didn't stop along the way and ransack our things, we followed our moving truck.

Along the way, Father explained the details of his new appointment to create the Regional Development Bank. Maracay would be the headquarters and Father the president. Later branches would open in every state capital. The government provided 50 percent of the start-up capital and local businessmen supplied the rest. In return, the bank offered low interest venture capital loans to local entrepreneurs.

The creation of this glorified position was only an elegant way to get rid of Father for not being "instrumental" in corrupt dealings and becoming an "honest nuisance." My father's mission now was to convince local merchants to donate 50 percent of the capital and, in return, get working capital loans at reduced rates.

In this town, Father was regarded as important, an organizer who made true on the promises of the politicians without dealing under the table. He was happy with recognition, not money; that's what made him different.

Around that time, I read an article in the paper about my father. The article reported him as the founder of the Internal Revenue Service, author of the first book about income tax in Venezuela, Director of the Central Bank, and founder of the Regional Development Bank. I guess that made Father a useful man, but to me he was much more: my father and friend. What made me most proud was that he was an honest man.

* * *

The year passed, the bank was already operating, and each one of us was doing his bit, except for me, playing the wrong note by not getting good marks. This time I blamed the heat. One day the inevitable phone call from school arrived, inviting Father and me to a 'friendly' meeting at the principal's office.

"Doctor Márquez, please come in. Have a seat. You sit here, Luis Carlos. The reason I called you here is to review Luis Carlos' performance and his attendance record. I regret to inform you Luis Carlos is not achieving the minimum grades. If he persists with this behaviour, he will fail all subjects by the end of the school year."

Father was about to say something when the principal interrupted and said, "Pardon me. One of the reasons why this is happening is that Luis Carlos is absent from class more often than not."

At this point my Father jumped from his chair, slapped me on the right side of my face and shouted, "So many sacrifices I make to send you to school, and this is what you do! Not even come to school!"

Embarrassed, Father grabbed my arm and yanked me out the door, "I will take care of this, Professor Santiago. Have a good day and thank you for letting me know."

I was stunned! Father had never hit me before. He was a gentle man. I mean, he was the most caring, loving, and guiding father ever. The situation made him break his code. I had let him down. I felt miserable. His words hurt me more than the slap on the cheek, because disloyalty to our very own had a special price. How could I have betrayed him?

On the drive home, we did not say a word. That evening after supper, Father approached me, sat on the chair beside me, and began to talk in a soft voice. "Before I was your age I ran away from home. We lived on a small farm. No school, no hopes, a mule, coffee beans, and tropical rain. If I had stayed, I would have been a farm hand and you a coffee bean picking boy. I didn't want that. I am a self-made man who happens to believe learning is the hope for those born without fortune. I didn't have the opportunity to have someone support me while I studied, like you do. I had to make it happen myself. I went to live with relatives, because my father was not there for me and my mother was already gone. Aunt Carmelina, who was not my aunt, and her brother Father Carrillo, who was the parish priest and not my uncle, brought me up. To this day, I still don't know if they did it because I was family, or out of Christian charity, or because I was good at running errands. I had a wooden bed and a small trunk. I went to the public school, ran errands, assisted as altar boy, and later taught grade school. I was given a bit of food, some old clothes, used books, and some time to go to school myself. That was my life at your age! I finished high school when only a handful of kids did."

My mother passed by and wanted to join, and he signalled her to go away.

"I enrolled in law school in Mérida. To survive, I taught Literature and History at the local high school. Luckily, university was free. When I finished third year of law school, I was already working as Secretary of the Civil Court in Mérida. I was nineteen. My point, Son, is I had to work hard to be able to study. You are lucky studying is your only activity."

At that point, tears ran out of my eyes. I realized then he didn't mind providing for me. What tore his heart apart was that I didn't take full advantage of the opportunity and betrayed his trust. I felt so ashamed!

"Look, Father, I promise I will work very hard the reminder of the year to pass all my subjects."

I could tell he was not listening and continued to say, "Luis Carlos, I have decided to send you to a military school in the United States, to see if we are able to make something out of you."

I embraced him, ran to my room, and sat sobbing on my bed. I didn't know what to think. I was fifteen, my father told me I was a failure, and I was being punished with the dream of my life. Is this the way life was supposed to be? It didn't feel right.

Later on, I was sitting on the patio thinking about my life there, and Mother approached me and said, "Your father tells me you are not doing well in school. Why?"

"Well, Mother, it's very simple and very stupid. What happens is that I don't get up on time and I am late. If you are late at school they don't let you in."

"Luis Carlos, please get up early!" my mother said, with a tone of desperation.

"If you fail school, you will disappoint your father. You know how he feels about learning, being responsible, and, most of all, being honest to yourself."

"I know how disappointed he is. I know he doesn't trust me anymore."

"You did it to yourself, Son," my mother said. "Your father is even thinking to send you abroad to one of those correctional schools where they send incorrigible boys," she continued to open my wounds further.

"Mother, they are not correctional."

And she continued, "I am terrified to think you would be going away by yourself. What if you get sick? Who is going to take care of you? And, who will wash your clothes?"

"Mother, they have a clinic and a laundry!"

"Okay, I don't want to think about it. Please, please, get up early, Luis Carlos, and go to school!"

"Yes Mother," I said. "You are not thinking about me. I want to go abroad and learn English. Some of my friends have been since they were thirteen." I continued, "What I don't want is to feel I am being sent there as punishment, like a convict, or if Father couldn't afford the cost. Anyway, before all that happens, I have to pass all my exams this year."

"I still want you to stay," Mother said, caressing my head.

Times were particularly tough. Whenever I felt sad, I sat at Sis' piano and tried to figure out the chords of *Blue Moon* and began to write a piece that began like this:

"My life is small, but my pains are too big to be ignored..."

I had some talent but no one noticed. I couldn't distinguish between sorrow and happiness. I had seen how less fortunate students lived in tiny cramped rooms and had to go outside to sit on folding chairs under the street lamps to be able to study and have a little peace. I had my own room and I didn't even appreciate it. I began to study on the street under a lamppost on the corner near our house to experience how it felt. I wanted to learn to appreciate. I wanted to recover my self-respect again!

The phone rang and I answered.
"Hey, Luis Carlos, this is Enrique. I have not seen you in weeks. Are you sick?"

"No, I am alright."

"Do you want to meet me at the corner?"

"Okay, I will meet you, but I can't stay too long, Enrique. I am doing everything possible to raise my grades before the final exams. I have to make a miracle to pass this year, but I do want to talk to you. Father is sending me abroad. Imagine: abroad! Come to the corner at seven. I must tell you about this."

* * *

Enrique was my best friend. At the time we were both fifteen, the age to validate dreams and draw a map of the future. What career to follow? What girl to marry? Where to travel? At this age, life is 80 percent dreaming and 20 percent doing. One is a kid but is expected to make decisions as an adult. Maracay was a very small town. Activities were mainly related to the Air Force base. Military men were everywhere; even Enrique's father worked for the Air Force. Enrique was the oldest of five children.

"Well, Man," Enrique was talking about women. "Listen; for me there are four types of girls: pretty and dumb, pretty and smart, pretty and poor, and pretty and rich. I am going to marry a girl who is pretty, rich, and smart. No less!"

"But you say there are four types," I commented.

"Well, now there are five," he said and laughed. "What about you?" he asked.

"I don't know. Well, I know she must be slim," I say.

He did marry a rich girl, but it didn't last long and he ended up with a young, poor, and dumb girl. It didn't matter, though, because by that time he was old and rich. He always had his own opinions; that's why he became a publisher.

"We live in an oil-rich country but do not share the wealth," Enrique told me one day, while discussing our fortunes and misfortunes.

"That is because we live in a Third World country, Man," I said.

"What does a Third World country mean?" Enrique asked.

"Well, it means we are not civilized and do not have a sense of justice," I answered.

We were thirteen years old and it was 1954.

Now I am 68 and the memory of this conversation still puzzles me. Nothing has changed since then, except that I have been places and seen more. We had a good friendship but, like many, drifted away.

* * *

After much struggle, I passed six out of seven subjects, all except Literature, because the teacher stressed she couldn't give a passing grade to a student who didn't know how to spell. I couldn't write one word without misspelling it. She didn't give me a passing grade, even though all the questions were answered correctly!

That week Father took me to his meeting at the Central Bank. His colleagues were tickled and set up an extra chair especially for me. I witnessed the agenda and was asked to sign the record at the end. After the meeting, Father and I visited a client who owned a General Motors dealership. At the entrance we were stunned by a yellow Cadillac that was featured right in the middle of the showroom like a magnificent jewel. Father asked me how I would like to own one like that.

"It would feel like a dream," I said.

The date to see the representatives of the American boarding schools was set to August 1956. Father and I went to Caracas to meet with the men from the three schools I selected: Wentworth, Miami, and Riverside Military Academies. Some friends from San Bernardino were already in these schools, which should have made my adjustment easier, whichever I chose.

The appointments were made by letters, and confirmations came attached to the school catalogues. I already had a very good idea which school I preferred. We met Major Alvarez, at hotel El Conde, and as soon as we arrived, the desk clerk let Major Alvarez know Father and I were there.

Two minutes later a Brilliantine black-haired olive skinned man greeted us with a Cuban accent and the ample smile most people have when they want something.

"What a pleasure to meet you, Doctor Márquez! And you must be Luis Carlos, if I remember. Please follow me."

We went to Room Number 308 and the man let us in with a courteous gesture.

"Please, have a seat. Have you brought the application forms we mailed you?"

"Yes, here they are." My father handed them to him.

"Thank you," Major Alvarez said, looking at each one of the forms, assessing us financially and otherwise. "And why, may I ask you, do you think about Riverside as your school?"

"Tradition," I said. "It seems it's one of the oldest and most reputable schools in North America."

"So it is," Major Alvarez said. "We celebrate 80 years this year. Riverside has a student population of 1,500 cadets, most of them also taking military training."

At that time Father said, "I would like to review the financial considerations."

"Of course," the man smiled. "It's all-inclusive. The total cost is US $1,500, covering tuition, books, room, board, uniforms, and even weekend transportation to and from the town of Gainesville. In addition, every school year the student body is moved at no extra cost to Hollywood, Florida, our installation for the winter months. This aspect is very popular with the students."

The last statement hit me right-on. I visualized myself in Florida surrounded by a blond, a brunette, and a redhead, all of whom, by the way, were crazy about me and told each other what gorgeous eyes I had.

Major Alvarez continued by saying, "I do have your application, so when you are ready to formalize your enrolment, please mail us a cheque to the attention of the treasurer, payable to Riverside Military Academy. You should get a letter of confirmation within days, stating your acceptance to the 1956-1957 academic court. It has been a pleasure to meet you, Luis Carlos. I hope to see you at the school this coming September. Thanks for coming, Doctor Márquez. You have a fine young man here. I am sure we will enjoy having him in Riverside."

Father shook the man's hand and we left. Out of courtesy, we went to the other two interviews, because Father and I had already decided. It was simple; Riverside offered more for less, Georgia and Florida.

When the arrangement was finally formalized, I called Victor and Brody, my childhood friends from San Bernardino, who were attending Wentworth and New York Military Academies, to tell them I chose Riverside and was also going to school in the States like them.

* * *

I took off on a journey to rescue a part of me that was wandering around far away, for the first time to meet my future. This one event made me very much what I am today.

This time I was not taken to the airport. It was too painful for Mother, Father, and Sis. We did have a final hug, though, embracing in a circle, signifying our unity. It was a confusing moment, although for my own good. We couldn't let go that easily.

At the airport, Victor and Brody were already lining up for the flight to Miami, wearing their neat Levis jeans and Bass loafers that I liked so much for so long. They saw me and waved as I took my place in the line.

The Pan Am flight to Miami was ready to take off and a knife split me in two. One half couldn't wait to get there and the other couldn't bear to leave. The magnificent Constellation was sitting on the runway, waiting for my dreams to buckle up. The plane took off, leaving the blue Caribbean behind.

As we took to the air, I jerked my homebound half by the hand and I came together again, bursting with joy, anticipation, and adventure. Victor, Brody, and I were sitting a few seats apart. We couldn't get seats near each other.

I was so enchanted that even the airline food tasted good. My flight companion was an older lady who kept asking all kinds of questions. She reminded me of my mother and, at times, Grandma. I guess she was also figuring out whether I looked like her son or grandson. We had at least the remainder of the flight to find out.

I was fifteen, on my own, and in charge!

So far I had only been on a plane once, when Father took us to Barbados on vacation in 1948. Then, the plane was a simple twin-engine DC3; and I had also seen a Constellation only once, when Father brought us to pick up Don Rafael Paris, who was coming from New York on business. But somehow, I knew one day I would also be in one.

I made sure to sit by the window, to see the clouds float under the plane like a huge bed of cotton candy. We were flying at 18,000 feet and in those days that was high. The clouds underneath looked so soft, it gave me the impression that if I fell down, I would bounce.

I ate and drank everything the stewardess offered and smiled at her, ten times more that she did at me. I bet she thought I had a crush on her or something.

We arrived at Miami airport, and everyone rushed to Immigration. I tried to do the same that everybody else was doing. Immigration officials frightened me. I was afraid of authority in general. I had nothing to be scared about. All my papers were in order, but I was still shaking. The sheer size of the place and the profusion of American symbols were overwhelming. I managed to pass the immigration and customs officers, in spite of my insecurities.

After settling at the hotel that evening, Victor, Brody, and I went to Dolly Madison, an ice cream parlour. Victor promised to take me as soon as we arrived. It's supposed to be 'the place.' I was not impressed at all. Two girls sitting in a booth looked at us, but... nothing. We didn't attract the slightest attention, even from them.

The following morning I went shopping for the pair of Levis and Bass loafers I had been dreaming about for years. I had to go by myself, because Victor and Brody had gone to school already.

The next day I overslept and missed my 12:00 pm flight to Gainesville. In frantic fear to fail my report date, I took the first Greyhound bus available to Gainesville. What I didn't know is that it would take twenty-four hours to get there. On the way, afraid to miss my stop, I kept asking the driver every two hours, "Gainesville, Georgia?"

The driver smiled and kept answering, "Not yet."

We changed drivers three times. Around midday the following day, we arrived at a bus station, and finally the driver shouted, "Gainesville!"

I hurried and took a taxi. "To Riverside, please."

* * *

The magnificent red brick building appeared, just like in the catalogue, wrapped by green ivy, a luscious lawn, and willow trees. This could be one of the happiest days of my life. Major Moony was expecting me and took me to the depot. My military gear and books were issued. Just imagine a fifteen-year-old boy like me, who wore baggy khaki pants shrunk way too short over my ankles, now wearing a sharp military uniform, topped by the R.O.T.C. (Reserve Officers Training Corps) patch on my shoulder and the brass Army crossed rifles on my collar. In time, the uniform faded and became a symbol of seniority, but we first-year cadets had to wait a few washings to acquire this sign of distinction.

My gala uniform was a bright royal blue, with shiny brass buttons and a military cap crowned with the school's American eagle brass shield. Work overalls, sweats, winter jacket, helmet, canteen, and combat boots completed my outfit. Very impressive!

Also a real M-1 rifle used in WWII was assigned to every cadet. The M-1 was the first semi-automatic rifle ever issued to infantry soldiers anywhere. General Patton qualified it as "the greatest battle implement ever devised." This equipment would make my next two years bittersweet. It required many hours of shining, brushing, cleaning, oiling, and detailing to keep it up to standard. Everything fitted well, except my rifle and helmet, both too big for my size and made me look like Sad Sack of the comic strip by the same name. I was ranked as a "junior" and began to take subjects requiring little knowledge of English: typing, drawing, math, sports, and military training. I lived now in a barrack: two adjoining rooms separated by a washroom. Each room had two bunk beds, four lockers, a table, and four chairs. The barracks were all connected by walkways.

Bugle at 6:00, breakfast at 7:00, general formation inspection at 8:00, class at 9:00, lunch at 12:00, class from 1:00 to 3:00, sports or military training until 5:00, dinner at 7:00, study hall at 8:00, and tap at 10:00. By the end of the week I had no energy, to the point that some Saturdays I preferred to spend the day in bed.

In the dining room we had to keep full etiquette. Our forearms had to touch the edge of the table. We had to excuse ourselves before sitting or leaving, use cutlery even to eat chicken, wipe our lips before and after drinking, and, of course, not make noises while sipping soup or drinks. There were cadets, wearing white gloves and sabres, on dining room duty, just to watch our every move like owls, ready to catch any little mistake and point their accusing finger, embarrassing the hell out of us.

Out on military training, 'Manoeuvres and Concealment' was my favourite subject. Every year we conducted war games, which almost made my 125-pound body collapse. I wore the complete infantry soldier's outfit, slept in the freezing forest, hid, and ran through enemy fire. The explosives were not real, but if you were to be hit by one, it could have caused serious damage. The war games reminded me of my hide-and-seek game at La Quinta Anauco, because it was just as rough.

We swam in the indoor pool once a week.

Sunday was special, full of events. It began with breakfast at 8:00 am, followed by the most rigorous inspection of the week, in full gala uniform. Every item had to sparkle, including our M1 rifle, which, by then, I'd learned to take apart and assemble with my eyes closed. The Sunday parade took place at the football field from 10:00 am to midday, after which we had steak or chicken for lunch, luxury compared to the normal meals. The townspeople, as a tradition, came to watch the parade. Ex-alumni and families, who came from miles around, were invited to join us for lunch, and their presence as guests of honour was acknowledged. I dreamed that one day I would also be there with my family, to experience such a special distinction. After lunch, we could choose between going to town on the school bus and returning at 5:00 pm or staying and having a good nap.

I used to write Mother, Father, and Sis every week, telling how homesick I was, how much I missed them, and what my wonderful life was like otherwise.

* * *

In Gainesville, signs separated white and black folks. It became clear to me the town was segregated. What used to really get my attention were the 'coloured' signs posted on designated public schools, churches, waiting areas, and washrooms, and the fact blacks had to sit at the back of the bus. It didn't look right.

The town boys didn't like the privileged cadets, nicknaming us "River Rats." But curiously, when they noticed I was Latin American, automatically I was classified as a different breed and placed in No Man's Land.

* * *

1956. My first Christmas away from home. I was invited to spend the holidays with the Jaffa family in Detroit. Richard and Jimmy Jaffa became good friends and asked me to join them up north. The Jaffas were an upper middle class Jewish family.

Father thought it was a fantastic idea, because it gave me the opportunity to stay with a typical American family, share their customs, and enhance my English. On December 15, 1956, Richard, Jimmy, and I took the commuter flight from Gainesville to Detroit via

Dallas. I knew Detroit as the important city where most American cars were made, "the automobile capitol of the world."

Richard's dad and mom were at the airport to pick us up. Richard's parents impressed me. In the parking lot, I noticed Richard's dad drove a burgundy Cadillac, a lawyer like my father who also cared about his image. It seemed "anybody who was somebody" drove a Cadillac these days. The Jaffas' home was very warm and cozy, broad-loomed, fireplace, and very well appointed with paintings and crystal everywhere--a dramatic contrast with my simple, plain home, our eternal leatherette living room, reupholstered time and time again, and our dining and bedroom furniture, several times enamelled.

That evening we had a taste of Richard's mother's cooking, which was delightful. Exhausted, that night we took a warm shower and slept like angels. The bed was soft and thick. I was in Detroit!

We visited Carol, one of Richard's friends who lived nearby, also a Jew. She invited her best friend Rachel. Richard and I arrived around 7:00 pm.

"Carol, this is Luis Carlos, my friend from Venezuela."

"Hi, Luis Carlos. This is Rachel, my friend. Why don't we go to the studio?"

Carol sat near me, and Rachel near Richard. The choice looked very spontaneous, but it was arranged beforehand. I was convinced I had to win every girl I met, or at I least give it a good try. I told Carol my lines about my origins and she told me I had a beautiful accent.

After a while, we went down to the basement, Carol brought canned pops and began to play singles. Dancing gave us the license to get closer. To my surprise, I could even do the steps I watched on TV. We danced some more and then Carol played a slow dance. That was the sign. I embraced her waist and she clutched her arms around my neck. I drew her closer and, in the most natural way, kissed her as we slow-danced. No words. We were fifteen, pretending to be in love.

Life was no different from a dream then. At the end of the evening, around 12:00 am, each one of us gave his girl a final goodnight kiss and walked home. I still remember Carol, a small, shorthaired, freckle-faced girl in bobby socks and penny loafers. When I returned to Riverside, I wrote her a long letter explaining how 'impossible' our love was.

She answered, "Why impossible?"

To me, she was as distant as a star. I never wrote her back. I was convinced we were worlds apart. Years later I asked myself the same question, "Why impossible?" and found no reason. I wonder what turn our lives would have taken if I had an answer then.

* * *

I shopped with Richard for a pair of brogue shoes and a red crewneck sweater. I believed every man should own a red sweater because it gave life a nice twist, especially during Christmas. It was so cold that I bought shoes one-half size too small and a sweater a bit too tight.

The following day we visited Alfred, who lived in a palace. His family owned an automotive parts manufacturing factory. Six cars lined up in front of the house, a super, split-level, modern bungalow with areas as big as tennis courts. Through the back sliding glass doors, I could see green patches of lawn smothered with snow, but still so green that I wondered if they were real or fake. Alfred showed us the lower levels of the house and we arrived at what was supposed to be the kitchen, which looked more like a huge restaurant. I thought a headwaiter could pop up any minute, with a menu under his arm and ask: "Do you gentlemen prefer a table or to sit at the bar?"

Out of plain curiosity, Alfred's sister showed up and introduced herself as Nathalie. I looked at her and said to myself, "This is what a rich, spoiled girl looks like." I was prejudiced, I know, against the over-privileged, because I didn't think they had a 'fair' share. She was wearing a baby blue cashmere sweater, black torero pants, ballerina slip-ons, and a red silk bandana. She had blue eyes and contrasting natural blond hair. Richard and Alfred excused themselves and went to Alfred's bedroom to fetch a jacket, leaving me with this man-eating kind of a girl.

She asked me, "Luis Carlos, do you care for some iced tea?"

"Yes," I said, and before I had time to blink, I was lying on the wool-carpeted floor.

She turned on this huge stereo, really soft, lay back with her legs crossed and her face tilted very close to mine and said, "You have the most beautiful eyes I have ever seen."

All I managed to say was, "They come from my father," and changed the conversation to a stupid subject.

I have this animosity against very rich people for no reason at all. Every time I see them, this thought crosses my mind: "You don't have enough money to buy me." I think it is some kind of inferiority complex I disguise as grandiosity. I feel threatened by them and, even without provocation, turn aggressive. I wonder what would have happened if I'd said to Nathalie, "I think you have the most wonderful lips too," instead of changing the conversation to a stupid subject. But again, it would not have been me.

Richard and Alfred appeared and asked me if I was ready to go. I got up, looked at Nathalie with a clowning sad look, and wrote her off as one more item on my nostalgia list. When I stepped outside, Alfred and Richard were already inside a red Cadillac El Dorado convertible, the car this kid drove to high school! I thought of my simple life back home, sat in the back seat, and enjoyed the ride anyway.

It was snowing outside, and we drove downtown and picked up this girl with short hair.

We continued to Alfred's family cottage and took turns banging her. She was very willing and enjoyed it, and I was baffled because I couldn't make out if she was a 'prostitute' or just a 'loose' girl. Nevertheless I didn't bother to ask.

Alfred went with her first, and then Richard, and with me last. While I was at it, I heard Alfred and Richard giggling outside the room, looked up, and saw them peeking through a screen. I was too busy to care!

On the way back, they asked the girl how was it with me. She smiled and said, "He was the best."

I thought that was cool. For a while I kept thinking I could be the father of a child in Detroit. I was terrified, then worried, distressed, and sad. What an oversensitive kid I was! Am I still?

I attended the Jaffas' Hanukkah celebration and found myself in a private chapel, watching how they pray in front of lighted candles. I didn't understand a word but appreciated their willingness to show me the intricacies of their religion.

* * *

The vacation came to an end and we were dispatched to school again. I wrote home describing the wonderful time I had and sent a thank-you note to the Jaffas.

In January 1957, I reported to Hollywood, Florida, for the spring quarter and began to take proper subjects: Algebra, English Literature, and American History. My uniform had faded and I was beginning to feel a little bit senior.

Around this time, during the American History class, a remarkable thing happened. The old teacher asked those who believed a question to be true to raise their hands. The whole class of 29 raised their hands, all except for me. I realized the compromising position I had taken; but when he asked who thought the question to be false, I raised my hand anyway, as the whole class looked at me like a freak.

The old man declared the answer false, and I was the only one who answered correctly! Everyone was astonished.

Chances are if the majority feels you are wrong, you are wrong--most of the time, but not all the time.

* * *

The bully of the Latin cadet community, Larrazabal, seized a small Cuban guy, wrapped a belt around his neck, and squeezed tightly. The kid turned blue, fell on the floor, thrashing his legs like a dying chicken. Everyone froze. Larrazabal released him, but the kid continued to thrash his legs. We were petrified to realize he could have died, a bad joke that almost turned fatal. Since that day, I despise abusive bullies, bosses, governments, or anybody who takes advantage of the weak.

On Saturdays we went to Hollywood Beach to soak up the sun, watch the girls, and dip into the cool water. I continued to get passing grades, go to Sunday parade, and write my family every week. But good times go by fast, and we were back in Gainesville again.

During the last week I attended an orientation seminar, and the facilitator showed us how to approach admissions offices to secure our university application packages. I discussed the idea of Industrial Engineering with Father many times and described it as a field dealing with efficiency, a combination of engineering, management, and economics. Out of the list of American universities they gave me at the seminar, I selected three: New York, Georgia Tech, and Rensselaer. When I received the admissions packages, I found out I didn't qualify to any of the three; my grades were too low. To make up grade points, I ended up applying to Kilgore Junior College in Texas.

* * *

Now it was time for my summer vacation. Riverside had been my home for nine months, and so far it had been a marvellous
94

experience, but I was anxious to see my family again. Father's extra money arrived. I bought 'L'Air du Temps' for Mother and a pink dress for Sis. I couldn't decide what to buy Father. He wore his belt, wallet, and shoes until they almost came apart, so I decided to get him a new wallet and matching belt.

I had my last breakfast at school and turned in my trunk at the storage room. The taxi was already honking at the steps of the school and I was coming down the stairs pushing my heavy suitcase. "Wait!"
"Where to?" the driver asked.

"To the airport, please. I am catching a twelve-thirty flight."

"We have plenty of time," the man said as we drove off.

I looked back, thinking how fortunate I was to be going home, but my eyes turned a little watery as I left.

When we arrived, a black busboy came along asking, "Need any help?"

"Yes," I said, walked to the counter, checked my bag, gave the boy a dollar, and sat at the side to wait for the flight boarding time. My bag was checked all the way, so I didn't have to worry about that anymore.

The flight left right on time. My next connection was Atlanta, then Miami, Habana, and Caracas. As I approached the Venezuelan coast, my heart raced. The plane began to descend, and I could now see the Caraballeda towers approaching. The lights looked like candles on a giant cake. The runway appeared like a treadmill.

Thud! The tires hit the ground. The engines reversed, announcing I was home again! Immigration and Customs was slow, the baggage belt went around forever, around and around, but eventually my bag appeared. The sliding door opened and, on the corner, I heard Father, Mom, and Sis calling my name. They embraced me and looked at my uniform, over and over. I looked imposing.

As we approached the parking lot, a yellow Cadillac appeared, the same one Father and I saw in the middle of the showroom at the dealership the previous summer. I looked at Father with a questioning face and asked, "Is it the same one?"

"It certainly is," Father answered with the sneaky half-smile he had for special occasions and moments of happiness, as he pushed the key to open the trunk.

I always hugged Father whenever I was overwhelmed by him. This conspiracy had been between us for years. At that moment, I couldn't help but think, "Screw José, Javier, the Jaffas, and the Acarigua farmers. My Father has his own Cadillac now, and it's the top of the line!"

As we climbed the Autopista (highway) towards Caracas, I began to relate the details of my adventure, faking an accent. Sis caught on and said, "You have a funny accent now."

Father snapped, "Of course, he has been almost a year in the United States!" Father was proud and convinced that my short absence guaranteed my foreign accent. I felt guilty about fooling my family and eased out of the feigned accent.

We continued on the road to Maracay, and when we arrived, my heart shrank at the sight of our modest home. The car covered the entire front, too big to fit in the driveway.

* * *

The following day I called Enrique in Maracay, and Victor and Brody in Caracas, to let them know I arrived and make arrangements to meet.

At home, that June evening felt like Christmas as we opened the gifts. Happy faces all around. I couldn't be more fulfilled than I was then, delivering a successful school year and knowing Father was doing well. I was claiming my share of happiness, which everyone is entitled to have once in a while.

From my bedroom I could see Father's magnificent Cadillac. So big! It reminded me of the Packard once parked in front of the Berlins' house in San Bernardino, so out of proportion, which, by the way, was the same yellow color. It seems we hadn't changed that much after all.

Enrique was also on vacation and we met to review our dreams. I told him about my stay up north, without going into much detail because I didn't want him to feel left out. He was holding a day job and going to public school at night. His family was still struggling to get by. But our friendship was not based on who was up or down; we just shared the realities we had. You may call it true friendship.

Sis had a new friend now, Glenda, a relative from Father's side, a beautiful girl, thirteen like Sis. Next door visiting her aunt, there was also a very interesting girl, Marla. She attended school in Boston and was now on summer vacation like me. She had beautiful olive skin, shiny black hair, and wore Bermuda shorts and white ankle socks. I chose Marla over Glenda.

I was flirting with Marla when Hector, one of my friends from Riverside, appeared in Maracay, driving a glitzy, red MG convertible. He was visiting family and stopped to say hello. We were all impressed when he told us about how fast the little car was, and then came up with the crazy idea to race it against Father's Cadillac. That got me stirred me up. I was certain I could beat him. We laughed and said, "Let's do it."

Father was having his siesta, so I got the keys and started the car. In no time, the car was going 100 kilometres per hour, leaving Hector way behind. Why did a tragedy not happen? The higher powers of nature should know; this was one of the stupidest things I had ever done.

The following weekend, Enrique was invited to a fifteen-year-old's party and took a couple of friends and me along. Before the party, we went to a bar and ordered a bottle of rum to 'warm up.' Getting to the party sober was not cool. Once there, I took a few more drinks and out of the blue asked the honoured girl to dance. We went round and around, waltzing.

Suddenly, the room began to swirl, I got sick, placed the palm of my hand over my mouth, and ran. I threw up on the way, leaving a yellow trail of indignity behind me. The girl began to cry in the middle of the room. Once in the washroom, I kneeled before the toilet and let my bitter guts spill out, while angry people banged on the door. In time, I had nothing left inside, took some air, waited until the banging ceased, opened the door, and ran to the street.

That night I dragged myself all the way home, guiding my right hand against the walls and leaning on my right shoulder to stay upright. I got home and found I didn't have my keys. Waking Father was not an option, so I climbed the wall, walked across the roof, and when I was about to jump to the patio, I saw Father pointing a gun at me, yelling, "Quién anda ahí (Who goes there)?"

I yelled back "Vale, soy yo (It's okay, it is I)!" and jumped and zigzagged in the direction of my room, scared stiff to think he could have killed me. He didn't say a word, no use I figured. Why another tragedy did not occur? Again, the higher powers of nature know.

* * *

Undeterred, I continued to do more stupid things that summer. Enrique and I got invited to his cousin's beach house in Ocumare, one hour's drive from Maracay. That chilly morning we tied our backpacks to the grill of my motorcycle and climbed the road to the coastal mountain, spinning like an Amazonian water snake, up into the dense forest, then down to the coast. The road's slanting curves ascended to the mountain peak, and then plunged from 7,000 feet to the coast. It was too hot, and we didn't wear helmets.

We arrived at the mountain peak and parked on the curb to admire the view, take a sip of water and a bit of fresh air, thinking the hardest part of the trip was already over. The rest was downhill and easy. When we resumed, a truck ahead of us (a sixteen-wheeler) was taking almost the whole road. The hydraulic brakes made an airy noise each time, making me anxious. I had to do something.

"Enrique, the first chance I get, I will overtake the sonofabitch."

I saw a short clearance and raised the throttle. It seemed to stretch forever. I was already midway, parallel to its gigantic wheels, when the road grew steep and I accelerated even more to get it over with.

Before I had a chance to overtake the tractor, a 360-degrees horseshoe turn appeared out of nowhere, like the road changed its mind and decided to come back. Coming uphill, another tractor-trailer showed its huge Mack snob face. I got scared, but my instincts told me, "Don't stop!"

I opened my eyes wide, accelerated to the max, and went for the small opening between the two fenders. The great forces of nature intervened, froze the trailers for a millisecond, and allowed the bike to go through. I found a cliff to my right, the edge of a curve going down like a waterfall on my left, and the rest of the upcoming trailer in the middle. Again, my senses told me "Don't stop!" I let nature ride us down. As if in slow motion, the two beasts passed.

I stopped at the edge of the cliff and collapsed to the ground. Enrique's face was as white as paper and I assume mine was red like a tomato. We both took a deep breath and stayed there for a while, looking at each other and the valley below, without saying a word. That day somehow, we were allowed to continue living.

* * *

Little by little, I got into Marla's head and we progressed into 'sweethearts,' but my time ran out. September was here and I was to return to school. Marla and I parted ways with the promise to write, and she gave me a photo with the inscription "Love you forever," knowing well that very few things are forever. I placed her picture in my passport wallet and said goodbye to my true friend Enrique.

I hugged my dearest family again and allowed the fragrance of their skin to linger on. Being the second departure, this one seemed more natural than before. I left believing that everything works out in the end.

Chapter 7

Riverside was like home away from home. It was my senior year, taking regular subjects and making higher grades. My English was more fluent. I felt more at ease in my second year there. My uniform was well faded and I was now getting the respect senior cadets get. I looked forward to Hollywood for the winter and already packed my trunk to be shipped to Florida.

This year Father wanted me to go home for Christmas, even though I was just home six months before. The trip was expensive, but he insisted it was affordable. Anyway, the reality was I had nowhere else to go. Besides, in my family no one knew what was next, so being together while we could was important.

The date arrived. It was December 15, 1957, and I was coming home! The flight went quicker this time and Father was busy, so nobody came to pick me up at the airport. Sometimes it was just not possible. I took my taxi to Maracay and, arriving home, I found Christmas arrangements were well under way.

That year we watched the fireworks, enjoyed Mother's food, and opened our Christmas gifts at midnight as usual. Also, we planned New Year's Eve at cousin Angela's house. On the 31st of December, 1957, in the afternoon, we left Maracay and arrived in Caracas at around 5:00 pm for 'the merriest night of the year.' New clothes, countdown, midnight hugs, fireworks, and wonderful food.

After dinner, Father was relaxing on the porch. "May I borrow the car?" I asked Father several times, "May I? We have a small party in San Bernardino."

"Okay." Out of pure frustration Father handed me the keys, "Stay at your Uncle Marino's apartment in San Bernardino until you hear from me. We'll spend the rest of the night here."

"Thanks Father." I kissed him and ran.

Father loved me more than I will ever know. I could feel he was proud. Later I picked up the Golding brothers, thrilled to show them Father's Cadillac, and when the party was over I went to Uncle

Marino's as agreed. Next morning, Father burst into the room and woke me up. When I saw the expression on his face I realized something was very wrong. He was in an awful rush.

"What? What?" I asked.

"Hurry--give me the keys."

"Father, what is happening?"

"Give me the keys! There is an uprising. I have to attend an emergency meeting. Don't go out of the house. Whatever happens, stay indoors."

The government was being taken down by the Air Force. I called Mother to let her know Father just left for his meeting and I was all right. I turned the radio on...

"Canberra fighter jets have been sweeping the skies of Caracas, bombing government buildings," the radio announced.

Later in the afternoon the coup failed and the government regained control. One may think terrible things happen on rainy days, but that January 1, 1958, the sun was shining bright.

During the meeting, Father was given a bundle of cash, equivalent to what our house was worth along with instructions to "hold on to it." Father spent that night trying to figure out for what purpose the money was given to him, pacing back and forth as he did during complicated situations. Nevertheless, the following day he asked me to accompany him to deposit the money in his bank account.

That night he didn't sleep, thinking about what "hold on to it" meant. I recall Father asking me several times, "What do you think they meant by 'hold on to it'?"

The week continued in relative normalcy, and at the end of the week Father decided to return the money to the same person who gave it to him. Everything returned to normal again and we returned to Maracay, Father to his bank, and I back to Riverside.

On January 8, 1958, I kissed Mom and Sis goodbye. The taxi rolled on until I saw no more of the two dearest women in my life. I asked the taxi driver to stop at the bank, hugged and kissed Father and gave him a final look. His eyes turned glassy. The taxi started and Father shrank into the distance, a small little man with his hand extended in a wave. It felt strange to see him disappear like that.

My father was conscious of life and worried sick about everything. This extreme awareness made him, and also us, anxious, as if something was about to happen any time. It was part of 'This Márquez Thing.' Sometimes something did happen, like the October 1945 Revolution, but then everything came back to normal again. Father fought two simultaneous battles: the world's and his own. Most of the time he won, but he looked much older than he was and less happy than he should have been. I could sense the struggle but failed to understand it.

Back in Riverside, we exchanged stories about Christmas and dared to describe the revolution as a colourful event. In five months I was due for graduation and felt invincible.

In the meantime, back home, the 'Patriotic Junta' called a massive demonstration on January 10 and a general strike on January 21. The Navy revolted on January 22, and the dictator Marcos Pérez Jiménez was overthrown on January 23, fleeing the country with what was left of the nation's treasury. The news that day reported 300 dead and 1,000 wounded.

Heartbroken, Father declared himself hunted; constituted a private tribunal; and appointed himself judge, jury, main witness, and defendant. He declared himself guilty and delivered the penalty of exile. On January 24, he took his family to Aunt Alicia's and boarded a flight to Barbados. My poor Father was now stranded on an island, hopeless. And only a few days previous, he had returned the money so crucially needed now.

Equally disillusioned, Don Simón Bolívar, after liberating a territory twice as big as Western Europe, wrote a few days before his death: "I am old, sick, tired, slandered and badly paid. I only ask as a reward, to rest in peace and the preservation of my honour, which unfortunately is what I cannot get."

This passage sadly reminds me of Father's last days.

My father was an honest man, as much as any man can possibly be, considering honesty comes to us through fear. My father was terrified to see us suffer and willing to go through any situation to protect us. On January 23, 1958, the government overthrown, Father exiled himself to Barbados. For years, I tried to rationalize this decision, coming to the conclusion that it was done more out of loyalty than necessity.

This is the way idealistic men act, with unconditional commitment. Father and I wrote each other every week for five weeks. The last letter I wrote touched on survival, sensing a major decisive moment about to take place.

"Hollywood, March 5, 1958

Dear Father:
I hope you are doing well when you receive this letter. I have been thinking a lot about you and the best way to resolve this issue. Foremost, I do not want you to worry about me. All my expenses are paid until graduation day in May, and then I can take a job here in the United States, as soon as I graduate. I already talked to the Jaffa family from Detroit, you remember the friends I spent the Christmas before last at their home, and they have promised to help me to continue university there. They have very powerful friends in Detroit, who own many industries. The most important thing now is you, how to keep you safe and healthy. I am thinking the best place for you to be would be here in the United States with me. I am wondering about what would the most practical way be to go about that and conclude that you should come now and stay here in Gainesville until I graduate, and then we both could go to Detroit and work this thing out together and later on bring Mother and Sis. Please let me know what you think

about these ideas, because we should act fast. Please take care of yourself.

Benediction, your son that loves you,

Luis Carlos

PD: Today I turned seventeen, and I am grateful to have a father like you."

Two weeks went by, without any news from Father, not a good sign. I knew instinctually that something was wrong to prevent Father from writing in two weeks.

I went over the context of my last letter to him time after time, wondering if he understood that he was the most important person in our family and his health was paramount. Our letters were written on weekends and mailed on Mondays, arriving in Barbados or Hollywood one week later. By the following Monday my uncertainty became unbearable. I was confused. Confirming my doubts, the following day I was summoned to the office of Colonel Beaver, the academy's vice-president.

"Cadet Márquez reporting, Sir."

The Colonel said, "Please sit," and continued. "We have been contacted by your family, informing us that your father is very ill in Venezuela. We have made arrangements for you to travel there at once. Major Mooney is going to accompany you to Miami, to request an emergency passport at the Venezuelan Consulate, and purchase an airline ticket for you. All the expenses have been already covered. I wish you an uneventful trip. Of course, you are welcome to return to the school after this matter is resolved."

As soon as the colonel finished, I established something was very wrong. My father was supposed to be in Barbados, not in Venezuela. He was in good health, not very ill. My presence had never been required this way before. Knowing how my family functioned, this was an extreme case; otherwise they wouldn't have required my presence. Nothing made sense, except that Father was near death or already dead. Besides, I knew in the bottom of my heart that Father would eventually get into something he could not handle, not even pacing and pacing, but still I refused to accept it. "It could not be!"

I didn't comment. I found it unnecessary.

"I will pick you up at 10:30 at the main gate to take you to Miami. Be ready," Major Mooney said.

"Yes, Sir," I answered in a faint voice, my head tilted down, as if speaking to a bottomless well.

Major Mooney and I rode to Miami. We didn't speak during the trip. We both felt if we did, we had to explain, and neither of us wanted to do that.

In a couple of hours I was holding my emergency passport and airline ticket and heading to face my reality, which I tried in vain to dismiss. During the flight I reviewed the situation a dozen times, arriving at the same conclusion: Barbados, Venezuela, illness, death. I concluded Father was already dead and understood that, out of compassion, no one dared to tell me.

Paradoxically, our first trip abroad including Father was to, of all places, Barbados. I was seven and Sis four. At that time life was bright; we enjoyed the island to the max. We went to the beach, had meals on the terrace and afternoon tea in an old castle. Father bought a linen suit, fine cotton dresses for Mom and Sis, and shoes made in England for the whole family. Ironically, his last trip had to be also to Barbados. I imagined him pacing and pacing, getting more desperate as time went on, until he could not take it anymore. I felt for the first time, life had let Father and me down. If we had more time or more money, things could have turned out much different. I also felt I'd contributed by writing my last letter. With good intentions, I felt I put forward the wrong proposition,

"The most important thing now is you, how to keep you safe and healthy. I was thinking the best place for you to be will be here in the United States with me."

Such an offer was unacceptable to him. I was convinced my message and the fact that he returned the much needed money, less than four weeks prior to that, killed him.

I felt guilt and rage and cried while looking at the cotton clouds below. When I arrived in Caracas, my cousin Rafael was waiting for me. His grim-looking face told me the story.
"Don't lie to me. He is dead. Isn't he?" I said, anticipating him.

"Yes, he is."

No more to be said, like the last page of a book. We got into the car, took the highway to the city, and on the way Rafael related the events of the last hours. My father's funeral took place at Graciela Márquez' house, in the same place we were during the October 18, 1945, Revolution. Very important people were present. Father was buried two hours before. Following the funeral, some people accompanied Mom and Sis to Aunt's Alicia house, where they were staying for the time being.

Very little else was said.
When we arrived, Mother was sitting in the middle of the room. When she saw me she burst into tears and said something incoherent. All I managed to say was, "Mother, why are you crying?"

The question was out of context; the answer was obvious. But that is all I could think of to say. I still don't have a clear understanding why I asked that. Maybe I didn't want to accept what was happening. I knew it was impossible, but the thing I wanted the most at that time was to have Father with us. And, I know it sounds absurd, the thing I dreaded most was not to be able to continue my education. The imprint that "those without fortune (not born rich) had no other choice than to have a good education" was so embedded in me by Father, that it superseded the horrible fact of his very own

107

death. How was I to continue my education now? How was I not to defraud him once more?

A dozen people, among them Dr. Gonzales, Father's dear friend, stayed. After a while, he called me aside and whispered, "Luis Carlos, don't worry about your studies. I'll take care of that."

I was unable to respond. But I did say to myself, "Some people are blessed with faithful friends. Father was one of them."

This wonderful man became my mentor and protector, until the very end of his own life. He took it upon himself to make sure I had all the opportunities I needed. He was the most important legacy Father ever left me. He remains in my memory as the man waving his hand from across the room, always ready to help. The most faithful, trusted, and loyal friend anybody could ever have had. Because of his good heart I still had a future.

After a while, people left, one by one, expressing a last thought about how sad this day was. Everybody highlighted the fact that my father was an honest, brilliant man and died too soon at 43.

That night, I looked up at the stars and could not stop crying. I thought, in a way, "Better that I didn't get to see him." The sight of Father dead would have been unbearable. In this way I wake up every day with my last memory of him as he was in a last picture taken in Barbados that I found in his passport wallet. He was sitting around a table having a couple of drinks with some friends, smiling. I wonder what day this picture was taken and by whom.

I used to fantasize someday finding him alive as if nothing happened. Like the day in 1944, after Mother was treated for her 'sadness,' when he picked me up from my exile over at Aunt Alicia's, I would not ask any questions. Father would now be 93.

Sometimes, I too make crucial mistakes, invite tragedy, and get myself into hopeless situations, following the tradition. The higher forces of nature must have spared me from catastrophe, because I should have died at least a dozen times. I have more lives than a cat!

"Why could he not be protected like me?" Sometimes I think he might have chosen his end, because he must have known in Barbados he didn't have a chance, didn't even know the language! I reconstructed Father's last hours, pacing back and forth.

Out of desperation, my Father hanged himself on the island of Barbados on his 43rd birthday, in silence, leaving a huge emptiness behind, two months after his arrival and a few days after I turned seventeen. The soldier fell; the battle of life was lost.

I am convinced if he'd kept the money given to him in January 1958, he would have come out alive. His most outstanding quality, honesty, killed him.

As well, my mother broke down and gave up without him. What else could she do? They were not two but one. At 40 she fell into depression, staring at the sky, looking for answers that never came. Why? Reasons were important to her. She stopped living, piece by piece, for the next 48 years. She spent the rest of her life searching, eventually falling into dementia. Her time came, Sis tells me, while sitting in the chair where she spent most of her later years. She also left in silence.

I picked up the suitcase, placed it on the bed, and opened it, a strange feeling tampering with Father's personal things. Inside, I found the remains of his life: some clothes, two pairs of shoes, toiletries, documents, his watch, and his passport wallet. Father carried few things, like a man on the run, on his final trip.

I was searching for a message, something helpful, something meaningful. I examined his clothes and his Tissot watch, and set them aside; they all reflected his conservative style. Next, I studied the documents, one by one. Four caught my attention: a life insurance certificate, the deed of the Guanarito land, a financial statement, and the passport wallet. I looked closer at the life insurance certificate and noticed it was issued by La Seguridad one year before.

Instantly, a feeling of guilt engulfed me: Even in moments of extreme sorrow, I was still driven by my own interest first. It was pitiful. My father lay dead and here I was looking for life insurance money. To justify it, I added a thought disclaimer, "That shows how desperate the situation is."

I finished reading it, placed it aside, and said to myself, "Tomorrow I should call the insurance company to find out more."

I continued with the deed to the land in Guanarito, which was much more complicated. I read it a couple of times and interpreted it as a "conditional buy and sell" contract. It contained a clause whereby the seller had an option to buy back, for five years, by refunding the original amount received. As far as I knew, this hadn't happened. The retract clause was valid for three more years, after which the deed would be final. The last document was a copy of a balance sheet, which Father filed as a requisite for public office. On paper, it seemed we had some assets, all of no use to save Father's life.

* * *

The next day my Aunt María called, to find out if Sis and I were willing to meet with her. She had news relating to Father, which she wanted to share with us. Anything having to do with Father was important and took priority. We arranged to see her the next day.

Sis and I arrived at Aunt María's house and she greeted us as amicably as the few times we had met her before. My Aunt María was a replica of Father: almond hazel eyes, aquiline nose, and that intellectual air that she exhaled from every pore.

She made us feel relaxed, served coffee and cake, and began to relate some passages from her life. She read us two poems, part of her latest series. In one of them she made reference to Father, her dear brother. When she sensed the time was right, she told us that we had a brother about seven and a sister about five. Their mother was Teresa Gutierrez, the maid who came to our house in 1947 who became Father's mistress.

She felt we should meet them and Father would have wanted it this way. I was inclined to comply, but still we told her that we preferred to take no action without mother's approval of such a delicate matter. We agreed to tell Mother and get back to her as soon as possible. As we expected, Mother never accepted our meeting the kids. The discovery made me more aware of Father's desperation in Barbados.

I continued to review the findings, hoping to clear our situation. But in the end, only three effects were helpful: the financial statements, the life insurance, and the title to the land. All in all, it was a fairly substantial estate, and it seemed incomprehensible how Father could have succumbed because of lack of funds nevertheless. I had no idea how the funeral, my trip, and Mom's and Sis' expenses were being paid. I didn't dare to ask. I was terrified of the answer. I was the man of the house.

Dreadful considerations kept coming into my head: "How am I to finish school? Will I be able to go back to Riverside? If so, will I be able to concentrate and graduate?"

I had no answers. I decided to wait for developments and the answers to come and then decide in terms of what Father would have wanted me to do. To encourage Mom and Sis I told them, "Don't worry. Everything will be all right. Besides, I will finish school in a few weeks and will find a job. The family will go on. Trust me."

Just like Father used to say, as if he or, for that matter, I, really knew.

We continued to stay at Aunt Alicia's house. Mother was outright pessimistic. I didn't blame her. The fact that we were not the only ones in Father's life was enough to destroy her. From then on, she wasn't able to cope, even with the simplest tasks. She didn't have the will. Thinking about daily things became very hard for her; doing them was just impossible. We moved from Aunt Alicia's to Cousin Angela's home, until new developments should arise.

The following day a miracle happened. I received a telegram stating that the Board of Directors of the Development Corporation had awarded me a full scholarship.

"In recognition of your father's great dedication and outstanding contributions to the organization, I have the pleasure to inform you that the Board of Directors have endowed the recipient with a full scholarship to allow him to continue his education, until such a time as the recipient receives a professional degree, without limitations, including round- trip air tickets to return to Riverside and finish the school year..."

I was to sign an agreement, pick up my round-trip air ticket and first month's allowance and go. I realized the souls of my brother Alvaro and Father and the hand of Doctor Gonzales were all behind this resolution. In addition, that same day another telegram came from the government informing Mother that she had been awarded a "lifetime pension" from the Ministry of Finance, also in recognition of Father's "important contributions to the country," the same country that two months ago persecuted Father (or so he thought) and drove him to his death on the little island of Barbados.

I wept when I read these letters and so did Mom and Sis. The scholarship was enough to sustain me through university in the United States. "What irony, more than enough money to sustain the whole family for the next five years!"

They were willing to pay all this money to a dead man's son, and a lifetime pension to his widow in recognition of her husband's efforts, but they were not willing to pay anything to keep him alive. The country's social norms wouldn't allow a member of a fallen regime any compensation after the fall.

I felt repulsion about the social norms and guilt and shame about using the money. I felt, like someone forced to do something indecent to save my life. Nevertheless, I kept the scholarship in honour of my father. I was not going to let my morals stand in my way this time, as Father did when his turn came. I kept half of the scholarship and gave half to Mother. The rent from our house, the scholarship, and Mother's pension were enough to keep the family going for five years.

For a while I didn't have the courage to visit Father at the cemetery. Not a place for him or for me to meet. I kept his memory clean and fresh within, and there is where it belonged. Blessed are those who are well remembered; they live longer. But when the time came to go, it became impossible for me to leave without saying good-bye to my Father, as I always did.

"Taxi! Al Cementerio General del Sur, por favor. Too much traffic today?"

"It gets worse every year," the taxi driver said.

His radio was playing *Hola, Soledad* and I said to myself, "It's so true; sometimes we feel so lonely." There was silence for a few minutes. I was watching the cars honking, zigzagging, turning, and crossing lanes back and forth in an effort to save a few minutes. Another moment of silence and a motorcycle cut off the driver.

"Carajo! I almost hit the son of a bitch! If you hit one of them, you are doomed for life. He would argue that you tried to kill him on purpose, because you hate bikers; and taxi drivers are their worst enemies, because they have to suffer the traffic we create. Anyway, I am prepared for this. I am faster than they are."

The cab driver himself changed lanes without warning, and changed lanes again, stepped on the gas and stopped.

"Visiting someone, at the cemetery?"

"Yes, my father," I said.

"I see," he said.

"If you are getting him flowers, the ones on the left lane are the best. He will like those better than the ones on the right lane." He continued, "What happens is that the ones they sell on the right lane are those left from the day before. We call them the 'forgotten' flowers."

Until then, I had no intention of buying flowers. I didn't think it was necessary, but I decided to do it, and why not buy the better ones? The ones on the left lane did look fresher.

When we arrived at the front entrance, he stopped on the curb, closed the meter, and said, "Son diez bolívares."

"Sure." I handed him fifteen and told him to keep the change. At the same time, I thought, "This is a lot of money," until I realized it was the equivalent of three dollars.

He reminded me, "Remember the flowers on the left lane are the best."

"Okay, I will remember," I said. I closed the door behind me and waved to the driver. I felt like beginning a new chapter of my life.

Once inside, I walked toward a sign that read 'Oficina.' I walked in and found an older man reading the paper. He looked at me and continued to read. After so many years in charge, he was able to distinguish the ones who came to buy from those who came looking for information. I made a small noise, like coughing, to make him aware of my presence, but he continued to ignore me. He reminded me of people I dislike, those who ignore us when we need them most. I deserved to be acknowledged. Then, I asked with a firm voice, "Can you please tell me where Block 37 is?"

Without looking at me he murmured, "Look at the map on the wall," and continued to read. To my frustration I couldn't read the map. When I was about to approach him again, to my surprise, he put the paper down and said, "I will take you." I guess he figured this was the only way to get rid of me and continue to read his paper in peace.

As I followed him along the narrow paths leading to my father's grave, he turned around and asked: "You are his son, aren't you?"

"I'm sorry?" I said, pretending not to hear his question.

114

"You are his son," he repeated, but this time not asking.

"What do you mean?"

"Well I have never seen you around here before," he said.

"No one has visited your father for five years. I can tell the ones that forget from the ones that never forget but never visit."

The old man startled me, because my father was buried two weeks ago. Was he visualizing the future? Now, I was passing judgement on myself: Am I the kind who forgets? Or am I the kind that never forgets but never visits?
"Here we are," the old man said.

"Manuel María Márquez h., 1915-1958." He pointed. "You may see me on the way out if you want to make improvements to your father's grave."

"Sure," I said.

He turned around and left.

I stood there looking at the naked stone, noticing it was so bare! Then I read the one next to Father's. It belonged to my grandmother and said: "María Pacheco de Molina 1870 - 1953." They were buried in the same lot, which had two niches. Father was buried in her lot, because there was no money. The irony was that my father and my grandmother never got along well; they were always directing poignant sarcasms at each other. By Destiny's will, they were now lying side by side, for who knows how long. If they knew this was going to happen, they would have complained.

I looked to my left and there was a skinny stray dog looking at me with eyes wide open, a unique breed, a little bit of everything. He looked hungry and thirsty, and his tongue was hanging out.

Then a noise of flapping wings came from the right, a black sparrow landed on my grandmother's grave, turned its head and looked at me. A backlash hit me and I began a journey back in time, accompanied by my father, my grandmother, a stray dog, and a blackbird. Surprisingly, it all made sense.

I returned. I was looking at my father's grave in the public cemetery, where people that had no fortune were buried. There was no sign of love or respect for the dead or money buried here. Everything was dilapidated, dirty, and abandoned. It all made me sick.

"Why dump the remains of Father this way? If there was no money for a private cemetery, would it not have been better by cremation? Would it have made any difference to him, anyway?"

Somehow, even today I feel guilty and ashamed that my father is buried there, under those awful conditions. I wished he could have weeping willows, green fields, and flowers around him, and water to keep them fresh.

I cared about Father, but was the sorrow I felt about him or about me? Was I saddened because he was not alive, or because I didn't have him anymore? Anyway, all that was left were memories and stories; they needed no specific place. Why should this matter? I don't know, but it did. Why did I feel anguish? I don't know, but I did.

* * *

April 15, 1958. I kissed Mom and Sis goodbye and returned to Riverside to graduate. The flight was lonesome and the future challenging. The word had spread, and all my friends, without asking too many questions, encouraged me. I thanked them for their support and for not duelling on the subject. I was back to finish high school in honour of my father and move on with my life. I studied hard to catch up and when exams came I was well prepared and made all the passing marks.

The graduation ceremony was scheduled for the last week of May. The night before, I brushed my gala uniform, polished my shoes and insignias mirror-bright, and arranged everything for the important date.

That night I dreamed I was lost in a horrible neighbourhood. I didn't recognize the place or the people and could not find my way out. My dream was similar to my real life, uncertainty all around.

The following day, I marched into the auditorium to the front rows where the graduating cadets were to sit. The rest of the student body followed, then the relatives of the graduating students. For me, it was a day of mixed feelings: proud, happy, sad, and lonely. No family present and no father to feel proud of me. I filled the emptiness feeling very proud of myself, all by myself. And, I became conscious that circumstances don't matter; on the contrary, they could give us enough reasons to want to succeed.

I also have to confess that of all the roads I'd been required to walk, the hardest and most painful was the one I had to walk through my father's death. I was so attached to my father, I felt like a kite whose line had been cut and has flown away to the unknown. From that day on my life became 'before and after,' a direct consequence of that event that dictates every step of the way, until the present day.

After the graduation ceremony was over, I reviewed it again in my own private version. I saw Alvaro, my brother who didn't make it, sitting in one of the rows wearing a cadet uniform at the age of seven and Father sitting beside him at the age of 43. They were both smiling.

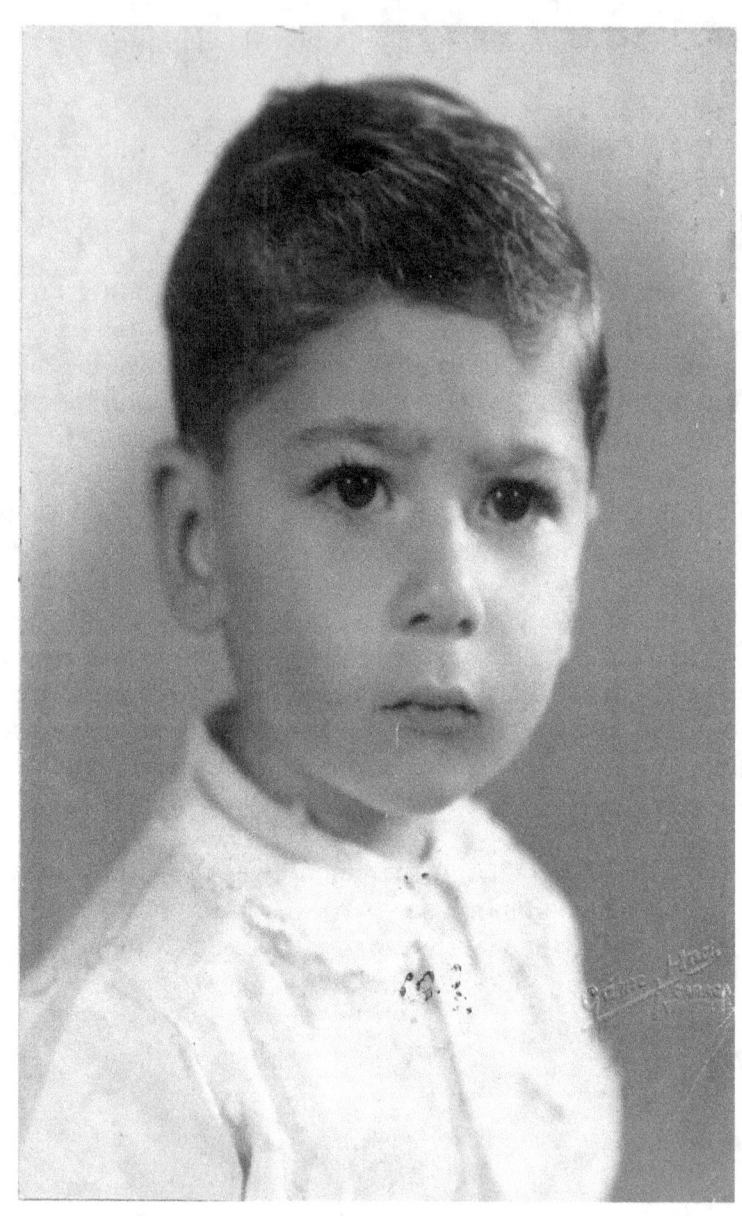

The author, Luis Carlos Márquez, age 5 (1946)

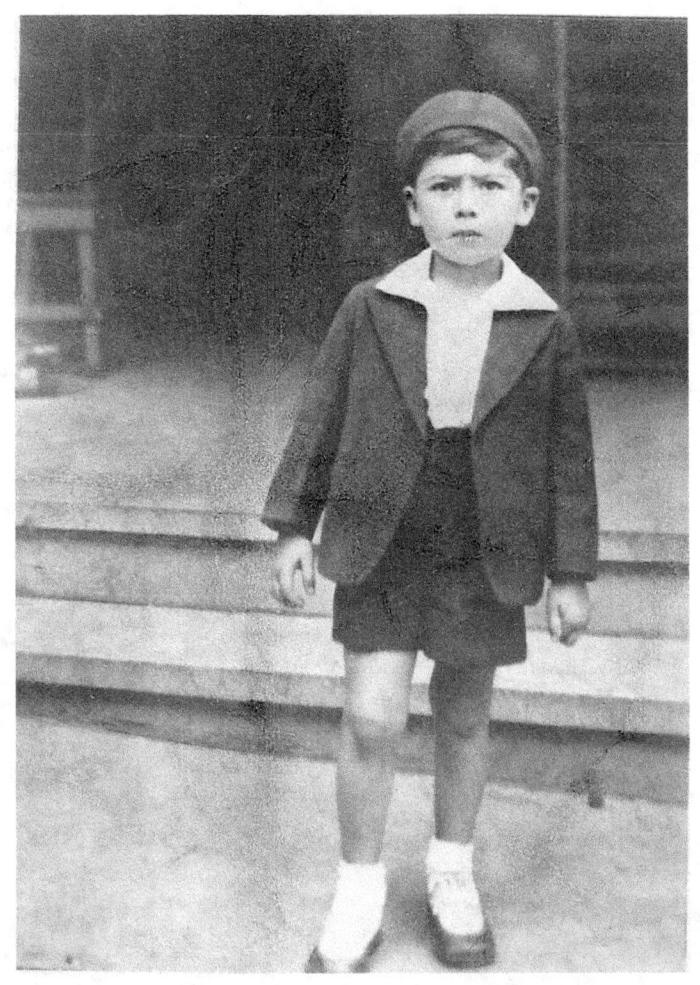

The author, Luis Carlos Márquez, age 7 (1948)

The author, Luis Carlos Márquez, age 17, Riverside (1958)

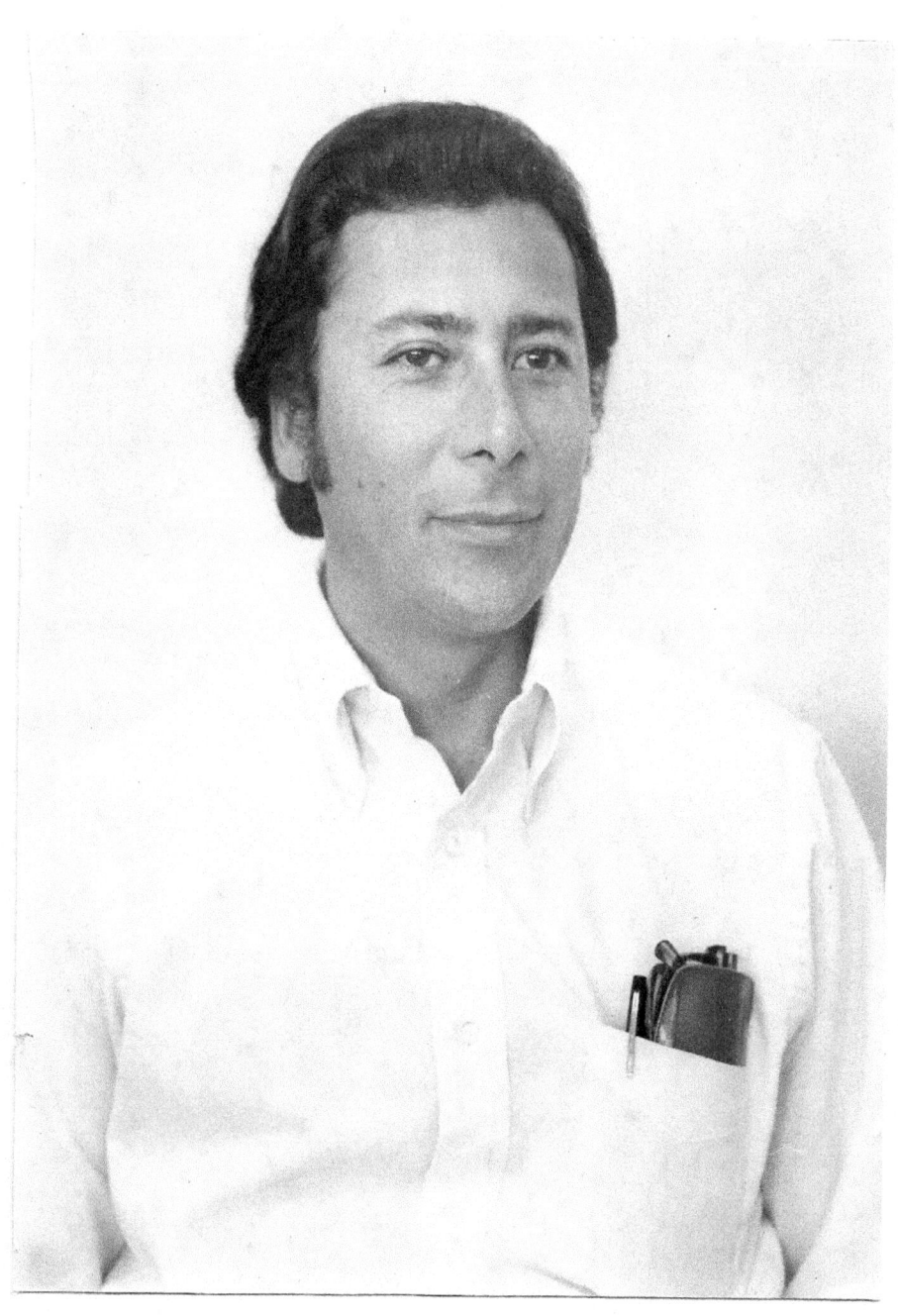

The author, Luis Carlos Márquez, age 27 (1968)

The author's father, Manuel Maria Márquez, age 40 (1955)

II
The Price of Silence
(Memories 1959 – 1969)

She came into my life, when I was too young to know better
Ten years ahead of me
A ray of fresh air, a breath of life from the sea
She came at dawn, when I needed her most
And I paid the price of silence.

Then vanished with my sons, behind a curtain of lies
Leaving me behind
While the sun kept shining bright, for everybody else
She is always here, like a stigma from the past
And I pay the price of silence

No more…

Chapter 8

~

Guilt is the cancer of the soul.

~

I felt a compulsion to live the rest of my life the way Father would have lived his, including his pains and joys. I was part of 'This Márquez Thing.' His tragic death changed my life forever. For some time the puzzle was like a broken mirror; the pieces didn't fit.

For years I blamed the country for failing to protect him, and began to admire those countries that protect their own people. I also blamed my mother for not being with him in his time of need, for not having been able to persuade him to make a better choice, and for losing our family home, in spite of the fact that I sent her part of my scholarship for that specific purpose.

It took me a long time to understand that blaming was not the answer. At the end of the day whatever happened, happened, and there is nothing we can do to change it. No one can live somebody else's life or save anyone from his or her own destruction. It's upon each one of us to make things happen, one way or another, because everything could be changed by us or by Nature.

At first, I didn't have the courage to endure the inevitable psychological ordeal required to live, and just recently I have come to terms with that reality. For instance, it took me a long time to accept: argument for its own sake (it is futile), arrogance (it reflects ignorance), honour conflicts (they disguise egotism), grudges (they cause self-destruction), saying everything is unnecessary, and so on, and on and on...

Most of all, I loved my father. There is a fundamental reason why I loved his story, how he placed others' wellbeing ahead of his own, and the countless ways I loved him. Of course, some aspects about him I disliked, but since those were subject to personal choice, I disregarded them. Because who was I to judge? I was his refuge and confidante. During hard times, I was the place he ran to hide whenever overwhelmed, to feel a little safer, despite that I was just a child.

* * *

After graduating from Riverside, I came home and found Mom and Sis had moved to a small apartment in San Bernardino, on the same street and right across from our former house, in the same building where my Grandma María lived for years. It was a nice, quite modest apartment on the fourth floor. I recognized the same furniture, placed very much in the simple old way. I was glad to find they had managed to put together a home again. I was back, with my goal accomplished, and ready for my summer vacation.

This new encounter with life was refreshing, like spring after a long winter. Everything smelled fresh again. The apartment had two bedrooms, one for Mother and one for Sis, a washroom, kitchen, and living room. Mother placed a cot for me in her bedroom. The atmosphere was relaxing, and coming back to San Bernardino at seventeen was just what I needed. Most of my old friends were still around: Rafael, Victor and Brody…

Life did not stay still. Victor's grandpa died the previous April and Brody lost his front buckteeth, biting an 'arepa,' a Venezuelan corn muffin. Victor and Brody also graduated that year from high school and had to find jobs, because their families couldn't afford college.

Rene died at seventeen, my schoolmate at La Salle who lived across from Don Chucho. It made me realize how fragile life is.

Another surprise, Enrique, my old friend from Maracay, moved, of all places, to San Bernardino. He rented a room there, worked as a bank teller during the day, and went to journalism school at night. To this day, I still have a hard time understanding that coincidence, because Caracas was then not a small city and Enrique ended up, out of pure coincidence, right beside our house, which was rented, and across from the apartment where we were living. The odds of that happening (without being planned) were very small, but it did.

Enrique and I now had more chapters to share and many things to confide. He told me about his dream of one day becoming a famous publisher, like Armando de Armas, who owned a chain of tabloid magazines. I told him about how lucky I was to have my scholarship and my decision to become an industrial engineer, like Father wanted.

Enrique, cautious about image, told no one about the room he rented and fabricated a story about living with his rich aunt. The so-called rich aunt was in fact a spinster, who also rented a room in the same house. Convenient for the story, she did well, because she worked as an executive assistant for Shell Oil, to the point that she drove a spanking new dark green Cadillac Coupe de Ville, which fit the image of a rich aunt. Enrique asked me to keep the secret, which I promised to do. To drive the point home that summer, when the lady took a two-week vacation to the Caribbean, Enrique sneaked out the car keys from her room, and for several days we drove the car all over Caracas. From that point on, there was no doubt in everybody's mind that Enrique indeed was living with his rich aunt!

That summer, we went to La Rinconada racetrack, where Enrique's younger brother worked as a gatekeeper and let us in for free. The little money I saved was bet on the horses, hoping to strike it big, which never happened.

Brody and Victor by this time were forced to find jobs. During their stay in the United States, at least they managed to learn English, which allowed them to find better jobs. Brody became a flight attendant for Pan Am and Victor worked as front desk clerk for Hotel Tamanaco, while Enrique had to work as a cashier at Banco Unión and study journalism at night. I was the only one on vacation from college and didn't have to work, but I was also the only one who didn't have a father. Life is full of contradictions.

* * *

Each one of my friends had a sister, and this time I was surrounded by girls. Not that I was overly preoccupied by this, only fascinated. I thought they were such a wonderful invention!

Sis was now fourteen, and had developed as quite an attractive young lady. She inherited Mother's brunette hair, huge, very expressive brown eyes, and an ample sweet smile, which she put to good use, making people think they had to do what she wanted for their own good. Many guys around the neighbourhood now noticed her and called me "Brother-in-law."

Two guys in particular, were infatuated with Sis and began to befriend me to get on her good side. They were about five years older than I and had their own cars. One, William, lived on the street behind us in San Bernardino, already studying architecture at the Central University but not making very good grades. His father owned the oldest and most exclusive toy store in Caracas, La Mina, where Mother, like most middle-class ladies, used to buy toys. Billy, as everybody called him, was very popular among the girls, but Sis had total control over him.

The other one, Alfredo, was the oldest son of a well-known army general. He studied in the United States and lived in Santa Monica (the neighbourhood where we lived during Father's last government job, before we moved to Maracay). Alfredo drove around in an Austin Healey sports car and came all the way just to see Sis.

Incidentally, around that time, Rafael, my cousin, came to visit, saw Sis, and called me aside and said, "Luis Carlos, your sister is wearing her pants too tight. You should tell her." I hadn't noticed. I didn't see anything wrong with it, because in the States girls wear their pants tight and nobody thinks anything of it. It is considered fashionable. Our country was more conservative.

Soon, summer was over and I had to get my things ready to start college. The only confirmation of acceptance I received was from Kilgore Junior College, a small community college in Texas, well-known for their petroleum science courses, the basketball team, and the Rangerettes cheerleaders, dressed in their red and blue miniskirts and kicking their heels up high.

In mid-September, 1958, I boarded the Pan-American flight back to school. So many changes at once made me grow up in such a short while. I had put on some weight and looked older. Once more, I kissed Mom and Sis and promised to take my vitamins and to write. The going-away scenes were becoming more frequent. For a few years I would be split, a foot here and a foot there.

On the way to the airport I felt a little sad to leave my family and friends but also fortunate to have the opportunity to go to college and, even more, to go abroad. This was not supposed to happen. I felt my life was very complete. I had a few friends, what was left of my family, and the opportunity to continue my studies, a luxury my friends didn't have.

This time I stopped in New York for three days on my way to Texas to try personally, for the last time, to be accepted at New York University and to visit New York, at least once, since the air ticket allowed me the stopover without additional cost. At the airport, I made a reservation at the Alamac, a reasonably priced hotel that had made its mark among the penny-pinching Latin American clientele. On arrival, I paid the taxi driver the exact fare, considering the fact I was a student, but he was not about to forgive the distinction. He threw my luggage on the street and called me a "cheap son of a bitch." I knew from the movies that New York taxi drivers were a breed of very unfriendly animals, so I did not take it personally.

The hotel was okay and well situated for the price. I showered and went to a nearby steak house for dinner. That night I lost my passport somewhere along the way. I was in big trouble now, because my student visa was stamped on it.

Then, what I thought to be impossible occurred, one of the many lucky things that have happened during my life. I received a call from the New York Police Department notifying me they had my passport. Someone had found it and turned it in. Of course I was thrilled, but most of all amazed, that in such a gigantic city there was an honest, good soul and an extremely well organized police department. I figured they must have gone to the trouble of checking my inbound immigration record into New York to find out in which hotel I was staying. Marvellous!

The next day I went to the police station and the officer who handed me my passport said: "Kid, you sure are lucky to have found your passport in this city!"

I said, "I know. I have a guardian angel that looks out for me." He looked at me, puzzled.

That day I went to my appointment with the admissions officer at New York University. She told me I didn't have enough 'quality points' to be accepted at the engineering school. I knew it, but still had hoped to overcome that deficiency with my brilliant personality. It did not happen. I took that rejection well; I knew it was justified. I just had to try harder at Kilgore and transfer to a higher ranked university later.

From there, I went shopping at Macy's for a new pair of Levis, Bass loafers, and a cardigan sweater to look just like the guys in *The Many Loves of Dobie Gillis* TV series for my first year in college.

The next day I took the Delta flight to the Southwest, because I had no other place to go.

Once there, I found the people friendly and the weather as close to home as possible. The fact that it was an oil and cattle state made it similar to my home country. Being on my own with enough money, not in the care of any boarding school or family, gave me a unique sensation of freedom. I interpreted my scholarship as a job, and had every intention of doing well for my sake, Mother's and Sis,' and for Father's memory.

Kilgore ended up being a very pretty southern college town, complete with a main street cinema and a few family restaurants, with chicken fried steaks, mashed potatoes, gravy, carrots, and peas always on the menu and ever-playing jukeboxes.

Being my first year at college I decided to live in the dormitory. I went to the registrar's office and paid my tuition, room, and board. The procedure was simple. I didn't have any complications. This community college just wanted you, period, like the army.

I came back to the dormitory, gave the housemaster a copy of my receipt, he assigned me a room and handed me the keys. His name was Mr. Johnson, but students called him 'Dodge.' I never found out why. He was a tall amiable man, also coach of the Kilgore basketball team, and gave me the impression that if he got mad he could throw you around like a basketball. He lived in a small apartment on the ground floor by the TV room. I went back to my room and unpacked the few items I brought with me. "A man on the move must be a light traveler." Later, I took a walk to the city centre, which was about fifteen blocks from the dorm.

Walking alone, in a small town, was a unique experience: no one to guide you, no friends, family, or knowledge of the place. Fortunately, the feeling was temporary, although shocking at first. I was in college now, on my own. Every step of the way was full of first discoveries.

Turning left, I found a string of houses, beautiful green lawns, a Baptist church on the corner, a small cafe, a rooming house, and a stretch of street becoming more commercial. I stopped at a music store, window shopped, and delighted myself with the tremendous array of record covers: Elvis Presley, Johnny Mathis, Frank Sinatra, Vic Damon, Dean Martin, Peggy Lee, and so many others. By then, I had adopted music as the best companion one could have. With music around one never feels alone. Unlike life, music doesn't have to be understood, just enjoyed.

I turned left again, crossed the street, and went into a Walgreen's pharmacy, where I got some shaving cream and toothpaste. I was the only person walking; everyone else was driving. Cars went in and out of parking spots along Main Street and people went in and out of stores, minding their own business. While walking, some people looked twice at me and made me feel a little uncomfortable.

A trendy metallic blue Buick, with white leather seats and lowered body, driven by a young lad, turned around three times. Two girls were also in the car, and the one in the back seat, gave me a one-block head-turning long gaze. I found out later, the car belonged to a guy who was a high school student and his father the richest man in town.

Incidentally, that day I saw real cowboys there in Texas, men in Levis, cowboy boots, and Stetson hats, really hilarious.

Time for me to start back to the dorm; suppertime was at six.

All and all, I was happy.

The next day at nine I went to my first class, English. I was the only foreigner in the room. I took it as an advantage, because my point of view was going to be unique. I didn't see anyone astounding, except a little blond girl diagonal to me who kept looking back.

After class, I went to the cafeteria to get a cup of coffee and browse around. I found two guys sitting in a booth, drinking coffee and speaking Spanish. I recognized one of the accents as Venezuelan and the other one as Mexican. I approached them.

"Where are you guys from?" I asked.

"I am from Venezuela and he is from Mexico," one of them replied.

"What a coincidence! I am from Venezuela too. Do you mind if I finish my coffee with you guys?"

Gabriel, a small guy with a head full of curly black hair styled like Elvis, a chain smoker and black coffee drinker, was from Caracas and lived on in a small garage apartment. Felipe, who liked to be called Phillip, a tall guy from Brownsville, Texas, with a round moon face, olive skin, and also a full head of straight black hair, very Mexican, always in Levis and white tee-shirts with no belt, lived in the college dorm, same as I did.

We talked about where we came from, our impressions of the campus and the people. We were all in Kilgore because we couldn't be accepted anywhere else. Gabriel knew a little more about the

131

college, because his brother at one time attended an oil technology seminar. We finished our coffees, promised to meet again, and went separate ways. We were freshmen that year and as time went on became very close friends.

* * *

Studying became my job, music and fashion my diversion. I followed the trends. To keep me company, I bought a small record player and began to collect romantic ballads. Gabriel, Phil, and I became inseparable. The three of us were away from home for the first time, lived with limited resources, and were very homesick. Friendship, small talk, and small things take on a bigger dimension when one is lonely.

I recall spending hours decorating my room. A simple decision, like how and where to place my records and my record player, or whether it looked better open or closed, took a long time. When I was satisfied, it gave me a tremendous sense of accomplishment.

I injected an extra sense of aesthetics into everything, a futile attempt at trying to arrange my life. It gave me a temporary sense of stability.

* * *

It was late November now, 1958. I was used to my life here. I had been in Kilgore since September. Studying, listening to my music, attending classes, sipping coffee at the cafeteria, watching the girls, walking to town, and every now and then, visiting with Gabriel and Phil.

I wrote home every two weeks. There was not much to say. We seemed to be in the middle of limbo, not wanting to touch on the past and not daring to mention too much about the future. The future without Father was full of uncertainties. We felt like we were hanging on a thin limb about to break. The fact that our future depended on my scholarship scared me. So much depended on me, and to think that it was only beginning worried me.

Walking from campus to town was sort of a humiliating ritual. I think I followed it purposely, perhaps to show the world how I dared to punish myself for things I had not done. I could have bought a student car but didn't.

Three months had passed. Carrying the responsibility and being away from home were hard. I tried not to think much about it, instead reaffirming that I was not the only one. I discovered that most American kids dreamed about going to college away from home. They wanted to be free.

I was free and very privileged to have an education abroad, but I have to admit I missed the warmth of home. Missing Father was even harder, but I knew that there was no cure for that. I was heading toward a lifelong struggle, but it was worth it.

On special occasions, Gabriel, Phil, and I went to the Mexican Village, a restaurant owned by a Mexican-American couple, an old man and his wife. I remember his silver hair and the missing middle finger on his right hand and, most of all, the hot tamales, the tacos, and the Budweiser beer.

Talking to Gabriel about Christmas, I mentioned that my scholarship covered one trip home per year, which should be the next summer. Gabriel was in a similar situation. We agreed to stay and celebrate Christmas and New Year's together, and maybe go to the Mexican Village.

But life was sometimes good to the innocent. As a surprise, Phil invited us to spend Christmas in his parents' house in Brownsville. We decided to hit the road that Christmas. We got ourselves three seats on the Greyhound bus that covered the Southwest Texas road from Kilgore to Brownsville.

Very few things compare to the freedom one feels when travelling by land, close to the earth. It seems the natural thing to do: by car, train, bus, or even horseback. Looking out the window of a Greyhound bus makes you think, review life, and make plans for the future. It's just about one of the best ways to do it. Every bit of your life passes by that window, as if it was happening at that very moment. Everything looks so clear, so real: the past, the dreams, and the hopes. Even the background music that one hears in the movies is played in one's heart, with all the resonance of the great halls, while looking out that window.

As I looked out the window I reviewed my story: the Andes, Caracas, Acarigua, Maracay, Gainesville, Barbados, Kilgore, and back to my seat on the Greyhound bus. I was astonished how much had happened in such a short time.

December 1958. I was seventeen. Gabriel and Phil sat two seats away from me, in the same row, but across the aisle. That evening, the sun was beginning to set, and we must have been traveling south, because gorgeous pale, yellowish-red rays were flashing on my window from the West. Looking at those rays blinded me, as life sometimes did.

In one of the small towns a girl came on the bus and sat beside me. The girl looked at me with her big green eyes and said, "Hope nobody is sitting here."

"Nope," I mumbled.

She smiled, placed her bag under, and reclined the seat. After a pause, she looked at me and said, "It's chilly here."

She went for her bag and took out what looked like a red poncho. I am a firm believer there is a message attached to every woman's smile when it's directed right at you in a certain way. You just have to read between the lines, of her lips. And so I read:

"I like you."

"I am pleased to be with you."

"I give you permission to kiss me."

She wrapped herself with the poncho, turned her body towards me and gave me that type of smile. We were so close, that I was able to feel her breath against my left cheek, and the warmth of her blood.

The time was so right. There, silence spoke for itself, but I interrupted and said, "You are beautiful."

She smiled again, leaned her head against the side of the seat and closed her eyes. At that moment I heard a voice say, "Kiss me," and I did.

I gave her the warmest kiss ever. She responded with her sweetness, and we enjoyed our tenderness for miles ahead, freed of conventions. When the bus arrived at her destination, about halfway to mine, she arranged herself, got up and said good-bye. I could see from the edge of my window her parents waiting at the station. She hugged both. I always admired this kind of family, warm people. I wonder if she remembers this passage of her life as I do, a beautiful moment of natural attraction.

We passed towns, stopping now and then at the unique Texas coffee shops, with their jukebox always playing, the green-uniformed waitresses holding their green order pads, the glass of water on the table as soon as one sat, and their own very special welcoming smile. The men sitting at the counter sipping coffee, turning their heads slightly, and giving you that look, followed by the inquisitive thought: "I wonder where this one comes from?" Those old Texas coffee shops!

We arrived in Brownsville late in the evening after twelve hours of travel. Phil's family was waiting at the bus station. His father was tall and dark-skinned like Phil, as I expected. His mother was short and a little overweight, I took it because of the good food. Phil warned us about her beans, tortillas, and those unforgettable tamales.

Gabriel was, by this time, a little hysterical for not been able to have a smoke for hours. Everyone greeted us with a most welcome smile, a handshake, and a hug to show more affection. I was glad to be at Phil's house, wonderful to feel their warm Southern hospitality!

Phil's house was a modest two-bedroom bungalow on the unpretentious side of town. The house told their story about being Mexican-American: a little shy, a little self-conscious, aware of class, and living in the Southern part of a country where many people had difficulties digesting certain non-White foods.

After a short conversation about our trip, Phil's mom served dinner. I could tell Phil was very proud to back up with tangible facts the stories about the marvels of his mom's Mexican cuisine. We ate everything on the plate with delight, down to the brown chili sauce. Afterwards, we sat in the living room and Phil's dad pulled out a Tres Cuervos tequila bottle and four glasses. We toasted several times, after which Phil's dad asked me, a little concerned because I was gulping too fast, "Have you ever had tequila before?"

"Sure, it's no big deal," I said. Then the room started to spin. That is the last thing I remember about that night. The following morning, I looked embarrassed, and when I met Phil's father for breakfast, I had this to comment: "Yes, it's a big deal!"

It took the rest of the day for my stomach to settle and accept any regular intake.

Esther, Phil's cousin, invited us for cake and coffee that afternoon. Phil drove us in his father's Chevrolet, a cool drive compared to the walking we did back in Kilgore. Esther and her younger sister were obviously delighted to receive visitors from Latin America, the "real deal."

They made us feel special.

Honouring old-fashioned Spanish hospitality, they first showed us around their house. Even their small dog followed us around, wagging his tail. The bungalow was tidy, American-style, but in their hands it appeared a bit 'borrowed.' The insane thought that some Americans considered them just 'wetbacks' kept creeping into my mind.

After a while, Phil disappeared. Gabriel went with the younger sister, and I ended up with Esther in the common room. I kept looking at the color of her skin, thinking that being a Mexican in the U.S.A. must be uncomfortable. In addition to being so visible, one is neither this nor that. At least I knew what I was, or so I thought. But the funny thing was that at home I also felt like a second-class citizen.

It was humiliating that many Americans didn't even know where Venezuela was. I had to explain it was on the northern edge of South America, right next to the Caribbean. And every time oil was mentioned, they asked me if I had an oil well in my back yard! In the U.S.A. this was entirely possible. In Texas, some people did have oil wells in their back yard, and they owned them. In any event, I had to explain that the oil and everything under the soil belonged to the State, and we poor people had no ownership, even if our house was sitting on it. The explanation made me feel as if I was talking about a mother who steals her baby's milk. Then I changed the subject and I talked about the fantastic weather and the beautiful beaches we had back home.

Esther sat at the piano and began to play *Blue Moon,* the song that followed me everywhere like a dark cloud over my head. I tried to sing along, but it didn't come out right. Since we were alone, I thought it was my duty to kiss her, and I did, and she kissed me back and I didn't know what else to do…

The following day, we, the men, crossed the border to Reynosa Mexico and did a bit of what men do. The excitement of being able to go to a bar and be allowed to order a beer legally was in itself a thrill and made the whole trip worth it. In Texas we had to be twenty-one to do the same thing. We had a few beers, flirted with the Mexican waitresses, and had dinner at the cantina. The American and the Mexican sides of the border were as different as night and day.

Phil and Esther were doing everything possible to make our stay enjoyable, and were succeeding, but somehow I still didn't feel comfortable with the concept of being Mexican-American and continued to feel strange. At that time, I was prejudiced about anything not 100% authentic and had a hard time accepting one could be transported to another country and remain genuine. What a ridiculous thought!

Now, when I look back, I think what it would have been like if I had gotten serious with Esther, married her, become an American citizen, and settled in West Texas. And it all seems very natural.

The way back seemed faster. We went through the same towns and made an effort to remember in which one the girl I met on the way to Brownsville got out. I couldn't remember.

I reproached myself: "The only thing left of our passing through this life is our memories. At least I should learn to conserve them!"

"Kilgore!" the driver shouted and we were at our second home again. Gabriel patted me twice on the shoulder, as a signal to get out. We picked up our suitcases and shared a taxi. Phil got out at his garage apartment first, and Gabriel and I continued to our respective rooms. During the following week, I thought a lot about what it meant to be a Mexican-American. I wrote to Mom and Sis about the trip and how much I missed them. School would begin in a week.

* * *

Time moved faster and things were changing. In January 1959, I received news that Sis and Billy were getting married. Sis was fifteen. I wrote Mother that I thought she was too young, but they married anyway, and soon were expecting their first baby.

I wrote Sis a letter wishing her and Billy total happiness, and excusing myself for not attending. In reality, I was very sad for Sis marrying without even finishing high school, but I didn't say anything.

This was a direct consequence of Father not being with us. Billy was twenty and studying architecture, but still very irresponsible. He was kept by his father, spent most of his time drinking 'Cuba Libres' (rum and Coke), and running around chasing girls in his baby blue Volkswagen.

Once married, Mother arranged for him to get a job at the Health Ministry, headed by one of Father's cousins, and enrolled him in night school. Later the minister awarded him a scholarship to continue architecture at Washington University. It took him one year to graduate, come home, and work for the ministry again. During their stay, a beautiful baby girl was born in Seattle, Washington.

For me, life continued: classes, exams, music, and my walks to town. So far, I was doing well in my grades. Spring came and the town became a beautiful garden. That March in 1959, I turned eighteen, and it was exhilarating to know that in some parts of the world I was "of age," but not in Texas!

That same month, one year previous, Father passed away. So far, I had managed to temporarily sidestep that reality. I enrolled in the spring semester and decided to remain in the college dormitory.

Coincidentally, around that time I developed some very disturbing symptoms. On occasions, when I was sipping coffee from a cup, my hands began to shake. It was more noticeable when I became conscious of it and made extra effort to control it. Then, breathing turned harder and the tremor in my hands grew worse. I was convinced people around me noticed. Then I used to freeze and had an uncontrollable urge to get away from the place. As soon as I was in the open and breathed fresh air, the sensation went away and I was able to calm down. Other times I felt a tightness in my stomach, became short of breath, and an uncontrollable cough overtook me, as if I was choking. These symptoms of anxiety became part of my life. I was convinced this was a delayed effect of Father not being with me anymore.

A silent sadness was corroding me from inside. Whatever it was hit me hard. I began to oversleep, miss classes, and spend more time listening to music and watching television than studying. Very few other things interested me anymore, as if my energy had been drained. Thinking and lingering went on for days. At one point, I came out of my room only at mealtimes and went back to bed again.

Over the next two years, this pattern went on, from bad to worse. Today these would be called a 'panic attack' and a 'depression episode.' Then I just called it 'This Márquez Thing,' like Father's.

Chapter 9

By the end of spring 1961 I was failing most of my subjects. My scholarship was in jeopardy along with my chances of getting a degree and assuring Mother's and Sis' survival. I was going down the drain into the sewage of failure. I had to do something.

When one loses the kind of father I had, one enters a dense fog. I began to look for ways out, but I kept bumping into blind alleys everywhere, turning and turning. The more I tried, like being in quicksand, the deeper I sank, and the more misplaced I became. I needed someone to pull me out and show me the way.

At one point the fog became so dense that I disappeared. It became very difficult for me to understand that no one was to blame for my father's death, not my letters nor the country nor even himself. I was simply lucky enough to get help in my time of need; he was not. It took many years to clarify this. I needed help.

The rest of the year was a total loss. And those *'Rangerette'* cheerleaders kept attending class in their short skirts, with the excuse that they didn't have time to change. How was one supposed to concentrate?

* * *

I needed to go home and renew myself. As soon as summer break came, I blocked my open ticket to May 26, 1961. When I arrived at Mother's door, she almost fainted. Billy had just graduated from the University of Washington and was now working as an architect at the Ministry of Health. He, Sis, and the baby shared an apartment with Mother, in a subdivision called Los Palos Grandes. I was back in Caracas only trying to figure it all out, not expecting any dramatic changes. I had enough of those already!

I just wanted to clear my mind, put everything in place again, continue with college, and provide for my family and myself. The strain was excessive, and the load had to be rearranged.

Aunt Alicia now lived three blocks away from Mother. It was not a coincidence, because they always tried to live near each other. One afternoon I was visiting her, having a cat nap on my cousin Humber's bed before dinner, when he arrived and said, "Hey, Carlu (like they sometimes called me)! Do you want to go to a party tonight?"

"What kind of party?" I asked.

"The neighbour's birthday party. She is an architecture student at the Central University."

"Humber, I don't think so; yesterday I was out late and still feel it," I told him, turning around on the bed and sinking my head into the pillow again.

"She is a party girl and there will be others. They are all very pretty you know," Humber insisted.

"How old is she?" I asked.

"I think she is eighteen," he replied.

Later, we had pot roast and browned potatoes for dinner, cooked by my Aunt Alicia, who knows how to cook.

"Are you going to the party with me or not?" Humber insisted again at the end of the dinner. It sounded like an ultimatum and his persistence puzzled me. *Should I maybe go?* I asked myself.

"Okay, I'll go. Just let me go home and change, and I'll meet you at seven."

* * *

Now, we were ringing the bell at the house next door and a girl dressed in white lace opened it.

"I am glad you could make it. Come in."

"He is Luis Carlos, the cousin I told you is going to university in the U.S. and here for the summer. I brought him along. I hope you don't mind."

"Not at all. Pleased to meet you, Luis Carlos. Please come in," she said, with a soft voice, waving her hand as a welcoming sign.

Later, standing in the middle of the living room, I didn't know what to do. I got this funny feeling in my stomach when I was among people I didn't know. I grabbed a drink from the first passing waiter, just to feel I was holding onto something, a Scotch and soda. I hate Scotch and soda, but it was the 'in' drink in that circle, and a glass in my hand made me feel a little more secure. The next step was to start a conversation with someone.

There was faint music playing. I glanced around and saw this woman in a green dress sitting on a chair. She looked like Audrey Hepburn in *Breakfast at Tiffany's*.

I approached her. "Are you a friend of the family?"

"Oh, yes," she answered. "The birthday girl is a friend of mine. She is an architecture student, and from time to time I become her tutor. I am an architect," she added.

"Where did you go to university?" I asked her.

"Sao Paolo, Brazil," she said.

"I hear they have one of the best architecture schools in the world, and of course you speak fluent Portuguese. Don't you?"

"Yes, I do," she replied and smiled, with that half sneaky smile that only women can make. I noticed she had a double dimple in her cheeks when she smiled and also one in her chin, which gave her the cutest expression.

Now we were both standing and sipping Scotch. It seemed natural to ask her. "Would you like to dance?"

"Yes," she answered, with that smile again.

While dancing with this woman in the green dress, I 'detailed' her. She was rather short, maybe five-feet-three. I was not sure, because she wore very high heels. Her eyes were large and sort of greenish. She had an ample smile. Her nose was parted at the tip and wanted to point upwards, like many German noses. Her hair was pulled towards the back in a fashionable way and crowned with a bun, which made her look a bit taller than she was. Her dress fit her well and was made of very good quality silk chiffon. Her legs were rather short for her torso but as well shaped as a ballerina's, probably the product of many hours of ballet training as a child. Still, she had a very low waistline.

She was pleasant to the eye and responded with a well-trained smile and an upwards, picaresque look, which made one feel admired. I drew her close for the slow song, one of those very old romantic boleros that I like so much. I felt comfortable holding her. She seemed to be what I call 'the right size,' the type of woman you hold close and fits like a well-tailored jacket, no pressure or pulling, just flexible and soft.

In very little time, we were talking as if we knew each other for 100 years. I told her I was still studying engineering in the U.S. and had at least two more years to go before graduation. She didn't seem to mind; on the contrary, she liked it.

Now we were singing *Happy Birthday* to the hostess, laughing and giving a mischievous gaze to each other every time we had a chance. After a while the party dwindled down, we exchanged phone numbers, and promised to call the following day.

On the way home I read the business card she gave me: *"Concejo Municipal Distrito Los Teques, Dra. Chica, Architect,"* after which she wrote by hand, *"Home (212) 236 - 532."*

Some numbers change people's destiny. This was one of them.

The very next day I called her at work and my life plunged into deeper waters than I was able to safely swim. I was aware that this woman was much older than I, at least ten years, but there was a fascination about being the object of attention of an older woman; it only added to the allure of the situation. I began to play a very dangerous cat-and-mouse game. I was the mouse and I was playing with fire, only I didn't know it. What an exciting, fancy, naive, and youthful fantasy!

I phoned her a couple of times and then went to visit her at the house she shared with her parents in La Floresta. We talked about each other. I told her, in my dramatic way, about my family, my father, my dreams, my beliefs, and why I considered being honest to oneself so important. She told me, in a very casual way, her family had been raising cattle for almost 100 years on lands near a small town called Upata, and by coincidence her brother was studying animal husbandry in Texas. By the end of the evening, I realized we were already involved. From then on, we called each other every day.

* * *

A long time ago, around 1810, the Venezuelan government gave a group of German immigrants the rights to a piece of malaria-infested tropical forest. This wonderful, dedicated, and hardworking people turned that forest into a heaven. Little by little, they erected a small town, a replica of a German village, with all the details of the original style. Their descendants continued to build and expand, until they turned the town into a colourful and successful tourist destination and a marvellous example of their culture. The following week, we spent the weekend at La Colonia Tovar.

I invited my friend Enrique to double date with Chica's cousin, who was staying with her for a while. For the occasion, instead of bringing her own green and white Chevy, Chica borrowed her older sister's car, a magnificent brand-new, pearl-coloured Oldsmobile '98 Coupe 442. Chica insisted I drive the fantastic machine, and I was delighted. I looked like I had made it in the world!

By enormous coincidence, we met Eduardo, my long-time friend from San Bernardino, on the road. He was also on his way to La Colonia Tovar with some of his friends for the weekend. They were parked at the side of the curb resting for a moment. I didn't waste any time to show off my entourage.

"Take that jalopy out of the road!" I yelled, waving my hands to attract his attention. He was startled!

We continued along, passing green forests, orchards, dairy and strawberry farms. The air became fresher as we climbed, and Chica continued to charm me with her smile, appearing even more beautiful.

The little town was very picturesque. We parked at the top of the hill, walked down past the town square, and stopped at a little restaurant in one of the side streets to have sweet hot chocolate and pretzels. The trip, the car, the company, the day, and her everlasting smile were intoxicating. It all looked like a master painting. From then on we became one and I acquired a sense of completeness.

As much as I wanted it to last, my summer vacation was over. This time, Chica took me to the airport, and I went away with the promise to write. By mid-September 1961, I was immersed again in my studies. The previous year was disastrous. I had to repeat almost all the subjects.

But now, all of a sudden, I felt renewed energies. Injected with an infusion of new life, I became enthusiastic again, and my grades immediately started to rise. Chica's letters began to arrive, and I was moving forward again.

* * *

Around that time, I moved to a guesthouse run by a graceful old lady. There was a restaurant on one side that served only lunch, famous for its delicious Southern cuisine, and on the other a guesthouse that looked like a stable, with rooms running along each side of a long hallway.

The owner was the most adorable person I have ever known. Her private home was a white bungalow on top of a green hill, overlooking a golf course. She drove a baby blue Cadillac with white interior and every morning went to shop for fresh groceries. Two black ladies dressed in white uniforms, complete with lace aprons and headpieces, always accompanied her. She was thin and wore small, flowery cotton dresses and a straw hat over her light blue silver head

146

in summer. She was about 75 at the time and a delight to observe, especially how she went about everything she did with such delicacy.

I decided to have her as a model of casual elegance for my later years, even though she was a woman.

* * *

Christmas was approaching and I had a few days off. Chica and I decided to meet in Houston, and she would also bring her brother Alberto. I didn't have enough money for the trip, so I pawned a gold I.D. bracelet I bought for my eighteenth birthday. They gave me up to one year to pay it off.

It was 1961. On the fifteenth of December, full of joy, I was in a Greyhound bus on my way to Houston to meet them. It'd been a long time since anybody cared to wait for me, anywhere. They arrived first. I got out, hugged Chica, introduced myself to Alberto, and went straight to a Howard Johnson they'd booked.

"So, how was your trip?" Chica asked.

"Fine, fine. It took two hours, that's all. What about yours?" I asked.

"Good, but long. Are you glad to see me?" Chica asked.

"Yes! Yes! I am," I was happy to see her. I was.

At the Howard Johnson, we had two adjoining rooms, one for Alberto and me and another for Chica.

We spent the day window shopping and teasing each other around the mall about how much money we were to spend on our 'expensive' Christmas gifts. Because nights were cold, we didn't go out much. Instead, I stayed in Chica's room and watched TV with her.

On Christmas night, we sat for dinner at the motel's restaurant. During dinner, I saw flashes of Mom and Sis. They were dining at Aunt Alicia's house. Chica confessed she was also thinking about her family, like the time she was in Brazil, alone, because she couldn't come home for Christmas.

None of us were in tune with the city, and we had no idea where to go and too little money if we had known. Chica and I were just happy to be together, and Alberto felt a little awkward to be chaperoning.

On January 5, 1962, our vacation was over. Alberto and I took Chica to the airport and parted ways.

Back in Kilgore, I felt awesome, like never before. I had a new reason to live. Nothing had substantially changed, but I felt it did. I had a new attitude towards life.

Before Chica left, we agreed she would come back to join me the following summer for good. Perhaps, she'd take an English course at first and continue to do postgraduate work.

As soon as I met Gabriel I told him about the new developments and he told me about how he spent the Holidays at the Mexican Village, drinking Millers and feeling homesick. I went through the spring semester with enthusiasm, easily shooting straight arrows towards my goal. It seemed I had found what drove me forward: someone to love.

* * *

On a very hot day in August, Chica arrived at the Houston airport. I waved both hands several times before she was able to see me. Smiling, unrestrained, she approached me. She threw one hand around my shoulder, kissed me, and said, "I am so glad to be here!"

The great adventure began.

I am known to have difficulty focusing on reality, because I make my own versions. This time, I envisioned the most romantic future. Only nice things were allowed in the very special story that was about to begin: love, freedom, adventure, and never-ending happiness.

"So, how are you, my dear little friend?" I asked her.

"I am here. Am I not?" she replied, meaning 'I kept my promise.'

We took the downtown airport bus and got out at the Crown Plaza, where I already had a room for both of us. She was carrying a large suitcase and a good-sized handbag. I carried only the essentials; the rest of my things were in self-storage back in Kilgore, waiting for wherever my new address was going to be. That night was long and pleasant. There is nothing a woman who wants to have a baby will not do. It is probably the strongest drive a female has. Chica was 29 and in that frame of mind.

The following days, we looked for a place to live and found a lovely, reasonably priced, furnished garage apartment. I ordered my self-storage from Kilgore and began to enjoy family life. Chica registered in an English course at Houston University and I in South Texas Community College to upgrade my quality points.

Hunting for a car, we found a beautiful '59 red Chevrolet convertible. Because we had no credit, we offered the blue sapphire and diamond ring Chica bought in Brazil as collateral. The transaction was done through a bank that kept the ring in trust until the car was paid in full.

My new life took off in complete dedication. On Saturdays I would spend a good two hours washing and polishing our car until bright red. Ready for a weekend of cruising, grocery shopping, A&W hamburgers, and, once in a while, a drive-in movie. We were good to each other.

Not long after, Chica brought up the subject of marriage. "Don't you think we should do things right?"

To me, it didn't matter, because I was committed anyway. "I guess so, but it must be done in Louisiana, because here in Texas I have to be twenty-one, and I am not."

In August 1960, we were pronounced 'husband and wife' by the justice of the peace in Baton Rouge, Louisiana. I was nineteen.

Two years had passed since my father died.

You may think I took the easy way out. A woman walks into my life and I decide to marry. Well, you may be right. Life was easier that way. She was ten years older than I.

'This Márquez Thing' did it again!

In due time, I applied to the School of Industrial Engineering at Lamar University and was accepted. In the summer of 1962, Chica and I loaded the red Impala with all our belongings, and on a clear, Texas blue, hot, humid day, we made our move.

We left, spearheading, this time towards Beaumont. Houston was blown away by the wind, as a small postcard from a photo album. It swirled, and sat in the past, as one of the good times of my life.

We set up house in the 'married student' apartments, and I enrolled in summer school. Very few students were taking summer courses. It was too hot and considered a punishment. One could melt on the way to class.

In the meantime, to deal with the heat, we spent our days at home with the air conditioner on full-blast or at the pool across the street.

* * *

Chica was now pregnant and still insisted on attending City Planning School at North Carolina University, in spite of the fact that I couldn't transfer, because they didn't have an industrial engineering school. She enrolled anyway, in the Master of City Planning program, I guess to justify to her soul that she tried, even though she and I knew she couldn't continue when the baby arrived. She was already three months pregnant. I didn't discourage her, didn't want to get in her way.

By September, Chica, Alberto (her brother) and I began the long journey to Chapel Hill, North Carolina, by car. We drove Alberto's two-cylinder DKW, which was easy on gas but not comfortable at all, and placed Chica on the back seat to give her as much room as possible.

I can't remember the exact reason why we decided on a camping trip, even though we had no tent and not a clue where to camp on the way. That night around midnight, exhausted, we stopped at a park in a town I fail to remember. We drove down a short, narrow, dirt road and parked in what looked like a picnic area. Chica settled in the car with her head on the pillow she brought, wrapped in a blanket, and went to sleep. Alberto dropped a sleeping bag on the ground and laid on it, staring at the stars.

I placed my sleeping bag on top of a picnic table, afraid of the critters potentially climbing on top of me. Around 5:00 am, the roaring of a pickup truck coming up the dirt road woke us up. It was already bright and the sun was beginning to warm up the damp ground.

I smelled trouble, and told Chica and Alberto to act as if nothing was happening. As soon as the pickup approached the picnic area and was within speaking distance, a dreadful looking man shouted, "Good morning!"

I answered back in the same tone of voice, "Good morning!"

"How are you folks doing today?" he asked, while looking us over.

"We are just passing by. By the way, do you know of a coffee shop nearby?" I asked.

The man gave us some directions, decided not to do whatever was in his mind to do, and turned the pickup around, saying, "Have a good trip."

We followed his directions, came to a coffee shop, washed up, and had breakfast. I am still convinced the man in the pickup had something harmful in mind, but for whatever reason he didn't go ahead.

It took us two days to get to Chapel Hill. Once there, we checked into a small hotel. That same afternoon, we registered Chica at the university and the very next day found an apartment for her to share with two other women, also university students. Alberto and I spent the night at her apartment and the next morning started our way back to Texas, but not before Alberto kicked the house cat on his way out. Funny, he was taking animal husbandry and didn't even like animals.

We drove nonstop while taking turns. Still, the way back proved to be very tedious, maybe because we turned right back without taking enough time to rest.

At one point, I felt very sleepy and stopped to take a short nap. Out of nowhere, a mosquito cloud swarmed into the car. They were so many, and in such a blood-sucking frenzy, that Alberto had to run around, push me to the passenger seat, and take over in a rush to get us out of there.

I was left in Beaumont, to continue my life alone, and Alberto continued to Lubbock.

After a while, I moved out of the married student apartment and took a room at the home of a retired lady, who spent most of her time doing housework. We shared the kitchen and washroom, so I had to wait my turn every time.

I called Chica every day to follow the baby's progress. On February 3, 1963, she gave birth to our son, all alone in Chapel Hill because of her silly choice. The boy was named in her father's and my honour, but I will call him Utu. Within one month she boarded the flight back to Beaumont, realizing it was impossible to take care of the newborn while attending university.

* * *

Being a father came naturally to me, though I didn't look like one. I felt like one and was one. Chica turned out to be a dedicated mother, breastfeeding her baby and attending to every detail as a genuine act of love and devotion. Utu became a vivacious, happy, brown-eyed boy.

My studies, the baby, and Chica kept me busy. Life was good once again.

When the baby was one year old, and I was six months from graduation, Chica proposed to go back to Venezuela and open up the path ahead of us. Another separation, but I took it as a transition. I don't recall the details about the day she left. I guess my mind refused to acknowledge the fact.

I found myself alone again, and my two dearest ones far away. In the beginning, she and the baby stayed with her family in Upata, where they were well known and influential, and used their connections, including the governor of the state, to secure her a good job. Things are easy for some people.

For two years, Chica and I had been more away than together, which I tried to justify was for a good reason, and for the time being we wrote once a week and talked on the phone every other week. In her letters everything was going well. She liked her job, the baby was fine, and she bought a new car.

* * *

The sacrifice paid off. I was now on my way to becoming a professional industrial engineer.

The day of my graduation in 1964, I was alone, like when I graduated from Riverside in 1958, after Father passed away. In my version, Alvaro my brother and Father were both again sitting a few benches behind me. Alvaro looked seven, as the day I first met him, and Father remained 43, as he was in his last picture. They were both smiling. I was static.

That day, I felt like a colossal load was taken off my back. One of my biggest fears at that time was being married to a professional woman and not having a degree myself, unacceptable and humiliating. If I hadn't graduated, I would have felt like a 'fracasado', a failure, for the rest of my life, unthinkable in terms of Father's philosophy. Graduating from university was one of the most fulfilling experiences I ever had. The amount of work done, within the time span, was astronomical, so I felt.

I also have to admit, if I hadn't married Chica, with certainty I wouldn't have finished university. Thank you!

Chapter 10

May 1964. I arrived in Caracas on an unforgettable Saturday. My sister, Billy, and Chica were waiting at the Caracas airport. I came out of the exit with great anticipation and looked everywhere, as if my life depended on finding them. It felt like an eternity. I saw them. Sis waved and Chica stood on her tiptoes trying to see me, just smiling. We all embraced and kissed, as we do when away for a long time. This time was the start of a whole new life. In Venezuela when you have a degree, people call you 'Doctor,' which makes one feel a little superior, a different person.

I had not seen my son for ten months now. When Chica took him to Venezuela, he was one year old and didn't walk yet. I wondered how he was now and how he looked. I missed him very much during this absence. I asked Chica how he was and how he looked. She said he'd grown a lot and tried to describe him, but it was not possible for me to visualize him. We stayed overnight at Sis' house, and she tried to make our brief stay pleasant. Chica initiated lovemaking as soon as we went to bed, which startled me; it was so not like her.

The following day, we boarded the small Avensa twin engine DC3 to Puerto Ordaz. The plane taxied to the middle of the runway, and we stepped out to a hot reception. In place of an airport terminal, there was a small tin-roofed shack. Beside it stood a cart with mixed luggage, to which people scrambled, looking and dumping the ones that were not theirs. We waited for the cart to empty and the last two, thrown on the burning asphalt, were ours.

A black-haired, middle-aged, small man stood outside the gate. Chica said, pointing at him, "That is Bastardo, the employee who drives me around." He was missing a front tooth but smiled as if the tooth was still there. He fetched our luggage and guided us to the grey Ford Falcon station wagon Chica bought for us. I congratulated her for the choice of color. She smiled, because she knew how fussy I was about those small details.

We drove straight to her parents' home. Chica stepped up a little ahead of us, and I followed. Bastardo carried the luggage and, as soon as I walked in, Chica was standing beside a little slender boy (wearing gauze diapers and sandals).

Chica pointed at me and said, "Este es tu papá." The boy seemed to understand.

I was disappointed because I didn't see the cute chubby baby I left. Somehow I felt they hadn't taken care of him properly. He was too slender, his hair was cut too short, and I didn't like the bangs on his forehead. The boy walked up to me a little shy, stopped short, and I gave him his first big fatherly hug. Then, I greeted Chica's parents. That night, after a healthy dinner, we went to bed and in the morning started our way back to Puerto Ordaz.

When we arrived at the camp that morning, the security guard gave us a swift bullfighter's pass and let us enter. Three corner turns on the very narrow asphalt road and we arrived at the gravel ramp of what now was home, a small timber bungalow under the blazing sun of the Venezuelan Guyana.

"Here we are. This is home, for now," Chica said, almost apologizing.

Everything was different than I expected. "It is fine," I said, lying to myself a little bit. She was carrying Utu, while Bastardo and I unloaded the luggage. As we walked into the house, the old wooden floor creaked, and there was no furniture--only three hammocks, the baby's crib, a glass-top cast-iron table, and six wicker chairs borrowed from Chica's mother.

The settlement once belonged to The Iron Mines, a subsidiary of Bethlehem (one of those British companies that prospects in faraway places). When the mining operation began, they moved the housing complex to the mine, leaving this old housing settlement behind. The grounds were once well kept. Vestiges of the green lawns lingered in places, refusing to disappear, and some of the paint remained on the bungalows as scabby scales here and there.

With us was a young mother's helper, who had been handed down to Chica like a puppy. "Take care of her," her mother said. (At that time it was common for poor families to 'lend' their children to middle-class families as mother's helpers in exchange for room, board, and a chance to go to school.)

In the midst of all this, I was full of dreams for a bright future. That night we slept like the whole world belonged to us.

Chica's family influenced their connections, now on my behalf. The national corporation for which she now worked, owned, to my good fortune, a state-of-the-art steel mill in this region. After a short interview, I started my new job as an industrial engineer at Siderúrgica del Orinoco.

The following weekend Chica took me to see her office in San Felix. She was the municipal engineer who issued land zoning and construction permits. Her office was on the second floor of a 50's building, scattered with drafting tables and piles of rolled drawings. Six people worked under her and she kept the rubber seal of approval that made everything legal secured under lock and key. It seemed the whole effort was well worth it.

Next morning I drove the Falcon station wagon along the highway towards the mill, wondering why there was so much traffic. Then I realized the mill employed more than 15,000 people and everyone went down the same road at the same time, many of them on blue buses provided by the company, all resembling a gigantic blue serpent.

I showed my confirmation letter. The main gate opened. The guard pulled me aside and gave me directions to the Human Relations Department. They were expecting me, and a lady supervisor handed me the 'Induction Booklet' that contained the companies' policies. Next, my picture was taken and my employee ID card issued.

Showing me the way on a map, she said, "Please follow me, first to the Industrial Safety Department, to pick up your personal equipment, then to the industrial area, and from there to your department."

For a while I thought I was in the army. It took a good half an hour, before I was introduced to my new boss. The plant was enormous.

My department was in a bay at the center of the plant, surrounded by the 800-, 1000- and 1500-millimetre mills (named after the cross section of the steel rods they produced). The office was an open plan where 30 engineers and technicians sat. Each desk was equipped with a massive, very noisy Friden electrical desk calculator (that had more buttons and levers than a plane control panel) and an Underwood typewriter, just as massive as the calculator. Many of them were being used simultaneously and the noise was worse than a stamping operation. Mr. Buskobownick was the department head, a thick-lensed Russian/Argentinian gentleman. My direct supervisor was Mr. Rizzo, a bald, short, Italian fellow.

I had the feeling neither held university degrees. I knew people told stories about being in the War, working in high tech factories; and if you were in these faraway places, people believed your credentials. They wouldn't know the difference. Nevertheless, they were my bosses. My initial assignments were simple time-and-motion studies geared towards productivity. My salary was half of Chica's, which I understood, considering this was my first job and I didn't have as much work experience as she did.

* * *

So far I had not done anything to deal with Father's land in Guanarito. I only had the certified copy of the deed to go by, the same one Father left in his suitcase. Later, on a three-day leave to Caracas, I found in the National Cartography Department two very detailed maps of the Portuguesa State and Guanarito District where the land was.

As I looked at these maps, Father's words resonated in my mind. "Someday you will remember me for this land." I guessed the time had come to find out more. I studied the maps in detail and located the boundaries of the land. I was not due for a vacation yet, but I couldn't delay it any longer, because it didn't feel right. I took a month's leave without pay and invited Alberto to join me to help locate the land.

Saturday morning in the middle of June, and we were getting ready to part.

"We'll stop in Caracas, for a day or two, and get copies of the photographic flights. With a magnifying glass, one can even see the trees on an aerial photograph. We should be able to at least see the southern and northern boundaries, Guanare and the Madre Vieja Rivers, and figure it out from there."

I took the first driving shift, passed the bridge across the Caroni, and turned west, towards Ciudad Bolivar, Barcelona, and Caracas. It was a bright day and somehow I felt Father was guiding us. Eight hours drive and we were in Caracas. At the National Cartography Department, we found the aerial photographs of the land.

The next day, we arrived in Guanare and stayed overnight in a small hotel. The following morning we headed south on a muddy gravel road to Guanarito. It was the rainy season, and I'd never been there before. A rusty road sign read "Guanarito 30 Kms." One hour later, we arrived at a small dirt town, stopped at the 'bodega,' and asked were the registry was.

The Land Registry Office was only a tiny room. I solicited certified copies of the documents by which Father acquired the land in 1953 from a man called Alfredo Reyes, as stated on the main document. One hundred and fifty years of legal tradition! Layering the detailed maps yielded 7,500 hectares.

That night we stayed at the guesthouse, and the menu was only one course, 'Hervido de Res.' The next morning we rented a 'rapida' from Juan, and went downstream from the Guanare to El Tigre. One hour later we arrived at an improvised dock and walked to a little shack up the riverbank.

"Hola, cómo están? Yo soy Luis Carlos, el hijo del doctor Márquez. Estoy buscando a Don Alfredo Reyes." (Translated: "Hello, how are you? I am Luis Carlos, the son of Dr. Márquez. I am looking for Don Alfredo Reyes.")

A tall old man came out, dressed in a soiled linen suit and black rubber boots. His welcoming, weathered face invited us into the shack.

Inside there were two more men and women. I introduced Alberto as my brother-in-law. After the old man acknowledged having met my father, I expressed my concerns about the land. He explained at this time of the year, it was not possible to survey it, because of the floods. I would have to come back during the dry season, and he would be happy to show me around. In the meantime, he made me an offer to become 'partners' in a cattle-raising operation. When I asked him about the cattle and the pigs Father left, he explained that after six years, everything was lost, eaten by the jungle.

I wondered who the jungle was.

The woman prepared a thick, tasteless chicken soup accompanied by harsh rum. That rainy night we slept surrounded by the sounds of the jungle and the river's murmur. On our way back, I said to Alberto, "At least I did set foot on it!"

* * *

Now Chica was pregnant again, and on July 25, 1965, our second son was born. He was a fair-skinned, greenish-eyed, German-gened one, named this time after my father, with a little twist on Father's middle name, so the other boys wouldn't call him María and make him have to defend his honour. For this purpose, I will call him Ike.

With two decent incomes and very little expenses, we soon flourished. We purchased and moved to a small bungalow in the new section of town, a surplus from the construction days, bought a new black Ford Falcon for me, and a carved Spanish colonial dining set from Chica's aunt for the house. The dining set was big enough to furnish the whole social area of the house: a long table, twelve chairs, chiffonier, serving table, and cupboard.

I loved the family we were creating. Every day after work I watered the lawn. The black cat, given as a token by a colleague and whom I named Azabache like the black stone, followed me everywhere. Sometimes I would sit on a lounge chair on the front porch to read and he would jump on my shoulders and wrap himself around my neck like a scarf.

* * *

Because of my love of horses, for my birthday that year I got a quarter horse called Ruscio from the herd of Chica's father. On Sundays I used to spend a few hours on my own, riding Ruscio around the countryside. These solitary rides became my religion. They took me closer to nature, my nearest conception of God, and cleansed my soul.

One Sunday after a frugal breakfast, I placed my saddle and tack in the station wagon and said goodbye to Chica and the boys. On my way to the stables, I realized how much I enjoyed horseback riding and how nice it would be to have the boys join me someday. I hadn't ridden Ruscio for weeks, and he could be a little fussy at first, but after a while he always calmed down to a steady pace. The stable boy was not nearby, so I decided to saddle the horse myself. I had ridden horses for many years, but someone else had always dressed them. I brushed him a little, placed a blanket and the saddle on his back, and tightened the synch to his chest and the false synch to his stomach, very tightly. To make sure, I tightened them a little more.

I gave him his bit and bridled, mounted, and started our ride. I noticed the horse was a little frisky, as expected, and attributed it to excess energy and lack of exercise. I went around my usual trail and on the way back, approaching the stables, the horse went mad, bucking wildly as though in a rodeo. I tried to hold on, but within seconds I was thrown. I fell headfirst, with my arms extended, like diving into an empty pool. First the arms crashed, next my shoulder, and then my head. My whole body crumpled into the ground and I felt the impact like a million volts, light bulbs bursting into pieces in plain daylight, followed by a curtain of fireflies.

When I regained conscience, Ruscio was standing a little ways ahead, waiting and just looking. I stood up, still in shock, grabbed his bridle, and we both walked the rest of the way back to the stable.

On arrival, the stable boy asked me, "What happened?"

"I just fell from the horse, that's all!"

He took the saddle down and said nodding his head, "You shouldn't have tightened the second synch so tight around his belly. It's supposed to be loose, not make him feel like he was hanged by his balls. That's how they make bucking horses buck."

This is what I tried to learn back at Chuchu's farm, from Belandia, but obviously never did! I thought to myself.

My arms swelled, but I still drove to the hospital. My right wrist and left arm were broken and my neck's fourth, fifth, and six vertebrae squashed. The doctor said, "You are lucky your neck didn't fracture. You could have become a paraplegic…"

I had to wear casts, and my neck was never the same. Once more, I sensed my brother Alvaro and Father carried me along.

* * *

My dedication to self-destruction was relentless, subtle but persistent! Another day, while driving the Falcon east, on the way to the mill, I saw a convenience store on the opposite side and turned left. At that precise moment, a red pickup was trying to pass me. It charged like a bull through a cloud of dust, ramming the Falcon off the road.

I was still shaking, when the driver came to me and told me, "You just turned left without any warning!"

"I know," I said. "I am sorry."

Only the left fender of the Falcon was smashed, so we left it at that. I had the car repaired before Chica returned from her business trip to Caracas. If you ask her, she will tell you this never happened.

162

What made me turn without considering anything else? I just don't know…

That very same week, Azabache, my black cat, walked up to me, stumbling.

"What is wrong with the cat?" I asked Chica. "How is it possible that I was away a few hours and the cat gets sick?"

"The cat was taken care of as usual," everyone said.

The next day Azabache died. This I considered a dreadful sign, very bad luck; something was going to happen. Many years later, an acquaintance told me a neighbour in fact poisoned the cat, because it frightened his chickens. These were subtle messages of bigger changes coming my way, bigger than a horse fall, a car accident, or a cat's death.

* * *

That year, I met Domenic at the company's country club, an Italian-American supervisor at Orinoco Mining Company (a subsidiary of United Steel Corporation). Besides the usual chitchat, we talked about my job at the steel mill. In the end, he invited me to apply to Orinoco Mining for an opening as a Senior Analyst in his department. I was delighted. Orinoco offered better conditions, benefits, and subsidised housing.

I did apply, was called to interview and offered the job. The new position allowed me to expand my experience in the steel-making process.

After the mandatory three months' probation, I was confirmed in the job and allowed to move to a nicer house in the company's compound. Now, we had enough room to properly set up the antique dining room, for the boys to run around, and for me a larger lawn to water.

That year, I was given a beautiful, black, Belgian shepherd puppy for my birthday. I named him Carbon because of his black fur. Then, our family life was simple and joyful.

One weekend, I took the boys and Carbon to the Caroni National Park, a stunning waterfall and natural reserve situated on the Venezuelan Guayana. As we got out of the car, Carbon, exercising his natural instincts, ran to the deer pen and pursued. Immediately, the guard asked us to put him on a leash, because it frightened the deer. We went for a walk along the river, breathed fresh air, and laughed about Carbon chasing the deer. Back home, the boys told their mother about the adventure as if it was an African safari!

Some weekends we visited Chica's parents. The boys loved those trips, because they were allowed to roam free around the small town, basically in the care of the houseboy, who was only a little older. I was proud of Chica, because she loved the boys and felt fortunate about our life. It couldn't have been better!

Chapter 11

One day, Chica told me about this guy from Harvard who was assigned to work with her. "He looks very intellectual. I know you will like him," she said.

I met him. The only things about him that caught my attention were the freckles on his face and his horn-rimmed glasses. Other than that, he looked rather common. So I decided to call him 'Freckles.'

* * *

A few months latter, in 1969, I came home one day earlier than I was supposed to from a business trip. I arrived late, around 11:00pm. As soon as I opened the front door, Chica appeared and immediately said, as if she had to justify something, "We have company."

I never felt so strange in my life. Nothing is as disturbing as finding a man in your house and being betrayed by the mother of your children, because, entrusting their custody is the greatest responsibility a man can place on a woman. I looked left, towards the den, and there was long-legged Freckles from the Harvard Joint Centre sitting in my favourite lounge chair. I remember thinking, *You may have company, not me. What is he doing in my house? Why are they hiding in the den?*

I felt my territory had been violated, the animal way. I told him to leave at once and slammed the door behind him, then shouted at Chica, "You have broken a married woman's most fundamental rule!"

I asked how long he had been in the house, and the help told me since morning. Freckles left his camera behind and I tossed it to the street. Chica rescued it, reasoning that where we lived it could be stolen. What did I care? I was infuriated at her insistence. I explained, once more, how out of place it was for a married woman to have a man in the house while her husband was away. Then I realised I was talking to a woman who knew all this and stopped saying anything else. I came to think she was a different person.

I couldn't sleep that night, and swore to myself I'd get to the bottom of the situation. I had to find out what was going on.

The next day, instead of going to work, I went to Chica's office. At ten that morning she was not in and neither was Freckles. I went through every drawer in Chica's desk. In the middle one, I found a small paperback written in English and entitled *Sex, Without Guilt.*

This book was telling me the whole story. To top it all off, I found in the closet of my wife's office Freckle's clothes hanging, his shoes scattered, and some books piled in one corner. In my very own wife's private office! I didn't move anything and went home to think things through and make sure I was not hastily jumping to conclusions, though it was obvious.

That afternoon I called Doctor Gonzales, at the time Minister of Mines and Hydrocarbons, and told him, as I would my own father, what was happening. I expressed that I wanted to go away, and asked him about the possibility of a scholarship, to do my Masters in England. He encouraged me to send my resume and a letter soliciting it.

That night, Chica was scheduled to attend the Municipal Council meeting. I went to her office again to type my job resignation and the letter to Doctor Gonzales. About nine that evening, I knocked on the door for five minutes before anybody opened.

"I didn't hear you knock," she said.

"I have to use the typewriter," I said and went in.

Freckles was also in the office, and they pretended to continue a work-related conversation, like nothing had happened, but their behaviour was uneasy. I also felt uncomfortable but didn't care anymore. As far as I was concerned, everything was already over. I finished typing my resume and the letter and went home.

That evening, I locked myself in my room and wrote a detailed account. I didn't want my mind to play tricks or jump to wrong conclusions. Back from the meeting, Chica knocked on the door. I didn't open. Scared, not knowing what was up, she asked the boys to knock. When I was finished, I opened and she was outraged about my notes. She thought, I was denouncing her to the world!

* * *

The following day, I delivered my resignation, and that very afternoon took the flight to Caracas to see Doctor Gonzales. He ratified his willingness to help and get me to England, and assured me in one week my scholarship would be processed. Next, I went to the British Council, and applied to the Loughborough University Graduate School.

When I returned to Puerto Ordaz, the house's door locks had been changed. I knocked and, believe it or not, Chica's father opened, holding a baseball bat, and saying, "Go back to where you were."

I couldn't believe this was happening. In a split second, I decided to yield to every demand and end the marriage. I spent the night at a modest hotel and the next day went to see a lawyer. I explained my situation, signed a power of attorney, and asked to initiate the divorce, with the specific instructions to accept any condition and not claim any assets. All I wanted was my freedom and to go away. I had no idea the price I would pay for that decision.

The following day I returned to the house, and picked up only the few things I could carry in two suitcases. Everything I valued vanished overnight. I was confused and afraid. I went back to the hotel, parked the Falcon along the curb, brought the two heavy suitcases upstairs, and opened the room with a key attached to a huge blue plastic tag.

Now, I was sitting alone on the single bed of Room 22 at The Roxy Hotel. The room was clean and unpretentious, as I liked it: small, thrifty, and clean. There was a wrought iron bed against the wall, dressed in white, clean sheets, a blue blanket, and two pillows. The hotel was run by Italians. The air conditioner was on and loud. A huge washroom with a shower in one corner gave a sense of freedom, too big for the room. The granite floor was clean and cold.

I surveyed every inch of the room, like a cat probing his new territory, pondering how I got there at all, because it made no sense. I took a shower, had dinner in the small hotel restaurant, watched television for a while, and fell asleep.

My last reflection was, "I must learn to exist again in a different way, regardless."

When I woke up, the black Falcon was gone. I knew Chica took it. It was newer, and that was the one she wanted. The real greedy person appeared, claiming anything of value. I called her, and she justified my suspicion. We met, I agreed, and switched the registration papers. She took the Falcon and I the old grey station wagon, sealing forever a door behind us, without remorse.

That week I received my severance pay, picked up my suitcases, paid my hotel bill, and drove west to Caracas. This was the second time in my life I was forced to make a deliberate, conscious decision, to walk away from everything that mattered. I kept thinking how it all happened.

The trip was long, sad, and, the final stretch, endless. It was hard to believe a few days before I was the happiest human being. Around twelve that night, I arrived at my Aunt Alicia's and asked her to put me up for a week. As always, she did. The next day, I told Mom and Sis a short version of what happened.

I was very depressed. My conclusion at that time was: We humans are no more than animals, who expect too much from each other, and to feel better we create fairy tales.

The last time I was this sad was when Father died. Now I felt like dying myself.

* * *

I needed help. I went to see Doctor Poleo, the psychiatrist who had been treating Mother for years. He practiced from the quietness of his home, which, by coincidence, was near my Aunt Alicia's, where I was staying.

The waiting room was like a greenhouse, full of tropical plants and an artificial spring, replicating the peaceful sound of the forest. After a while, a short, bald, gentle-looking man invited me in. He was as serene as his studio.

"How are you, Luis Carlos?" he asked.

He addressed me by my first name, on account of his relationship with my mother. Short of breath and sobbing, I related what this woman had done to me, how I felt, and the decisions I had made. He listened, made notes, and asked a directional question from time to time. As I drained the pollution that was poisoning my heart, my senses came back.

At one point, he stopped and said, "She doesn't seem to be that kind of person," meaning, according to my description, she was too passive and not capable of doing the things I was blaming her for. I knew what he meant. Nothing is entirely true or entirely false. We seldom find or give away the true nature of things, especially in matters of the soul.

For a moment I hesitated, but put myself together again, and said, "I saw what I saw and heard what I heard."

In reality, that was enough for me. Her very last comment, our last words, summarized the whole story: "He is not going to marry me," she said, to which I responded: "Of course not. I am the only stupid man who could have married you!"

To this day, I don't know what she expected of me, but whatever it was, I couldn't deliver.

After a few visits, and a few pills, I felt strong enough to go away. I signed my scholarship contract, sold the grey station wagon, and left for England, thinking that because of my insecurities and her stupidities, we failed our marriage and denied our boys a proper family.

In spite of everything, I owe Chica a lot. She provided, one way or another, the fuel that drove me to finish my Bachelor and

Master degrees. It seems I need a 'bigger than life' challenge, or a 'traumatic experience,' to propel me toward achievements. She provided both.

Like my Father, I lived for others. To me, God, salvation, and self-reward weren't enough. All I ever wanted was a family where children could grow within an atmosphere of trust, harmony, sharing, and understanding. Was this too much to ask? I don't think so. But very few people in my life appreciated that.

Chapter 12

For the second time I ran to a strange land following a dissolution. This time, the woman with whom I built my family had let me down. Ironically, another heartbreak opened the next great opportunity. The prize of my tribulations was another full scholarship, this time to do postgraduate work in England. Was history repeating itself, driven by the spell of 'This Márquez Thing,' taking away and then giving?

* * *

On a rainy day in August 1969, I arrived at London's Heathrow Airport. I felt lost and didn't understand the British accent. I learned my English in southern Georgia and Texas; this was quite different. A lady with my name written on a poster was signalling. I'd forgotten my arrangement with the British Council to accommodate me upon arrival. "How well organized these people are!"

A very pleasant lady took me to the foreign student's hostel. I was to stay there two days. Meals, accommodations, and reading materials were provided, as well as one seminar on the subjects of Britain: currency, transportation, weather, and visitor requirements. All was well intended, well received, and appreciated. A little time was provided to browse around the neighbourhood, a brief visit to Piccadilly Circus and Trafalgar Square. What a city London was!

The next day after breakfast, I went to the railway station and purchased a ticket to Loughborough. I was told it was about two hours from London. During the trip, I was startled by the magnificent English countryside. "This is the perfect green forest country, since it is always raining!"

Before long the train arrived at a small, very colourful station (red painted doors and phone booths, just as one sees in the movies) and a man shouted, "Loughborough!"

At last I was here with a million possibilities, a new life, and a new beginning, the product of my misfortunes.

I stepped out of the train, inhaled the fresh air, as Father always did upon visiting a new place, checked out my luggage and called the first taxi from the two or three waiting in line, this time a black British cab. I directed the driver to the Loughborough University graduate student dormitory building.

On the way, I admired the green university town: beautiful!

I had been there before, only in America, the dear, gorgeous university towns of Gainesville, Kilgore, Beaumont, and now Loughborough, England. The fabulous feeling of being a student again was enough to stir renewed enthusiasm all over. I was 24.

The housemaster received me warmly and guided me to my new room, which was more modern that I'd expected. I had a large closet, even my own in-room sink, and a beautiful view of the campus. The washrooms were in the hallway. The building was co-ed, but separate floors were assigned. Darn it!

I settled my things and went for a stroll around the campus. What first called my attention the most was a pub right in the middle of campus, which students visited often before class! I had never seen that before; I could not believe it.

That evening I came down to the dining room at seven, the dinnertime. A few early arrivals were already seated: two Indian guys from Madras, a British guy from Sheffield, and one very beautiful green-eyed girl from Ireland. The very English meal gave me an idea what to expect in the future: split pea and bacon soup, shepherd's pie, cheese, crackers, and, of course, British tea.

Monday class began at nine. I found myself sitting in Professor Seaman's class, the head of the Management Department, a very imposing man: wire rims, white hair, whiskers, and a very deep voice. He introduced the other faculty. As usual on the first day, he gave us the schedule and a list of books. He explained the philosophy, context, and purpose of the Industrial Engineering and Management Program. For his own class, he recommended the most complete book I have read about management, *The Functions of the Executive*.

I felt most at ease at Loughborough, because they laid out the expectations clearly. The school year began.

* * *

I have great admiration for fine cars, exceptional design, workmanship, and performance. At the time, my dream car was the Jaguar XKE. I first saw the car in a magazine in 1951. Its looks, curves, and sensual appeal captivated me. Love at first sight, you might say; I was ten years old then. The unforgettable feeling is still with me. When I think about this car my temperature rises, my cheeks flush, my heart pumps faster, the wind sounds musical, the sky looks clearer, the mountains greener and life more exciting.

I became slender, taller, and rather handsome, and, as I grew up, I also admired the subtle changes the car went through: a little modern touch on the headlights and taillights, a tad wider frontal air intake, an integral one-piece safety windshield and wire wheels, all of which suited me as well.

The years went by: high school, university, work, divorce… One day I was in Miami with a colleague on business and parked our rental car in a stall near the door. Right beside it was a Jaguar XKE. I stopped. The car was beautiful burgundy with tan leather. It looked so distinguished that I could almost envision its owner, a very chic man, or, it never occurred to me before, a woman. It was improbable a woman could choose such a car, not because of gender issues, but sheer competition. She would never be sure if a man was admiring her or the car, and for a woman this would be very annoying.

"Someday I will own this car. It's an old love affair of mine," I said to my business partner, caressing the long front fender with my hand, as if I was caressing a woman's leg, preparing her to be mine. He half-smiled.

***

In 1969, the opportunity arrived. I had enough money to make the foolish move. The mere wicked thought of killing two birds at a time was, to say the least, exhilarating. "I deserve it and I am going to get it."

The following Monday I took the first train to London, a very pleasant trip across the English countryside.

As soon as I landed at Union Station, I rode by taxi to Henley, the Jaguar distributor in downtown London. Five minutes past five in the afternoon. The doors were closed. I knocked and a very well dressed gentleman came to the door.

"Yes?"

"I am here to buy a car".

"I am very sorry, Sir, but we are closed."

"At what time do you close?

"We close at five."

"Could you make an exception? I am coming from Loughborough especially for this."

"I am afraid you'll have to come tomorrow, Sir."

I realised it was hopeless, dropped my hands, and gave up. I said to myself: "This could happen only in England, refusing to do this calibre of business because it's five minutes past closing time. Banks do that!"

I considered getting a German 280SL Mercedes instead, but my love for the Jaguar was final and unconditional.

I came back the next day. The same straightjacketed man offered me a British green Jaguar equipped for export and immediate delivery, same model as the one I wanted. I looked at the car and decided it was now my opportunity to refuse. I said to him, "Thank you, but my car must be pearl white and with a red interior."

I placed the order, despite that the car would take six months to arrive from Coventry. The day I picked it up, the car was only one-quarter of a tank full.

"Where is the nearest pump?" I asked the same straightjacketed gentleman.

"I haven't the slightest idea," he answered, stretching his neck like a goose.

"I guess we all have our little insecurities and hang-ups, but I won't allow you to spoil any bit of my life's dream." I smiled within myself, and concluded that to understand some British behaviour, you must be British!

Back in Loughborough, I delighted myself looking at the car from all angles, admiring the workmanship and enjoying the fragrance of the new leather interior. I was very proud of my pearl white Jaguar.

Soon, I decided to ride the car to London for the weekend. I was driving south on the M1 in my super car and near midway drove off to one of the overhead bridge restaurants. I parked my awesome car, walked upstairs, and, still turning my head around, I admired the car at a distance. I took a window seat halfway across the bridge restaurant and ordered a sausage-and-eggs breakfast. From my window I could see the traffic zooming down the highway beneath the restaurant.

I finished my breakfast, paid the bill, went down the stairway and walked to the parking lot. I arrived at the spot where I left it and realized the car was not there. I walked back and forth around the parking lot, like Father did when he was nervous, and concluded my car had been stolen. I waved down a patrol car that happened to be passing and informed the two officers my car had disappeared.

The pair grinned at each other and asked me, "Where are you traveling to and where are you coming from?"

"From Loughborough to London," I said.

With loud laughter the officers suggested, "Why don't you try the other side of the road?"

At that point, it all became clear how silly it was, and I began to laugh as well. "How many goofs do you catch a day?" I asked.

"Quite a few," they said, with the same malicious grin.

* * *

It didn't take me long to be at ease with my work and my way around. From time to time, I spent weekends in London, shopped for colourful Scottish 'Pringle' sweaters, went to Carnaby Street, hung around Queen Street, and treated myself to a steak dinner at Piccadilly or Trafalgar. I also joined the University Diners Club and made a habit of inviting a lady guest to their black tie dinners. On these occasions, I wore a smoking jacket, tasted wine and brandy, and smoked cigars, while listening to the speech of an important guest speaker. All was essential training for a future executive, I thought. I also became a member of the very exclusive Playboy Club in London. What a monkey I was then!

* * *

At midterm I meet Joan, a sociology student at the University of Leicester: impressive, simple, beautiful, mild-mannered, comforting, and unpretentious. She was exactly my opposite, because at that time I looked artificial, arrogant, and pretentious, although people who took the trouble to look deeper, which not very many people did, found out it was only a disguise.

At first we became friends and later inseparable lovers. She was always on my mind. We gave each other the unique peace of mind companionable people feel, just being there. When I met Joan she was planning a vacation to Majorca. I was terribly jealous of the idea. I believed lovers should expend every possible moment with each other. It didn't make sense to me going separate ways on vacations. Nevertheless she went. It seemed harmless, but I still didn't like it.

Believe it or not, in August of 1970 when my vacation came around, surprisingly, I did the same foolish thing. Instead of going with Joan to Spain, I went with Javier, an Argentinian friend. I should have been with Joan and Javier with the nurse he was dating. Nevertheless, we planned a trip to Malaga for a summer vacation. I chose to take my car on the ferryboat that sails from Southampton to Bilbao and drive south to Madrid and Malaga. I asked Javier what kind of visa was needed to visit Spain, and he told me no visa was required.

The very first day of vacation, Javier locked us out, leaving the car keys inside when we stopped to top up gas. The car was constructed so tightly that it was impossible to open. Surprisingly, the solution came almost by magic, as many things have come my way. There was a Jaguar distributor near the gas station. I went there, explained the situation, and asked about the most practical solution. The person in charge opened a drawer and handed me a large ring with a huge bunch of keys. It seemed weird that they could have so many keys, but I wasn't about to ponder for long. There must have been more than 100 keys. After a few clicks on the driver's side, the door opened! I was so happy and even kept the key as a replacement.

Since then I know there is a key for the solution to any problem; you just have to look around and find it.

At the ferry, we parked in a very tight spot in the lower level, where cars were packed like sardines, and settled for twelve hours' sailing to Bilbao. When we arrived, Javier went right through immigration and, when my turn came, the immigration officer stopped me and asked about my visa.

"What visa?" I said. I didn't have one.

I looked at Javier, with a mixture of rage and puzzlement, and explained to the immigration official that my friend told me no visa was needed. He looked at me, astonished about the irrelevancy of my explanation. It so happened no visa was needed for Javier because, as the immigration official informed me, Javier was an Argentinian national. But Venezuelan nationals, like me, needed a visa.

I was caught in a matter of 'diplomatic reciprocity' between two countries, he explained. I told him this was going to spoil my vacation and asked if there was an alternative. The official turned me over to a higher-ranking officer.

After pleading for a while, he agreed to give me a temporary pass to go to the nearest Spanish consulate at the French border, where I was to get a Spanish visitor's visa stamped on my Venezuelan passport. We took off from Bilbao, pointing west to San Sebastian and further out to Bayonne, France, tempted to blow the permit, turn around, and head south to Malaga, Spain.

On the way, Javier suggested, "Why don't we just turn around and not waste our time going to France? They will never know."

"You think they will never know? On the way out they will notice that I never followed the instructions to get a visa. I've had enough from you, Javier. Because of you I am in this mess now. Every time you open your mouth it gets me in trouble. We will go to France and come back when I get my visa. After all, it's a few kilometres to Bayonne."

When we arrived in Bayonne that Thursday, the Spanish consulate was closed and the following day was a holiday. The next business day for the Spanish consulate in Bayonne was Monday!

"Dammit!" I said. "What do we do now? If we wait till Monday, we lose at least four days of our vacation, or, if we continue, maybe we make it to Andorra by tomorrow and get my visa there."

We decided to go to Andorra. The ride through the Pyrenees is one of the most beautiful views in the world. At least that thought was comforting. We made it to Andorra that evening and stopped at a small family hostel for the night. When we asked about the nearest Spanish consulate, the person was startled and didn't know what to say. Andorra is an independent tiny country that doesn't have any diplomatic relations. No consulates, Spanish or otherwise, in Andorra!

All stupid things in life are done out of malice or ignorance. This one was not done out of malice. Frustrated, that night we went to a pub, had dinner, picked up two girls, and left for Perpignan on Friday morning. We arrived at Perpignan at midday, called the Spanish consulate, and they said it would open at 3:00 pm that afternoon. At least there was hope. We had a wonderful lunch and a brief siesta in the car, in front of the Spanish consulate, waiting for the doors to open to get my Spanish visa. The consul was very accommodating. I paid the duties and left after he sealed my passport.

Finally, we were on our way to the border, Gerona and Barcelona, Spain! Looking at the map on the way, we decided to stop briefly at Sitges, a small resort town about 35 miles southwest of Barcelona, to make up for lost time. We planned to stay there for a day or two. If we liked it we would stay longer; if not, we would continue to Malaga, our original destination.

We arrived at Sitges in the evening and settled in a small motel facing the waterfront. That evening we showered, had dinner, and went to a famous discotheque, where we drank a few beers and danced with the Spanish and German girls. About 3:00 am we decided to leave.

A little ways down the road, we found two Irish girls walking towards their hotel, and we offered them a ride. One was a redhead and the other a brunette. We invited them to our motel and in the confusion I got lucky with the redhead. I'd never been with a natural redhead before; it was a colourful experience!

Next morning, they went their way. We decided to stay in Sitges for a while longer. That morning on the beach, we saw the two girls again. Hoping they wanted to sample more of the Latin tapas, we tried to be friendly, but they were indifferent, like nothing had happened the night before.

By the end of the week, we were broke and still had one more week to go, according to our ferry return tickets. Javier sent a telegram to Argentina asking for more money, and I went to my English bank correspondent to arrange a modest transfer. Within two days I received my money. Javier's money was to take much longer, so I covered his expenses for the rest of the week.

When the time came to leave, Javier's money hadn't arrived and I had only enough for the trip back to England. Javier had to stay behind and wait for his transfer. I pawned my camera and gave him some survival money, attached to the promise that he would retrieve my camera and pay me back once in England.

We parted ways and I started my trip back alone, towards Lerida, Zaragoza, and Madrid. It was so hot that August in Spain, I was afraid the tires would melt. Nevertheless, driving the Jaguar was wonderful. It seemed to eat the miles away.

In Madrid, I spent the night in a cheap pension and resumed my trip to Bilbao, via Valladolid, the following morning. When I arrived at Bilbao, I was exhausted. I took the ferry and went to sleep for the rest of the cruise, relieved once I was in Southampton and eventually in my room in Loughborough. It all seemed like a dream.

* * *

Life continued, understated, where I left off, collecting Pringle sweaters and velvet jeans and seeing Joan on weekends. I would ride to Leicester, or take her back to Loughborough, or we'd go together to London for the weekend, marvellous sweet weekends! I felt loved. I felt alive.

One day Joan invited me to go north to Leeds and meet her family. To me, it was the sign of total acceptance, which I had been long expecting, ready to make long-term plans with her. That weekend, we packed overnight suitcases and chose to take the train instead of driving. Once in Leeds, we took a bus from the train station, which left us three blocks short of Joan's house.

We walked uphill carrying the heavy suitcases. Midway, I could hardly carry mine and Joan was ahead, looking back at me and grinning, "Weakling!"

She was a strong girl, maybe stronger than I. Joan's family lived in a very English working class neighbourhood. All the houses looked identical, bricked and stringy, attached for blocks. It seemed they went to great lengths to make them look undistinguishable.

The whole family was awaiting our arrival: father, mother, and younger sister. No cats, no dogs. I could see honest good people in front of me, resembling Joan, no dubious signs at all, just kindness all around. I could sense she had said good things about me because of their attitude.

Soon we were having pot roast dinner with all the trimmings, including green peas, Yorkshire pudding with gravy, and Earl Grey tea with cream and sugar to wash it all down.

Friday night. That night I slept in Joan's room. The next day we spent some time chatting at the family's brunch table, mainly about life in my part of the world, which the family was most interested in hearing: my reasons for coming to England and my intentions about returning home. I reasoned my trip was a necessity in order to be more competitive in my world.

That evening Joan's father invited us to high tea at their local pub. Being Saturday, they had live music to which I danced, first with Joan and then, as a courtesy, with her younger sister. I let Joan's father pay the bill, to avoid any chance of him being embarrassed by my apparent wealth. Next day we had breakfast with the family and Joan's father drove us to the railway station. On our way back, it became clear to me that Joan and I had a fair chance of spending the rest of our life together.

My youthful dreams kept following me, this time my passion for dogs. I just had to have one and take it back to Venezuela, one of those romantic images I carried for years, which I had to paint. I remember an 80-year old man sitting in El Gran Café in Caracas, when this was a fashionable place, sipping his espresso. Beside him lay this fabulous German Sheppard. One could tell they were inseparable. It was so gratifying to see the tranquility of the dog and the serenity of the old man, so dignified side-by-side. One could tell they were at peace with each other and the world. The vision remained in the inner chambers of my mind.

More by impulse than by reason, I researched the English breeders and found an outstanding one, a lady called Evelyn. I contacted her and soon we were both picking the best of the litter.

Three years of hard work were about to come to an end. The last months of my stay in England were spent researching my thesis, seeing Joan, and, every two weeks, visiting the little puppy at the kennel. Soon I was taking back three of my dreams: a degree, a Jaguar, and a German Sheppard. But precious Joan stayed behind, temporarily, I thought.

Chapter 13

Bursting with dreams, I came back victorious in 1970 to the same place I was three years before, Aunt Alicia's, to start fresh where I left off, without any other repercussions, I thought.

I had a new fiancé, a new job, a new car, a new dog, and multiple versions of a life in mind. I pretended to have no past, except that the past can't be erased that easily. It is there forever to deal with.

My cousin Humber took me to pick up Larry the German Sheppard at the airport. The poor dog had been in quarantine for three days, and the veterinarian who was to clear him was nowhere to be found. The dog was a poor sight: smelly, thirsty, run down, and hungry. We took it, cage and all, and placed it in the back of a pickup Humber had borrowed from a friend. When we got home, we took him out of the cage, gave him water, bathed him, and placed some food on a platter. At first he didn't eat, but once left alone, he was eating when I came back. The next day he was happily running around.

I started my job at the Ministry of Mines right away. The first day I had to leave Larry chained, because my Uncle Humberto was afraid of dogs. Poor dog, he had never been chained before. I stayed at Aunt's Alicia one week, until I found a small apartment in Las Mercedes.

Mother had hoped to live with me, as many mothers do. I was driving her to the room she rented when she told me, "Carluchito (the name she called me whenever she wanted to be sweet), "I saw this apartment, which we could rent and move into together."

"Mother, I can't live with you."

"Why can we not?" she asked.

"Because I just can't."

What a clumsy answer that was! The truth is I was ashamed to live with my mother, too selfish and afraid to be a son. I didn't know how anymore.

I saw tears running down Mother's cheeks and I knew I had broken her heart and her dreams, once more. It was one of those little dreams that could have kept her half-going all those years. I was aware that I could have rescued her and made her life a little pleasant, like Uncle Marino did my Grandma María, but I didn't do it. I was too selfish, dedicated to my car, fashion, and narrow-minded women. How selfish and ungrateful was I being? Very!

I loved my mother in my own way, but I never did anything that mattered for her, and I didn't get to know her enough. There was always someone between us: Father, Sis, my wife, my children, and even myself. Always someone!

My mother broke down after Father died and gave up along with him. She did not die then, she just stopped living for the next 48 years. What else could she do? They were not two, but one. Sis was the one that made it up to her the best she could. Sis, the one born in May, the month of the flowers, always came through in our times of need.

* * *

My job at the Ministry of Mines was the required way to repay the time they 'kept me' in England. I was then the Industrial Engineer in a group of mining engineers and was assigned to a coalmine feasibility study, one of many projects that never materialized but kept the staff busy with the illusion that something was being done. This particular one was being conducted by an English engineering firm, and, to my amazement, I was chosen to go to England to review the final findings with the company. I was so thrilled I would get to see Joan again.

* * *

I arrived at Heathrow Airport, where the Vice President of Engineering himself was waiting for me and took me to my hotel in his limousine. As soon as I was in my room I called Joan at the university. One of the girls answered and told me she'd gone to London to spend the weekend with her roommate, and she gave me the address and telephone number. That evening I joined my engineering host for dinner and, as soon as we finished, took a taxi to the address without notice to surprise Joan.

Her roommate opened the door and shouted, "Joan, guess who is here!" Joan came running down the stairs and, without saying a word, embraced me, as if I had just come from the front lines of war. I was very overwhelmed and happy to see her too. I stayed for a few minutes and agreed to meet the next day.

I spent the week working and seeing Joan evenings and nights. I asked her to come to Venezuela to get married there, and she agreed. *That simple,* I thought. *I have done it once.*

Before returning to Venezuela, I ratified my proposal, and she agreed again. I was so happy! I asked her to get things ready and the first thing I did when I arrived home was to book Joan an open airline ticket. I called her with the details and asked her to set a date. A week later I received this letter:

"Dear Luis Carlos:

I have given your invitation to go to Venezuela careful thought. I have concluded that I can't go. However, you may come and visit me any time you wish. I will be here.

Love, Joan"

I never answered, but remember writing in my agenda:

"And I ran away once more

What I knew and did best

And pretended it never happened

Looking for a breath of peace

I fell in love again

But Joan never came..."

When my ego allowed me to think about Joan again, which took me a long while, I realized I was asking too much of her. I was asking what I couldn't do myself. I was asking of her to leave her family and her country, things she could not negotiate either.

With time, this idealistic illusion of what a mother country is may vanish. I realized that, after all, one's country doesn't necessarily has to be one's country of birth, and the 'so dear' piece of land we love as a mother can also be capable of good and bad. One's country of origin becomes pure nostalgia in time. Nevertheless, in the end there is still something about that piece of land that inspires us, regardless, especially when we are far away. There is something unique about the Old Country--the music, the air, the food, the people, the sea, and the sky--that casts an extraordinary spell on us.

Sometimes, contradictorily, we run from what we love when it's not what we wish it was and still miss it, wishing it was. I shouldn't have returned.

One thing I have done, while not being able to grow, is to pretend I am doing well even when I am not; this way problems seem to vanish. Being on the other side of the fence is compelling, but I always pay a price!

III
The Family
(Memories 1970 - 2009)

And we become stray sheep
And we need urgent help
And I choose her to help me instead
Because I think I need her most.

And we build sand castles together
And we tear them down again
Because we think we are eternal
We repeat, repeat, our mistakes.

And we part separate ways
To make our very own mistakes
And build sand castles once more
And tear them down again.

In our very own way...

Chapter 14

~

A family is like a river that inevitably disappears in the vastness of the ocean.

~

Caracas 1971. Soon after my arrival from England I leased an annex in Las Mercedes. The place was small but very well appointed with antique furniture, which I love so much because it adds character to my life. It even had a microbar like a hotel suite, offering comfort and elegance at the right price.

I moved in with Larry the German shepherd, placed him in the tiny fenced garden, opened the tap, filled his bowl, and went to sleep. The following morning, while getting ready to go to work, I heard a lot of barking.

When I opened the door, someone was running past the fence. It was my neighbor holding a gun and yelling, "Take it away or I shoot!"

"Hold it! He is harmless!" I said.

"I don't care. Take it away or I'll shoot the hell out of it!"

I convinced him to put the gun down and talk. "Look," I said, "he is on the other side of the fence and just wants to make a little fuss and feel he is holding his ground. It's their natural instinct but does not mean any harm."

Still shaking, he explained that he was terrified of dogs because when he was a kid he was bitten by one. I tried to convince him that as long as the dog was behind the fence there was no danger. No way! He still complained to my landlord about the dog scaring him to death and argued he couldn't walk to his own annex without confronting the dog. He didn't have the courage to pass by even if the dog was inside the fence.

In desperation, I chained the dog to the window's steel bars, placed some water in his pan, and left. When I came back the poor dog was frantic and the landlord dictated that Larry had to go.

I panicked and sold the dog to a breeder for a fraction of the original cost. Was it 'This Márquez Thing' again or plain stupidity? I had no business traveling with a dog, but because of my obsession I was willing to go through all kinds of trouble, including bringing a dog all the way from England. At the first sign of adversity I gave up.

As the breeder was leading him away Larry turned his head, lifted his ears, and looked at me, confused. It was like he was asking, "After all we've been through? Are you going to leave me here?" This happens to my dreams from time to time. One by one, I let them drift away, leaving me also confused.

* * *

During that time, I meet a widow through Sis. Like Chica, she was older than I. We began dating in spite of my scepticism to fall into the same trap again. Her name was Marcia. She had two sons and pretended to be an artist. Because I looked a little too young to be her boyfriend, she used to call me 'Nene' (Baby), which provoked foxy grins from her friends. In time she introduced me to a great bunch of people who met every weekend at Pedro's beach house.

The story goes that Pedro's wife divorced him and, to occupy his mind, he designed this beach house, which took him five years to build and all his spare energy. Every Friday night we all pitched in for supplies and car-pooled to Pedro's beach house, located on a beautiful bay called Buche, two hours from Caracas. I worked all week and beach-partied the entire weekend. This became my life for a while.

Marcia was a devoted mom during the week, which I admired. One day she had her appendix removed and, don't ask me why, I didn't go to visit her at the hospital. From then on she didn't want to see me again. Much later, I ran into her at a mall and almost didn't recognize her; she was ten years older and grey-haired. I understood then: we weren't a matching couple after all. That was the last time I saw her.

One weekend the group decided not to go to the beach. Instead, we met at a trendy Caracas bar, *Mario's*, famous for its red neon sign. There was a real Mario behind the bar, appointed by his mother, who owned the establishment.

I was sitting at the bar listening to the jazz in the background and sipping Scotch and soda, easily, with my other friends. Mario was across the bar helping his mother. Slowly, the front door opened and Mario said in a whispering soft voice, "Here are the two models I told you guys about."

As they entered the room, Mario welcomed them with his usual cunning remark, "Sofia, Bella. Welcome to Mario's!" Then he came around the bar, guiding them, and made a general presentation pointing to us, "These are my friends."

We moved along with our drinks to the small booths in the saloon and ordered two more drinks for the new girls. As I sat beside Bella, she crossed her legs and smiled. While looking at her thighs folded below her miniskirt, I couldn't help but murmur to myself, "This girl is built like a brick house."

Then Mario made a comment about Bella and me being relatives, because we had the same family name and both our parents were from the Andes. Hers were from San Cristobal, mine from Trujillo. To top it all off, she had a cousin also named Carlos and, according to Mario, there was a good chance that Bella and I could be related. Our first reaction was to joke about these coincidences. After a few minutes we cleared up the matter and concluded that, thank goodness, we were neither cousins nor even remotely related.

Talking, flirting, and laughing, our rendezvous continued, unveiling the layers of our personalities with the clear intention to impress each other, at least enough to make a connection. It didn't take much.

I told her about my father being a lawyer and my studying in England. She told me about her father being a general and her being an ex-beauty queen at the Miss Venezuela pageant. She told me about not having a boyfriend right now and I told her I was divorced. We both were pleased. We continued to reveal our little secrets, one by one, covered with little white lies from time to time. As the conversation continued we both realized, and it was written all over, that we liked each other a lot. One, two, three drinks and an effortless 1:00 a.m. arrived.

Sensing that it was time to go, I played one of my master moves. I asked her if she wouldn't mind giving me her phone number, so we could be in touch again. "I would be delighted," she said. Then, I mentioned my pen was in the car and asked her to walk out with me to get it.

Get it?

When I opened the Jaguar's door, she smiled. She understood our game. I wrote my number on a small piece of paper, asked for hers, and, like a ritual, ripped it in two. This simple act started a thirty-year story, which seems to keep going and going. It never ends.

* * *

Once home, I got out of the car, opened the gate, drove up the driveway, parked the car, and closed the gate. When I was about to retire, the phone rang.

"Hello. Is this Luis Carlos? This is Bella," she said without pausing.

"Bella, what a surprise!"

"Look, I am sorry to call you this late, but I wonder if you could do me a great favour. Remember I told you I am staying with Sofia, my girlfriend. Well, her boyfriend is here and they are quarrelling. I feel awkward being in the middle of all this, so I wonder if I could spend the rest of the night at your house. Would you mind?"

I had never received a similar request before, one I was not able to refuse.

"Well, Bella, there is no reason why not, considering there is still a small chance we could be relatives and that is what relatives are for. No?" I say jokingly.

"Fine. Write down the address and call on the intercom when you get here. Okay?"

"I could be there in a half-hour," I said.

I rang the intercom, Bella answered, and in no time she was in the car carrying a small overnight bag. We drove home. On the way she told me how difficult the relationship with her family was, and how she stayed out most of the time. I listened and tried to sympathize. I have difficulties seeing distress and not helping out.

The first thing that caught my attention about her was how vulnerable she was. Almost immediately, I assumed the role of protector, and for the next thirty years I faithfully carried out that responsibility. I still pretend to fill it partially, although I am not, and never was, totally capable.

At home, there was my single bed and a blue velvet couch. She slept on the blue velvet couch, but woke up in my bed. What was meant to be was meant to be. From that day on, our souls and bodies fused in ways that we could not then imagine. That morning before leaving for work, I placed a small note and some money for groceries in an envelope. When I came back, I found Bella had done grocery shopping, prepared dinner on the small hot plate, and hand-washed my laundry. I never experienced such a clear way of delivering a message before: *I want to stay and I can be useful.* I was startled.

We had dinner, did the dishes in the washroom sink and planned the rest of the week. That night I found out Bella didn't drink water, only Pepsi Cola. As it developed, we stayed together the rest of the week, much the same way. When the weekend came around, I informed the group that Bella and I were coming. That Friday we bought groceries, went to her parents' to pick up some clothes, and joined the group. We were to spend the weekend at the beach, and the group took her in graciously.

I looked at Bella going into the water. She looked gorgeous in her white bathing suit, like a mermaid. The beach liked her. She seemed to be in her natural habitat, the ocean.

What I liked most about her, besides being simply beautiful, was her sensitiveness of soul and unawareness of reality, not like anyone I had met before, a dreamer. She was running away and I was running away too. Maybe we could run together, I thought.

I told her about my marriage and how it ended, and how I had two sons whom I never saw, and how I had no intention of marrying again. She said it was all right. I was disarmed.

* * *

Just when I began to feel happy again the phantom of Chica appeared. She was more vindictive than ever and went to the courts, claiming three years of child support. She knew very well I left my share of the assets for that purpose, more than enough to cover the kids' expenses until their coming of age. In addition, willingly, I kept silent and didn't bring the real reason of our divorce to the courts. It was an unwritten agreement, which she was supposed to respect, but she didn't.

"Why else would I do it?" I asked the courts.

They ignored me and ruled as if this never happened. I believed in people then and acted in good faith, thinking I could trust her, but greed and vengeance took over and won. One evening, while I was out for a walk, Chica came. She broke the radio antenna of the Jaguar and cut the curtains of the annex through an opening with a pair of scissors. Her unwritten message: "I hate you because you left me!"

A month later the court impounded my car and garnisheed my salary. Mario lent me an old motorcycle his messenger boy wasn't using. Bella and I rode it, pretending it was an adventure.

* * *

It had been one year since I came back from England. I paid my service time to the Ministry of Mines and was in a position to take an offer from Shell Oil. I contacted Mr. Frederickson at Shell's human resources in Caracas. He remembered me and invited me to his office to complete the forms and take the required physical examination. The company offered me the position of Senior Analyst Methods Standards in Shell's Industrial Engineering Department in Lagunillas. It was the type of job any young professional would kill for: prestigious, well paid, with subsidized housing, a homeownership plan, a car loan, full health coverage, training, and full benefits. The company ran an oil camp community in the middle of nowhere, like a country club, complete with swimming pool, golf course, and the Cordon Bleu Restaurant.

What else could I ask for?

I quickly delivered my resignation to the Ministry of Mines and shared the news with Bella. She was sad to see me go, because she thought she would never see me again. I assured her, one way or another we would continue to see each other. In the meantime, I asked her to return home to her parents. She didn't fancy the idea and instead made arrangements at a boarding house in Altamira, a nice Caracas suburb.

The following Monday I was given my ID card and other placement documents. Another Enrique, a master in nuclear physics, and I started the same day and were sent to the oil camp in the same company plane. We connected very quickly and became very good friends. In the beginning we were lodged at the company's motel for a week, after which we were assigned our respective 'bachelor apartments.'

Our boss, a German-American expatriate, was good and helpful. There were three more Venezuelan industrial engineers about our age in the department, all of them married. My furnished apartment was the third in a lane of twelve. It had a covered carport that remained vacant, because Chica had had my car impounded.

The first thing I did was to apply for a company car loan. Everything was within walking distance but nobody dared to walk. It was a matter of prestige, and I also needed a car to visit Bella on weekends. The loan was approved and I purchased a tiny white two-door Opel coupe with red interior. Every weekend, almost dozing at the wheel, I did seven hundred kilometres one way to Caracas, which took me eight hours. I used to leave Lagunillas on Friday afternoon and return exhausted on Sunday night, sometimes so drowsy I almost drifted off the road.

We talked on the phone daily and saw each other on weekends for almost a year. At times it was frustrating, because the town had only one long distance line and I had to wait my turn, usually for more than an hour, and sometimes after all this trouble, to find out Bella was not at home. Many times during the rainy season there was no communication at all.

* * *

Chica, with that special women's intuition, found out about the relationship between Bella and me. She committed herself to destroy it, using the courts again, and to choke me in my new job. One day she proposed to bring the children to Maracaibo (Venezuela's second biggest city) "to see their father," I agreed to meet at Hotel El Lago. She and the children flew in on a Saturday around midmorning. I hadn't seen or spoken to the children in four years. When I saw them I didn't recognise them.

Utu was now nine and Ike six. We got reacquainted, trying hard to bring into focus what had been a faint blur for so long. The four of us sat in the hotel lobby and tried to make some family conversation. The boys talked about the school they were attending and I described my small apartment at the oil camp. We tried hard.

Chica was using an ancient control method: clamping the throat to suffocate the victim, from time to time easing the pressure to allow a slow death. Only this time, instead of her hands and teeth she used the children.

After a while, Chica sat the boys at a table for lunch and we took a place in a corner facing them to review our standing issues. I proposed before going any further, hoping she would show some

194

willingness to cooperate, to release my car, drop the garnishee on my salary, and recognise the value of the assets I left towards the children's expenses. If she agreed, I promised to see the boys frequently and follow the arrangement to the letter.

"It's the honest thing to do," I said.

She refused. Instead, she proposed we come back together, keeping separate accounts, and invited me to spend the night at the hotel to discuss the details. Jezebel! I have tried my best for years to understand this absurd proposition without success. How in the world could she propose such an artificial solution, entailing living together as if nothing had happened, knowing full well my point of view about a relationship purely administered by the courts?

I felt the 'sword of Damocles' falling on my neck again. I gave up on the conversation and proposed that since they came so far, I would take the boys to spend at least a day together and show them where I live. She realised she was not included, but still agreed.

On the way I initiated conversation, and the boys followed easily. I told them we were going to spend the night at my apartment, which was very small but I thought they would like it. To make it look like a little adventure, I told them we would cook our own meals and spend the following day at the swimming pool. They liked the idea, but with kids you never know. During the hour-long drive I told them a little about the company camp and how oil was extracted from the ground, piped to the refineries, and then turned into gasoline, kerosene, or lubricants, trying my best to avoid technicalities. I didn't ask personal questions they might interpret as prying into their lives.

We arrived on time and I showed them how tiny the apartment was, comparing it to a squirrel hole. I asked if they were hungry and they weren't. I guess the idea to cook our own meals didn't attract them that much. Watching television did, and I sat my two boys on a small couch until I saw their heads droop. After a brief snack, they were ready to sleep. I showed them the washroom, pulled out the mattress of my single bed, and laid it on the floor, then dressed the two halves and asked them in which half they would like to sleep. They chose the mattress on the floor.

In this part of the world, before bed, children asked their parents for 'benediction' and parents would answer, "Que Dios te bendiga" (God bless you). All I could say at this time was, "Goodnight," and I received no answer. We had a silent and peaceful night.

The next day we woke up around eight and prepared eggs, orange juice, toast, and coffee for breakfast. For a moment I remembered the baby bottles Mother used to prepare for me out of her leftover coffee, which, come to think of it, must have contributed to 'This Márquez Thing.' After breakfast we went to the swimming pool and the boys had a ball, splashing and racing each other. I went into the swimming pool a couple of times and experienced being a father again.

Also, for a moment I thought how wonderful all of us could have been, if their mother and I hadn't separated. It was far too late now to change that, mainly because of her attitude towards money and her insistence on misusing the law, knowing nobody has or ever will get anything from me by force. A real shame, because the boys could have had a father.

The boys had enough swimming. We changed back into our clothes and had a nice late lunch at the company's restaurant. Before we headed back to Maracaibo I drove them through the camp, so they could actually see the oil wells pumping, some even in the middle of people's gardens, only they didn't belong to the homeowners as in Texas.

Later on, I delivered them back to their mother and they flew away. I drove back to the camp, again leaving part of my life behind.

* * *

In the meantime, the daily phone calls and the weekly travels to see Bella were wearing me out. At one point, paying the boarding house became difficult for her and I suggested again moving back with her parents, but she refused. Then, I decided to bring her to stay with me at the camp for a while, just to figure things out.

* * *

It was Friday. I was on my way to Maracaibo to pick up Bella at the airport. I was looking forward to seeing her and discussing things. The flight was on time. I was watching the exit across the aisle, where she should appear at any moment. I became anxious and began pacing, like Father did when he got nervous. She was taking forever...

There she was! I waved, rising a little on my toes. She noticed and smiled.

We drove back to the oil camp, happy to be together again, looking and smiling at each other. No thoughts about the past or the future, just concentration on the present.

Once in the apartment, we made love as if we hadn't ever before, took a refreshing shower, and cuddled for the night after a nourishing dinner. We faded into sleep, reviewing the last few weeks, and avoided conversation on any type of decision-making, just behaving as if we were on vacation. The following day we had lunch at the company's restaurant and spent the afternoon at the pool. Her company, the freshness of the water, and the sight of each other made the moment sublime. Then, we bought groceries and felt at home again.

I wanted Bella to experience the limited environment and restrictions of the oil camp, because its people were chosen not by us but by the company. I went to work in the morning and came home for a brief lunch. Sometimes, after work, we used to invent some excuse to go to Maracaibo for a ride, and weekends at poolside took the place of the beach weekends.

We played house for two weeks, at the end of which I had to tell Bella to return home, because people were beginning to notice and it was against company regulations. She was distraught, but there was no choice. I sent her home that weekend. At the gate, she looked back with tears in her eyes, like a wounded sheep. It broke my heart to see her go, but I couldn't keep her any longer, for the time being.

At least we tasted a little of how it could be if we were living together. It reminded me of the day I left Larry (the German shepherd), because she gave me the same look. I felt responsible, guilty, and sad. From that point on Bella became my obsession, because I felt I'd let her down. I began to worry about: Where would she live? How would she manage to buy food and her Pepsi colas? I realized how vulnerable she was and began to count the hours till I'd see her again. But where would she be? How could I find her? For sure not at the boarding house or her parent's house; that much I knew. Then I received a letter telling me how sad she was to leave, how attached she was to me, and she gave me the phone number of her cousin Grisel, who would know at any time where to find her, in case I wanted to see her again. Grisel was in the same situation: no job and living away from her family.

That weekend, after eight hours of anxious driving, I arrived at Caracas. It took me three phone calls to locate Bella. The first thing I did was to buy her plenty of Pepsi colas and walk her to the rooming house where she was staying. It was not a pretty place. We talked and I tried to convince her again that the best place for her to be was home with her parents and to get a small job to begin a normal life. This time I was successful. I guess she already had her quota of hardships.

I took her home, she apologised to her parents and they took her back. We saw each other every day for the rest of the weekend. On Sunday I went back to Lagunillas, feeling I had achieved something. I had placed her on the right track.

While talking on the phone the following week, she told me about the job she took as salesperson at a ladies' shoe shop. I assumed her father, or someone who knew her father, helped her get the job. Nevertheless, I saw it as a great achievement and I felt proud of her.

My vacation was due and Enrique (the guy who started the oil job on the same day I did) talked about going to Bogotá, twelve hours' drive south. I had been to Colombia once, but only to the border town of Cúcuta, which didn't count as the real thing. I saw it as a great opportunity, to get to know a little bit more the neighbor country. On the way we would pass through Trujillo and Mérida where Father and Mother were born, and San Cristobal where Bella's father was born, which seemed to mean something. From there we would drive into Cúcuta, Bucaramanga, and, finally, Bogotá. I needed to get away from the routine for a while and said "yes."

We departed in Enrique's Triumph TR7 on July 7, 1971. The whole trip was through the mountains. The car was so close to the edge it made me dizzy. Enrique was having a ball, testing the qualities of the sports car against the turns. In time we reached Bogotá, a very traditional colonial city. The mark of the Spanish conquistadors was everywhere.

We settled into a small hotel and then went sightseeing, hoping to find a nice restaurant by dinnertime. We didn't. Back at the hotel, the desk clerk told us about one just around the corner. This is what happens when you don't know and don't ask.

The following day we visited Plaza Bolívar and the museum Quinta Bolívar. To be a foreigner in a country and to find a fellow Venezuelan so revered made me feel proud.

The next day we met two girls, who took us around the city and to the Monserrate cable car. From there one was able to view the whole city.

When the vacation was over, the drive back didn't seem shorter as it usually did, maybe because of the steep cliffs and Enrique driving 'grand tourism' style. I didn't tell Bella about the trip, as I did not see the point.

* * *

A few days later, Chica called to thank me for the good time the boys had during their visit to Maracaibo. Once more I asked her to lift the impound order on my car, and to my surprise she acceded. The following week I went to Caracas, picked up Bella and the release order, and recovered the Jaguar. To celebrate the occasion we gave the car a full service.

Later on I called Chica, thanked her for her understanding and proposed to take the boys to Coney Island amusement park, during my next visit to Caracas. I let her know Bella would be with us. If Chica minded, she didn't express it.

The following weekend we picked up the boys. Bella came out of the car, and I introduced her to my children. Without any hesitation Utu immediately took the front seat, leaving the back seat to Bella and Ike. Bella and I looked at each other, rolled our eyes, and smiled. Was he following his mother's instructions or his own instincts?

The day was well spent. The boys enjoyed the rides, the Shetland ponies, and the hotdogs. I was thrilled to see them with Bella. After all, they were part of a reality that couldn't be ignored.

The weekend came to an end and I returned to the camp, calling Bella as soon as I arrived. By then, I realized it was impossible to live without her. I thought about her day and night. I was well onto a road of no return. She needed help and I was resolved to give it to her, but the truth is I needed her more.

Convinced we could become our mutual saviours, within a week I made the decision to marry again. Amazing, how a glass of Scotch and a phone number, fuelled by loneliness, changed the direction of our lives.

Bella's family and mine were well known to each other, perhaps too well known, which apparently gave them the right to barge into our lives. As it happened, my Uncle Humberto and Bella's father graduated the same year from the Military Academy. They were not close friends but maintained a close link throughout their careers, and their wives competed with each other for status.

My Aunt Alicia supplied Mother periodic gossip, ignoring the fact that my Uncle Humberto had been discharged from the force for "dubious financial dealings." Everybody did it, but he had the bad luck to get caught. In contrast, Bella's father made it all the way and retired with honours and the rank of general. In addition, Bella's uncle once worked under my father at the Tax Administration Service.

The two families were intertwined and felt entitled to give their opinion about our projected marriage. It's true that all parents want their children to marry well. Mom and Sis were no exception, and they considered Bella unsuitable. They placed a cold barrier from the beginning. Bella always felt my mom and Sis didn't give her a fair chance to prove herself. Nevertheless, I decided to start a family of my own, again, this time forever.

* * *

That Friday, driving on the same road I had driven many times before, I didn't even feel sleepy. I was motivated by my lifetime goal. When I was near Caracas, I stopped by a phone booth, called Bella, and told her I was on my way. I couldn't hold back any longer and said, "I have a surprise for you." She insisted I tell her, but I replied, "Hold your horses; I shall be there in half an hour."

When I arrived at her house, I rang the intercom and she yelled back twice, "I am coming, I am coming!"

I could tell she was very excited. She came rushing, wearing her usual tight jeans, skimpy blouse, flowing hair to the shoulders, and riding boots. I opened the car door and she jumped on my lap, smacking a kiss on my lips.

"Now, tell me: what is the surprise?"

"Well, I just want to say that I have decided to marry you."

Her expression changed, her eyes opened wide, and her jaw fell open.

"Wow! This I was not expecting! I never expected you to marry me."

"This is the one reason I have decided to go for us. You have never demanded anything or placed any condition, were always flexible, never complained about the difficulties we went through, and embraced every bit. Now, you must promise me to take care of yourself. Not like those women who, after marriage and babies, abandon themselves and get fat."

She was moved. "Of course I will marry you. I promise to be a good wife and I won't get fat!" Then she laughed and kissed me again.

I felt so happy knowing we had a direction in our lives. Next day, Bella told her family and I formally asked the general for her hand in marriage. Like the old days!

I never believed in engagement rings. I like things simple and elegant, like Father. We got two white gold bands in a small jewellery shop and overlaid our initials in yellow gold script. Bella's had a "C" and mine had a "B." My size was eight and hers was six.

* * *

Federico was the owner of the Hotel Waldorf in Caracas. Every detail of the landmark reflected his personality. Some important Matisse, Degas, Monet, and Rembrandt originals were hanging in the entrance and in the main banquet hall, reflecting his love of art. The pastel colors of the walls mirrored his soft and honest disposition. The exquisiteness of the cuisine and extensive wine list exemplified his 'joie de vivre.'

He was a close friend of the general and the recipient of a host of favours in his days of power. Now that the general was retired, it was Federico's turn to show his appreciation, which on this occasion he overdid.

On October 9, 1971, Bella and I married at the Waldorf Hotel. That day, I left Lagunillas in the morning, checked in at the Caracas Hilton, left my luggage, and went to my appointment at Giovanni's.

"I am getting married today, Giovanni! Make me look good: haircut, shampoo, manicure, and the works!"

"Absolutely signore, I will make you look like a million dollari," Giovanni said.

Two hours later, I was driving back to the hotel with my million-dollar look. I arranged my Carnaby Street tuxedo, wingtip shirt by Luciano, silk socks, and grey ascot on the bed. I sent my

202

shoes for a shine and settled into a bubble bath, followed by an hour's nap. At six, I dressed, placed the small case with our two wedding bands in my pocket, and drove the Jaguar to the Hotel Waldorf. I parked the car in front of the main entrance and prepared to accept the woman I'd chosen to be with for the rest of my life.

* * *

I was astonished by the beautiful decoration Federico had provided. The tables were dressed in white linen with pink bows stitched over the sides. Each table had a centrepiece of fresh pink roses.

The main feature was a magnificent ten-layer wedding cake, also decorated with pink bows and roses, "Luis Carlos y Bella" written on it. Pink satin bows adorned the wood-paneled walls, complementing Federico's paintings. A string quartet was playing my favourite Strauss waltzes, my only request. The whole display made my soul tremble, and I thought how happy Father would have been if he was here.

Scanning the large ballroom, Bella's extensive family was anticipating the arrival of the other guests. Bella's parents were sitting at the table beside ours. The general was wearing his gala uniform, worn only on special occasions, and this was the first time after his retirement from the Army. It was a splendorous cream coat adorned with the general's insignias and trimmed with golden braided olive branches, regal gear, and red striped black pants. The highest Venezuelan honour, the Orden del Libertador, was proudly pinned on his chest. He looked magnificent. Bella's mother was sitting beside him, wearing a simple but elegant black dress, adorned with sequins.

Around the general, other prominent members of his family were sitting, dressed in formal attire. Bella's mother's family apparently was not invited. My mother didn't attend our wedding either. These two women, Bella and Mother, never accepted each other, oblivious or unaware of the suffering they caused me.

Sis and Billy entered the room and took a table near us. Doctor Gonzales, my dearest mentor, didn't attend, but sent a gift and a lovely note. Pedro and the group from the beach house arrived. Many other people I didn't know made their entrance. Nobody from my extensive family was present, except Sis and Billy. I must have lost them along the way, a little on my account, a little on Father's, and the rest on their own account. All lost forever, what a shame!

The waiters were setting up the bar and arranging appetizers galore around the main table. On the way I stopped the headwaiter and asked for a glass of Scotch.

"Sir, the drinks are not being served yet," he replied.

I was surprised he did not recognise me. "I need a drink now, please. I am the groom!" He caught the urgency of my demand and brought me a glass of Scotch and soda right away. I really needed it.

I sat with Sis and Billy for a while and asked about Mother. Sis apologised on her behalf and pointed out Mother was not up to anything emotional yet. I thought to myself, *She should have made an exception*, and changed the subject.

At that very moment, Bella and her maid-of-honour entered the room. Bella was wearing a simple but elegant satin pink ball gown and no accessories, except soft pastel makeup. Her flowing hair was a brilliant platinum gold colour chosen for the occasion, a pleasant and startling surprise. She looked astonishing, simply beautiful!

For a while we went from table to table, greeting, smiling, and thanking everyone for coming. When we were about to sit at our table, a photographer required us for pictures next to Federico's favourite painting and led us towards the entrance of the ballroom. Federico himself came in, joined the photo shoot, and gave his ideas about the best angles. In the meantime, appetizers and drinks were being served. The music was pleasant, almost imperceptible, but as soothing as the sound of nature itself.

As soon as we came back to our table, the justice of the peace and his secretary arrived. It was 9:00 pm, the time scheduled to perform our wedding ceremony.

Everyone was called to the farthest corner of the room, where a small mahogany table dressed in white linen had been placed for the purpose. Everyone gathered in a circle around the table. The justice opened the books and invited Bella and me to step forward.

Without any other introduction he said, "Please join your hands," and proceeded to read the duties of the spouses, as established in the Civil Code, Chapter XI. Then, he asked, "Luis Carlos, do you take Bella for your wife?"

"Yes, I do."

Turning to Bella, "Do you take Luis Carlos for your husband?"

"Yes, I do."

Joining his hands to ours, he said, "On behalf of the Republic and by the authority of the Law, I declare you joined in marriage."

The witness and the two of us signed the document and were handed the certificate.

The usual toast of champagne, a light meal, and delicious wedding cake followed. We continued our gracious pilgrimage to every table and made sure every guest felt attended.

Around 11:00 pm we went up to our room at the Waldorf, changed our clothes, and sneaked out to our suite at the Hilton. A long life of happiness was waiting for us.

The next day, late, we had brunch, loaded the car with our wedding gifts, and started the trip back to Lagunillas. A beautiful trailer house was waiting as our first home, set on green lawn at the top of a hill.

The day I married Bella (October 9, 1971) was by far the happiest day of my life. It fulfilled one of the dreams I had for many years, the kind of dream one elaborates in fine filigree to the smallest detail, the kind one replays many times during one's life.

There is desire, which is natural; there is need, which is necessary. And then there is love, the kind of love that is anxious, indispensable, compulsory, that one cannot do without or one feels as if one could die if one doesn't have it. Ours was a mixture of all that. This was Bella to me.

* * *

A few weeks later during a short trip to Caracas, Bella and I were driving the Cota Mil West and my cellular phone rang, it was Sis calling. "I have some bad news," she said. "Utu, your son, died in a car accident. His aunt was taking him to his grandfather's ranch in Upata when it happened."

Bella noticed the expression on my face. "Is there something wrong?" she asked.

"Utu is dead," I said.

"Oh! I am so sorry, Luis Carlos!"

Tears ran down my cheeks and then I kept silent the rest of the way. She respected my silence.

He was thirteen when his life ended. Images of the short while I was allowed to be his father rushed through my mind: Beaumont, Texas, when he was a baby; Upata, after a year's absence; Puerto Ordaz, where he grew to be eight; the oil camp, when he was ten; and Coney Island, the last time, at age eleven.

He died reportedly traveling in the passenger seat, when a front-end collision occurred and he was thrown out of the car and landed on the asphalt. He was not wearing a seat belt.

According to what Ike told me, years later, the body remained on the side of the road for six hours, because the coroner of the nearest town was nowhere to be found, until Utu's Uncle Alberto came and threatened to shoot the person in charge if the body was not moved to the nearest hospital immediately.

I never fulfilled my role as his father. Chica didn't allow us to have a normal relationship after we divorced. She did, however, allow him to relate to Sis and Mother, his aunt and grandmother. At least he enjoyed that part of the family.

I didn't go to his funeral. I figured if I was not there for him alive, I had no right to be there. My moral code didn't allow it. It was not a matter of being right or wrong, just a matter of being me. My father was not present at his father's funeral. I did not make it to my father's funeral, and I didn't go to Utu's funeral, probably because of 'This Márquez Thing.' I remember him as he was the last time I saw him, at eleven.

Later on I also learned he was scheduled to go to Riverside Military Academy, my old boarding school, that year. What could have motivated that choice? I like to think maybe to be near his father in some way.

Utu has a place in my heart, right beside Alvaro and Father. They were three beautiful lives that ended too soon. Strangely, I have never allowed myself to mourn Utu's death. He remains an unresolved chapter of my life.

* * *

The first days in the trailer were a fairy tale. Bella was the perfect wife. She strived to prepare wonderful meals, did our laundry, maintained the place tidily, and kept fresh flowers. She tried her best to do everything right with love and care.

Inexplicably, as soon as I married Bella, I became obsessed about her past. Somehow, before, it didn't matter, but once married it became morbidly important to me. I claimed ownership and believed I had the right to pry into all areas of her soul. All the insecurities and traumas of my life surfaced. As if possessed, I began to recreate the past. I blamed her for dating other men during our courtship. She reasoned that we were not engaged and, besides, I was the one who said I wasn't going to marry her anyway.

I became jealous of everything, even her wardrobe. I asked her how she got it and she said some items were gifts. I threw them in the garbage as if they were contaminated. I told her from then on I would be the only one to buy her anything. I replaced everything!

I thought I was moved by great love. Now I understand I was in the midst of insanity. Subconsciously, I was blaming her for Chica's actions. I submerged into a period of obsession, selfishness, and plain psychological revenge. I pounded her soul hard, over and over. It seems I waited until we reached the happiest time of our lives, to turn it into a disaster. Was this part of 'This Márquez Thing'? A compulsion to destroy anything that resembled happiness?

One day she gave up and, in a rage of desperation, took a whole bottle of sleeping pills in front of me. The cry was clear: "Is this what you want? Do you want to destroy me? I'll do it myself before you do it!" I drove her to the limit.

I took her to the company's clinic. The doctors pumped her stomach and retained her for observation. For the next few days we tried to live as much of a normal life as possible. That weekend we took a peace break and went to Caracas to have a breath of fresh air.

* * *

We were sitting in my sister's family room having drinks. Sis, Billy, and two of their friends were making jokes. Somehow, Bella interpreted one of the jokes as directed at her, stood up and told me to give her the car keys, ran out, and took off.

Everything happened too fast. I called a taxi and rushed to the hotel, afraid she could have an accident. Once at the door of our room, without warning, Bella jumped me and began pulling my hair. She'd lost it.

That night we didn't speak. The next morning we went to her parents and I told them she would have to stay until we could figure out how to put our lives together again. For a while Bella lay crying on what used to be her bed, just mumbling, "Please… Please…"

At this point, I realized everything was too much for her and me. I told the general the best thing, under the circumstances, was to take her to a psychiatric clinic and help her back on her feet because I didn't know how. He agreed. They admitted her that night to La Virgen María Rest Home and I returned to Lagunillas.

The following weekend I came to see her. We spoke, and I explained what was being done was for our benefit, to 'clear up' before making any further decisions. The doctor said she was not ready to leave yet and had to stay another week.

Bella was discharged as scheduled the following weekend. I suggested she stay with her parents under a separation agreement, to give us some time to figure things out. She agreed. I stayed overnight and that Monday we signed the separation agreement. We had been married for only three months!

I am not proud of this period of my life. By nature, I despised making anyone suffer, especially someone who trusted me and depended on me. 'This Márquez Thing' haunted me. There is no way I could compensate Bella for the aggravations of this period.

* * *

We stayed apart for one month and talked on the phone from time to time. The truth is we missed each other terribly. Sometimes it's necessary to be away, to find out how much one cares. At the end of the fourth week we decided to come back to each other again. I made arrangements to have Bella flown back on the company's plane. I promised myself to control my obsessions and told Bella it was probably best for us to go away. We talked about Canada as the best of Europe and America, the best of both worlds, and our best chance to settle and live in peace. She agreed to go away with me.

Immediately, a rush of merriness flowed through our veins. Without delay, with boiling enthusiasm, we placed ads on the company's bulletin and the local paper to sell everything.

Looking back, I placed her in the same position I once placed Joan and Chica, when I asked them to go away with me. Bella chose me above everything.

In search of a new start, we applied for a resident visa for Canada in 1972. We thought with my qualifications it wouldn't be hard to get. The gifts and the cars were sold. I resigned my job at Shell and we moved temporarily to Bella's parents', until our resident visa for Canada would be granted.

After three months, our visa hadn't come. Tired of waiting, we decided to fly to Toronto on a temporary visitor's visa, before our money ran out. To wish us a happy trip, the general gave us a going-away dinner party to which the whole family was invited. And to protect us from evil he gave each of us a small cross on a gold chain.

The following day we were on our way to New York to take the honeymoon we never had and continue to Toronto to restart our life. The best of my wardrobe purchased in England was packaged and sent into temporary storage to be shipped later to our final destination, an impractical attempt to retain my symbols, because the packers looted everything; very little arrived. I failed the insurance claim, because the company refused on the grounds that a detailed list was never made. Was nature giving me a humbling lesson?

* * *

The Park Plaza Hotel was one of the two hotels I knew in New York, Father's favourite, which this time seemed to be the perfect choice. It was almost directly across from the world famous Waldorf Astoria and near Central Park, convenient enough for people like us not to get lost in New York, or at least to have clear bearings to be able to come back.

Besides, if we were hoping to give ourselves a second chance, it might just as well begin with all the illusion of happiness that money can buy. I had gone through it myself in England for a while, and it worked. With an uncertain future ahead, it didn't make too much sense to go shopping at Macy's or Saks 5th Avenue, but we did! How could one come to New York and not be tempted to do so? How can you not succumb to the temptation to take a stroll on 42nd Street or Broadway to see the craziness? We did it all!

I bought Bella everything I bought myself. I got myself a brown set of American Tourister suitcases and a blue one for Bella. We filled them up with Levis jeans, shirts, sweaters, and Bass penny loafers. On our way to Toronto we bought colognes at the duty-free shop, Channel No 5 for Bella and Channel Pour Homme for me. I adore French fragrances because they make one feel good, regardless of the circumstances.

When we arrived at Toronto Pearson airport, we went through Immigration and Customs with no difficulties. Once outside, my thrifty mind clicked to select a reasonably priced hotel for two to three days. I spotted an advertisement at the airport for The Cambridge Castle. It quoted a very reasonable rate and the façade really looked like a medieval castle.

The hotel ended up being a dilapidated dirty old rooming house, frequented by the homeless and one-night stands, of the cheapest class. Not willing to take defeat, I paid for the night and went up to the room. The room was lousy, with cheap furniture, yellowed sheets, cigarette burns on the night table, soiled washroom fixtures, and old plumbing. My pride was hurt for allowing such a stupid choice to take place after so much travel experience all over the world. Me, a sophisticated and intelligent world traveler!

Before unpacking, we called Bella's cousin Ana (then a medical doctor in Toronto) and told her where we were. She recognized the place as one of the scummiest places in the city. Right away she told us we had to get out before we caught a disease. She would come to move us into a decent hotel. Very soon we checked into the Yonge Street Holiday Inn. I joked about my 'foolproof' travel method, which was supposed to start with a one- to three-day stay in a four-star hotel, then locate the most commercial newspaper, browse the yellow pages, get familiar with the neighbourhood and subway lines, and quickly move to a reasonably priced clean apartment.

The next morning, after a good night's sleep, I located a realistically priced executive suite building. That very afternoon we moved to 77 Dundonald. The suite had a kitchenette and fridge, so after unpacking we ran to the nearest supermarket to buy a few groceries, including the Toronto Star, which I was told was the most commercial paper.

Anxious to start our life as a newly married couple again, I rented a typewriter and began sending my impressive resume everywhere.

Around ten that night Bella complained about a sharp pain below her stomach, towards the side and the back. At first I thought it was one of those things women do to attract attention and maybe the pain was not that bad. Within one hour she was overwhelmed by pain and couldn't hold her tears. Soon she lost control. I called Ana. She asked me a couple of questions and right away told me to take her to The Toronto Western Hospital, where she worked. She would be there in a half an hour. The diagnosis was a kidney stone. We had bought travel insurance this time, and fortunately the cost was covered. She stayed three days at the hospital.

There seems to be a reason for everything. While at the hospital, Bella met this lady who shared her hospital room. The lady learned we just arrived in Canada and I was looking for a job, asked for my resume, and gave it to her husband who was the handyman at an industrial laundry. He in turn gave it to his boss, who at the last minute called me for an interview.

I fell into a job as Industrial Engineer without even looking. The company assigned a lawyer to represent our case before Immigration Canada. He brought up the application we introduced back in Caracas and soon enough we were granted temporary residency, which included permission to work, social insurance, and health coverage. This older couple, our first friends in Canada, played an unexpected role. We didn't realize at the time how exceptional this whole resolution really was. Too easy! True, we were young and well qualified, but also lucky and privileged. Later on I found out most people waited for months and sometimes years to get that privilege.

As soon as I started my new job, we moved to a small flat near *Roncesvalles Street*. Our first landlord was a Polish-Canadian lady.

212

We rented one bedroom on the second floor and shared the washroom and kitchen with another tenant.

To accompany Bella while I was working I bought her Louie, a stuffed yellow and white version of Donald Duck's nephew, and a small battery radio in the shape of toy soldier. In a humble, quiet, simple, complete, and unbelievably happy way, we began our new life. Without a doubt, life rewards those who dare. Within two months Bella surprised me; she was expecting our first baby. I was going to be a father and took it as one of life's blessings.

As soon as regular money came in, we felt the small flat was outlived and moved to a redecorated suite: modernized, with pastel colors, and appointed with compact furniture. The owner divided the house into beautiful efficiency apartments, complete with newly carpeted floors, kitchenettes, new washroom fixtures, and a built-in vacuuming system.

Later, I even convinced one of the partners at my company to be the cosigner of a car loan. We bought a used maroon 1970 Mercury Cougar convertible, leather seats and all. Finally we were geared up, to which my boss one day commented, "You moved far in three months, but also managed to get into debt, be careful. If you default, I wring your neck!"

* * *

I was very ambitious then and kept looking for more options in the Careers section of the Toronto Star. I nailed an interview and within ten months found a higher paying job, as a management consultant. During the first three months, I completed a couple of projects in Toronto and then I was promoted to a six-month project at the comptroller's division of a major oil company in Edmonton, Alberta. The company gave me the choice of a biweekly trip to Toronto or a family move to Edmonton. We chose the latter and moved to a furnished apartment, paid for by the company, in Edmonton.

The company was headquartered in New Jersey and from there managed more than one hundred consultants, converting man-hours into tons of paper, which in turn got converted into tons of money. In the end, the systems were delivered with their correspondent instructions and free maintenance for life. Oil companies paid hundreds of thousands of dollars for this privilege. To make this process happen, I was paid a high salary and treated like a king.

Alfred was my supervisor, a white-haired, nail-biting, very nervous man from Las Vegas, which was odd to start with. He wore a dark blue pinstriped suit every day, the only one he had, but in an immaculately sharp fashion, complemented with spotless white shirts and conservative blue ties. I don't think he had a college degree but he handled the clients well, at least according to our project director, who also was aware of Alfred's awful treatment of the employees. But nobody is perfect and this characteristic was overlooked.

One day his wife told Bella he thought I was "very intelligent," which I interpreted as "being able to grasp his vague instructions." We had our quarrels. For instance, he was most annoyed by the cologne I wore and complained it made the clients uncomfortable. I ignored him, simply thinking he had no taste. Another day we receive an invitation from the head office to attend a meeting in Toronto. Alfred didn't go and didn't want me to go. I made reservations anyway, and in time he passed me the bill. Nevertheless, we managed to survive each other.

* * *

The coming of the baby was a phenomenal event that was shared step-by-step by Bella's family. When the baby's arrival was imminent, the general arranged a visit to Edmonton. Her family appeared at our door around the fourth week of June 1973. Somehow we managed, utilizing the spare room and the living room. While waiting for the baby, they enjoyed the city and the Klondike celebrations, an annual fair and exhibition themed around the gold rush days.

On the twenty-ninth day of June, one day short of Bella's birthday, the baby arrived. We named her "Carla" in my honour.

In a few weeks Carla turned into the most beautiful baby everyone had ever seen; so they told us repeatedly. Wherever we went, within seconds, scores of people gathered around her carriage to admire her and she rewarded them with her toothless angelic smile.

* * *

I continued to deal with Alfred the best I could, and he kept biting his nails, as we flew through tons of paper and numbers. The goal was to first determine and then increase the level of efficiency of 1,000 clerical jobs. The project finished on time, after which the company placed us in Edmonton's best hotel, in waiting for the next project. The next project took its time to arrive. So, to make our wait easier the company sent us on a paid vacation to Mexico! I was amazed how much attention we were getting. We chose Ensenada, a small resort in Baja California.

The three of us headed south, first on a large passenger plane to Los Angeles, then on a nice air-conditioned Pullman to the border, and lastly on a small, colourful little bus, bumping and rolling into Mexico. On the road to Ensenada, the driver began to sing Mexican folk songs and pass a bottle of Tequila for everyone to take a sip. One bottle and another followed. When we arrived at the hotel, one man had to be carried out head first, his feet dragging in the dust.

As soon as the concierge saw our baby, he informed us about the hotel babysitting service. The room was comfortable and the food interesting. That evening we had 'enchiladas Suizas,' which even Carla liked. We spent most of the days at the swimming pool but one day requested the babysitting service and went to a famous old 'cantina' people said was standing there since 1886. Certainly it looked old, but the rest was a matter of imagination.

The week went fast, so we decided to stay one more week at our additional cost. The package had a fixed return flight date, not reimbursable, but who cared! At the end, we rented a car and drove to Los Angeles to board a plane back to Toronto.

Once again, Bella and I were feeling high. I was young, well dressed, educated, supposedly smart, and well paid, with a lovely wife and baby. But once more, we managed to spoil it. As soon as we came back to Toronto we began to spend beyond our capacity. We rented a 2,500 square-foot bungalow and furnished it with everything imaginable. Our family was just us two adults and the baby. We didn't need any of that, but it felt good. This lifestyle drove us quickly into deep debt.

I continued to complete three more projects on behalf of the company, and the work was completed satisfactorily. But soon the excessive debt of our lavish lifestyle caught up and debtors began complaining to the office. In an attempt to solve the situation, we moved into a smaller apartment. But I had so much short-term debt that I couldn't keep up; one day the office called me up and handed me a pink slip and a cheque.

In desperation, we came up with the foolish idea to come back to Venezuela, after all we had done to re-establish. The Cougar went to the bank and the furniture to the dealer. Bella, Carla, and I spent the last night in a Holiday Inn waiting for the morning flight back to Venezuela. Once more, my life went in a circle, delivering me to the same place I started from. It was not the smartest decision I ever made.

* * *

I met Winston in Puerto Ordaz when he was in charge of the local Ministry of Mines Inspection Office and now he was the National Director of Mines in Caracas. Once in Venezuela he made it easier for us to start again. He fixed me up in an adjoining office to his, with direct communication to expedite matters. In return, I helped him resolve problems related to a zinc mining project that had been sitting in limbo for a long time. He allowed me to assemble a staff and gave me an additional incentive: "If the mine opens, you and your team will fill principal positions in the new company."

Located in a small town on the slopes of the Andes, the project gave me the satisfaction to go back to my roots, fresh air and the most beautiful surroundings.

The three of us, Bella, Carla, and I, started from scratch once more. I had a one-year contract and temporary peace of mind. Full of enthusiasm, I rolled up my sleeves and began to build our nest again: linens, kitchenware, a TV, and a small blue Hillman, all on credit. The pale blue car looked very much like the real us: informal, unpretentious and easygoing. Our baby Carla filled our present and future. At that time our life revolved around her. She was adorable.

For some time we concentrated on arranging a home, picking up pieces of furniture here and there. One of our first acquisitions was a loveseat sofa upholstered in ivory silk chiffon, around which everything else was planned. A long journey was ahead. From time to time we commissioned or found a chair, a rug, a table, a headboard. This would become one of the undertakings that kept our family together, collecting interesting pieces of furniture.

One time as part of the mining project, I had to fly to Vancouver to discuss the results of a pilot test performed by an expert. I flew from Caracas to New York, to Seattle, then to Vancouver. The short stay in Vancouver made me feel sentimental about the Canadian way of life. It took me back in time, wishing I never left. Time went fast, the project and my contract came to completion, but the mine never opened.

* * *

The next job I could come up with was in a courier company, similar to UPS but much smaller. I tried my best but the owner, a hard working Italian, didn't understand me. All he knew was to maintain a fleet of trucks and deliver packages.

Truly he was making enough money without me, not because he was terribly efficient, but only because of lack of competition. He kept me for seven months, mainly out of curiosity, and then let me go. At the time, Bella was expecting our second daughter, Bebé, and I asked the Italian to at least keep my health insurance active until the baby was born and he agreed. Thanks!

Bebé was born during a period of unemployment. I refer to her as the angel who came at the time of the 'skinny cows,' not enough food or milk on the table for her. Regardless, with part of the severance money, we bought her the best of baby furniture and stuffed animals. It was a matter of pride. But time erodes everything. Our resources dwindled to the point of lacking the essentials. Nobody seemed to notice except Bella's aunt, who made it a point to drop in every Saturday with a 'mercadito,' a food basket.

* * *

Six months of endless job searching went by, answering every newspaper ad that resembled the likeness of me without any luck. In certain countries a person with high qualifications was not allowed to do menial jobs, even if one's life depended on it, and also there was no such thing as unemployment insurance. One survived until the severance cheque ran out, then went to the pawnshops, then to the relatives, while one's morale rotted.

One morning the paper reported a plane crash on the way to Margarita Island, with no survivors. Among the deceased were a young couple and their infant daughter, supposedly on their way to a marvellous weekend. I was saddened because they reminded me of my own family and how the most perfect life can turn into nothing.

I had been having a hard time, unemployed for six months. There seemed to be no openings anywhere, at least none that would fit me, even without being choosey. A week after the reported accident that had impressed me so, an ad appeared in the newspaper soliciting a "Special Studies Analyst." The job description seemed to be copied out of my curriculum vitae. I answered. I had no particular high hopes anymore, but this job sounded right for me. To my surprise, they called me after two weeks for an interview and immediately offered me the job and a good salary. The job was mine.

The Conglomerate, turned out to be one of the oldest and most respected enterprises in Venezuela, founded in 1812 (the year of the country's independence). My job was to perform feasibility studies related to new capital investments. Mr. Victor, my new British boss, was an older trusted employee of the owner's family for many years and reported to the CEO. To my absolute astonishment, once in the position I learned that of all persons Doctor Gonzales, my dear mentor, was on the board of directors as their most relevant financial advisor. Sadly, I also learned that I was filling the position left by the husband and father of the young family who died in the Margarita airplane accident.

It is amazing how some things turn out as if they were arranged and, sadly, this time had everything to do with this incredible coincidence.

* * *

One day I woke up in the middle of the night with a sharp pain running from my back to the front of my lower stomach. I was sure I was having a heart attack. How does one choose between waking up the family and dying? Well, just at the point when I was sure I would die if I didn't, I woke up Bella and the girls and told them, in a frantic panic, to call for an ambulance.

At the clinic I was diagnosed with a stone in my right kidney, the same thing Bella had the day we arrived in Toronto in 1972. No wonder she was in so much pain that day! After a few days and a lot of peeing the stone came out.

The day I was discharged, the doctor came to my room and informed me that my x-rays also showed a tumour in my left kidney. I was devastated. Just when I thought everything was over, this unexpected menace had to come up! I asked a few more questions about the density and size of the tumour, but he had no answers. He referred me to a specialist who ordered a computerised tomography.

The results came back defining a 1.5-inch 'aqueous diverticulum' in my right kidney, congenital since birth. I was in trouble like never before! By the results of the scan, it could be a malignant tumour in my left kidney, discovered by pure chance. The recommendation of the doctor was to undergo a 'computerized guided puncture,' which meant inserting a needle into my kidney and draining the liquid out of the tumour. What could be the outcome? No one knew.

Bella and I decided to call Ana, Bella's cousin, who happened to be the chief nephrologist at the Toronto Western Hospital. She advised me not to do anything and to come to Toronto as soon as possible to explore a safer solution. Anybody would have gone immediately on sick leave, but not loyal me.

When my vacation came due, I arranged to go to Toronto and find out what the future held for me, or rather, for us. The news made me realize how it felt to be responsible for others, Bella and two baby girls, ages one and four. The feeling was bigger and weightier than I'd realized before.

* * *

The family set up temporary headquarters in a mid-sized hotel on Front Street in Toronto. Ana was as helpful as always and arranged an appointment with the surgeon. The routine scans were done and traditional surgery performed.

"Do I still have my kidney?" I asked when I woke up.

"Yes, you do," the nurse said.

I went into a deep sleep again.

Bella and the girls visited me every day, always bringing a large cup of freshly squeezed orange juice. They bought me an Italian ebony walking stick and a navy blue cashmere blazer. I guess as a manner of celebrating still having me alive. It took an extra week in the hospital and another at the hotel to get me in shape to travel. After one more week at home in Caracas I was then back to work. I could have become a victim of cancer but my guardian angels didn't allow that to happen.

Upon my arrival, I was promoted to manager for having contributed my share of studies, but once the major expansion was achieved I was discarded very much like a Christmas tree.

My stay in The Conglomerate lasted four years. Where did I go wrong? My conclusion was I talked too much and at the wrong time. People don't like that. Memorable meetings came to mind when

I embarrassed the CEO in front of a dozen people. I didn't have a clue about my position.

Chapter 15

After I was let go from The Conglomerate a new odyssey started. Until now, the longest I had been out of a job was six months. This time it took me one year to get another job. Everyone became 'skin slim thin.' Pounded with idleness and unable to buy the essentials, the passing of time became unbearable; it felt like an eternity. My severance pay lasted three months. Then I began to sell, borrow, and beg. I started to take long walks to distract myself from the painful wait and attempt to comprehend what was happening. Again and again, I sent my resume to every conceivable place. The only clear fact was that nothing was happening.

I played games to try to keep the family in relatively high spirits. Every time I came home, I would pretend I couldn't find Carla and would ask Bella, "Where is my girl? Has anybody seen my girl? Maybe someone has taken her away!"

Then Carla would hide behind the furniture and make squeaky noises, "Wee… wee…" so I could get closer and closer and finally startle her to death.

"Here she is!" I would jump at her, laughing.

To keep us going, I referred to anything we could not have, as: "The first thing to buy when I get my first pay cheque will be…" Soon there were too many 'first things.' I was sure bad times could not last forever, but they were taking long enough. Never before were we in such bad shape as we were this time!

To keep my sanity, I became philosophical. Which situation was worse: A poor family going hungry or a middleclass family going hungry? On the surface there was no difference, but looking closer one found that a middleclass family had additional psychological burdens to endure. In short, it was not logical that a highly trained engineer should be unemployed. Despite that philosophical shenanigan, I still did not cope well. Some days I felt I was losing the battle. I am still amazed how we hung on to each other at that time. I guess we were still young.

When one is young, one assumes there is a whole life ahead and bad winds feel temporary. No repercussions. The one consolation I had was that the girls were still babies and not able to judge me too harshly. At times, thinking they didn't deserve that hardship made me feel horrible. In the end I knew everything was up to me. I had plenty of time to think and made it a point to review every bit. In doing so, I recognized in myself a clear tendency to rebel, find targets, antagonize people and make enemies. I added "see a psychologist" to my list of "first things to do."

* * *

When I thought everything was lost and my morale could not stand it anymore, a phone call came one morning around 10:30. "May I speak to Mr. Márquez, please?"

"May I ask who is calling?" I asked.

"I am calling from Savoy. Mr. Cornelious would like you to come to his office next Tuesday at 9:00 am. His office is located in Edificio La Joya, 1ra transversal de la Urbina, Penthouse 'A.' Our phone number is (0212) 555-3557."

"Absolutely, I will be there!"

I made her repeat the name of the company and the address, which I recognised as the most important chocolate manufacturer in the country, but the address didn't sound right. As far as I knew, the company was located on a main street, nowhere near the address she gave me. I rushed and checked the newspaper clippings of the jobs to which I had responded, and the date was scribbled on the top. This one was mailed three months ago! I told Bella about the interview and dismissed it as another one of those odd jobs I was getting lately but still had to accept to survive.

* * *

I was sitting in Mr. Cornelious' waiting room, realizing it was, in fact, the private office of the President. It came about that he had two offices: one at the plant and another one in this location.

When I was in his presence, he appeared to be a very amiable gentleman. He was of Dutch descent, soft-spoken and right to the point. We hit it off right away, and he handed me a written job offer by the end of the interview. In short, not only did he save me from further suffering, he placed me in a very special position. My job was to process, in accordance with the guidelines of the parent company, the operating and capital investment budgets and follow up on all the new capital investment requisitions. The job was interesting and the pay was better; it was perfect to help us recover from the deprivations of the past year.

With the first paycheque, I treated the family to a steak dinner. In time, we moved to a new apartment, with swimming pool, tennis courts, and gym and filled one of the two parking spots with a white Fiat Manta, a nice-looking little car.

I tried to bring the family to the same level of comfort they enjoyed while I was working for The Conglomerate, but without making the same mistakes. In 1984, our life became, what in our view it was supposed to be. That Christmas I bought a piano for the girls to reward their endurance and patience during the hard times. I was good at my job but soon gave in to my old weaknesses. The General Manager was supposed to issue monthly operational and capital investment reports. He was always late, and I didn't take late for an answer, so I pulled his ears every time, backed by Mr. Cornelious. I was the power behind the power and I used it!

***

Three years passed. Mr. Cornelious called me to his office and asked me to sit down. I guess he wanted to make sure I didn't fall when hearing the news. His frameless glasses were foggy and he was perspiring heavily; his saggy face looked much older than the day before. On that blue Monday, as soon as I opened the door, I smelled the rotten odour of disaster.

"The company has been sold to a bunch of speculators. I have resigned and the central office will be closed in two weeks. This is the way they do things: buy a company, strip it to the bones, resell it, and make high profits. No consideration is given to the customers, the product, or the employees, just quick profit. I will make sure you get the highest severance pay possible. Get ready to vacate the office in two weeks and please do an inventory of the files, which should be handed to the General Manager. He is the Interim President of the company."

I knew right away I was doomed. But foremost, I felt sorry for him, because he was the gentlest boss I ever had. I admired and respected his style: human, direct, and still firm. I could tell he was disappointed by the decision and worried about the company's future.

He had spent 30 years of his life building this company and guiding it to the top. It was a miracle to find him and a real tragedy to lose him.

Then, I felt sorry for myself and angry at what was happening: sorry to visualize myself hanging from branch to branch again and angry to see a wonderful man like him bite the dust. My luck ran out again...

Beatrice, the mother company, was sold. Mr. Cornelious resigned and the central office was closed. I could have been spared, but the General Manager cut my head off without hesitation. Without knowing, because of the way I treated him I dug my own grave. I wonder if any animal builds his own trap and falls into it, time and time again. I don't think so; animals are not that stupid!

* * *

As soon as I opened the door, Bella perceived the calamity in my face. I have this way of showing the bad news before talking. I told Bella about how they sold the company, how I got laid off again and then I said, "We are going back to Canada! I don't want to be trapped unemployed for one more year, like when I was let go by The Conglomerate. I don't need to. We shall be better off over there. The girls will learn a new language, continue school, and live a normal life for a change!"

Bella looked at me wide-eyed but didn't oppose the idea. I think she understood that sometimes one has to recognize when one has been beaten. She also knew that when I made a decision, it was carried out, no matter what. Truly, I had no more will left. I told the news to the girls by the end of the week and found a mixture of surprise and curiosity. Was I behaving like Father, moving around every time a crisis came instead of finding a solution? Most probably, yes.

The truth is I was not able to relate to people. I could have kept any one of my previous jobs. 'This Márquez Thing' denied me the stability needed to live in peace, and it was not easy to tame, like my cowlick. At the end of the story, I wanted to adjust, but I couldn't.

I had never done anything without the family before, and this time I was not about to do it. Besides, my enthusiasm was contagious.

"Why did we leave Canada anyway? Let's go back!"

* * *

The Air Canada flight allowed each one of us one suitcase and one carry-on. My handbag was filled with books and credentials. As soon as we arrived at Toronto Pearson Airport, I took the family to a small motel, which right away Bella didn't like. I kept the room anyway hoping that she could ride it out. In my view considering the price, it was not too bad, but again it was only my view. That's when the problems started. Bella and the girls sat on their suitcases and didn't move, just looked around the room and at each other, with disgust.

I tried to explain that things would get better as soon as I was able to get a job and other reasons, to no avail. In the past, I had spoiled them too much, too long. Now, I was harvesting what I planted. In their view I was ruining their trip. There was not much desire to 'suffer together' and they had no idea that this one was a 'survival trip.' It was getting to be too much for me to climb a mountain with three girls in my small backpack. I didn't want to see them suffer, so we moved to the same hotel where we stayed during my kidney operation, in downtown Toronto (Front and Church), nicer but pricier. I knew I shouldn't spend, considering we just arrived and I had no job, but love and my desire to please was more powerful than reason.

We settled in and went for a reconnaissance walk to Eaton Centre, in an effort to make things a little more pleasant. On the way back I bought the Toronto Star and tried to locate a temporary furnished apartment. But the multiple dives taken from various heights had taken a toll on Bella. She was not the same daring girl I had married. She was now a frightened little girl, in spite of my efforts to boost her confidence.

As soon as we got back, Bella fell into a panic attack and began to sob and shake saying, "Please don't take me to any ugly place, please don't."

It hurt me so much to see her broken down, that out of the blue I changed our plans entirely. "Look love, if you don't like it here we go to Miami. After all, I don't care where I live, as long as there is a job and we are together. Miami is a beautiful place, and the girls could grow up there with opportunities as well. I could find a job there and the girls would continue their studies. The same plan we have here in Toronto, but in Miami. What is the big deal? Let's have dinner now and later we can talk about it, okay?"

Carla and Bebé got scared at first, but later were quite thrilled when they heard what I had to say about Miami. Once more, Bella had managed to change my plan in the middle of its execution, a decision based on emotions, but I was convinced I could pull it off. My three girls looked happy now and began to look at this great adventure with more excitement, and that was important to me. I didn't know it then, but I was delusional.

That evening I made reservations with the airline and the next day headed to Miami. Most people travel for pleasure or business. I traveled out of need, to save my life, either studying or working. In Miami I did not want to make the same mistake, going to a cheap motel and get the family frightened again. I went ahead and made a worse one, checked into the Dadeland Marriot Hotel. Time confirmed what follows to be the most foolish of all things I have done.

* * *

To give myself an edge in finding a job and to reinforce my application for a temporary work permit, I hired the services of a professional resume writer who added some whistles to mine. Of course he charged dearly. I began my campaign, reviewing the newspapers and mailing hundreds of resumes, without any luck.

We continued to look for a furnished apartment that we could afford, but found none to the liking of Bella and in the meantime spent a fortune at the hotel. Since time was running fast, in my desperation I retained an immigration lawyer to handle my case on a professional qualifications basis. Of course he also charged a small fortune.

By then, we were two months at the hotel and I could not yet find a job or a suitable apartment, but I was not about to give up. I never give up. Soon the money ran out, and I was forced to sell the jewels I had bought Bella in my days of glory. Later on, I had to, and was able to, convince the lawyer to give us a partial refund. Making use of the new money, I convinced Bella to move to an efficiency apartment, which she agreed only if it was the one she saw on Brickel Avenue, the expensive one.

We spent almost all the money on our first and last month's rent and the apartment was not even furnished. But I never give up. At that point, I gave instructions to sell the car we left back home for whatever they could get, hoping that before we consumed the car money I would be able to find a job. By then it was clear it would have been much easier if we'd stayed in Canada, but those thoughts were morale downers and I tried to avoid them.

We slept on the bare carpeted floor and had no television, until such time as I could resolve small problems, such as: legally getting a job and some money to buy furniture. To make things worse, an army of red ants invaded the apartment. They settled in the carpet and ate us alive at night. I reported the invasion to the management and they sent an exterminator to spray some chemical. I was forced to explain when they saw the bare apartment that we were waiting for our "new furniture."

Every day we bought groceries and the newspaper in a nearby supermarket and every day I went downtown to mail my resumes. Dinner was our time to recapitulate and give each other hope for the following day.

After a while, I made a contact in a men's store, and the manager was brave enough to give me a written job offer as a salesman. I found out later the job was not sufficient for the purpose of immigration. I had to find 'a proper job,' one that made use of my professional qualifications. What a silly thing! How was I supposed to do that, just arriving? If I could find a job that made use of my professional qualifications, I wouldn't have to leave home!

Anyway, I continued to look and send resumes. To keep the family active and the morale as high as possible, we took walks along Brickel Avenue and spent some time in the swimming pool pretending to be on vacation. Many people settle in the United States illegally, but I wanted to do it right.

Just when the money was about to run out again, I received a call for an interview from a company that performed maintenance for small aircraft. The position was Logistics Supervisor. The General Manager was very impressed with my credentials and very sympathetic, because I reminded him of the efforts his parents had to make arriving from Ireland. My second interview was with the Maintenance Manager who was from El Salvador, which I interpreted as an advantage because I thought he could understand my position. Far from true, it was a total disaster! It became clear that he considered me a threat. He did everything possible to discourage the General Manager from giving me the job. My appeals did no good at all, and my last chance disappeared. Jealousy can take many shapes.

We were one month in the apartment and two months in the United States. By that time the money ran out completely. Our chances of continuing became zero and it was obvious we had to come back home. I had a meeting with the property manager and pleaded for the return of the unused part of the rent, to allow us to buy the return tickets. She refused. Stranded, sometimes one is forced to fight for life. This was one of those times. I went back to the immigration lawyer, who as a favour intervened and got us the unused money back.

* * *

We were now on our way back to Venezuela, strapped to collapsible seats on both sides of the front part of an Air Force 'Hercules.' Bella's brother-in-law, a captain in the Venezuelan Air Force, helped us get four cheap tickets, allowing us to cut loose from our ordeal, return home to rest, and find another way to continue.

Before we left the U.S.A, I did manage to buy each one of us a little something to take back as a consolation prize!

After eight hours of punishing, thunderous roaring from the Hercules' powerful engines, strapped at right angles into back-breaking cushion-less seats, with cold sandwiches and coffee for lunch, the Hercules arrived at Maracay Air Force Base.

We were all in high spirits when we met Carolina, Bella's sister, who was waiting to welcome us home again. The most eloquent thing to do was keep silent. But girls cannot keep silent. Carla and Bebé chattered about how they would tell the story to their friends. They agreed not to 'tell it all' and manufactured a version like "a three-month vacation trip to Miami," where they soaked in the golden sun, visited the 'in' places, and shopped for the 'latest,' their father for vintage watches and their mother for jogging gear.

Of course the story would include that the family was to stay in their grandma's luxury apartment until a suitable luxury condo could be located, so their Father could resume his business as usual. The girls had the ability to accommodate accounts, within the framework of possibility, therefore not classified technically as a lie but a very feasible plan!

In the meantime Grandma had moved to another apartment, not far from the one we stayed in before leaving for Toronto and Miami.

* * *

"We shall be there in a little while," I said.

"Hum. Hum," Bella said.

I knew what was in her mind: How to account for and justify our failure and how to ask grandma again to relinquish the comfort of her room? We'd developed a method to sleep on a standard size bed.

This would be the second time the four of us had to share one room and sleep on the same bed, using common sense, very much like sardines in a can. I would lie on the outside with my head at the bottom of the bed, then Bella with her head at my feet, Bebé's head at Bella's feet, and lastly Carla's head at Bebé's feet. Since we kept neat (always took a shower before bed) there was no offense to have each other's feet near our faces. Nevertheless, we turned our heads in the opposite direction. We always kissed each other good night before retiring to our dreams and hoping for a better day.

The arrangement was made successfully. Immediately I started looking for my next job. The first thing I did was to get a copy of El Universal, Caracas' commercial paper, and browse through the job openings section, which had been the key to my solution many times before.

The thought of Father's land returned, and this time it occurred to me to place a classified economy ad in the Land for Sale section of El Universal and try once more. I did that as a ritual every time I lost a job, and sometimes during the interval of getting fed up and getting fired. This time the ad was more brief and simple than the ones before: "Se venden 7,500 hectáreas en Distrito Guanarito, Estado, Portuguesa. Bolívares 150.00 por hectárea."

The set price was about 10% of the market value. Within three days, I received a phone call from a lady who introduced herself as Professor of Agriculture at the University of Milan. She was calling from Italy to inquire about the land and confirm the price. She asked three times as a sign of disbelief. She gave me her phone number and the phone number of her lawyer in Caracas, who would make arrangements to have someone see the land and follow her instructions.

Also in disbelief, I told Bella about this and, most of all, the fact that the inquiry was from as far away as Italy. That night I could not sleep. I had a premonition. Within two days, I was requested to deliver the lawyer a copy of the title to the land, which I did, making emphasis that the documents established a legal tradition of 150 years.

That same week, the lawyer arranged for an acquaintance of the professor to inspect the land, and I spent two days showing the men the forest, savannahs, and boundaries. As far as I could tell, he was satisfied, and the one thing left was the approval of the Italian professor, which I got next day with detailed instructions about signing the transferral and receiving the certified check.

I could not believe what was happening, but it was happening! 28 years had gone by since I took charge of selling Father's land. I had gone through countless similar motions before, without success. This time it seemed to be working. The signing of the transfer was scheduled for the following Monday, and the time was set for ten o'clock.

The four of us, Bella, Carla, Bebé and I, had a light breakfast that day and headed for the lawyer's office to sign the documents and receive the certified cheque. When I was signing the papers my hand was trembling and I hardly could contain my tears. When I received my copy of the document and the cheque, I couldn't breathe. I had never received an amount that large as one lump sum in my whole life.

We went to the bank, deposited the cheque in my account, which by that time was thinner than the x-rays of a skinny lamb. I promised the girls and Bella to take them to the best steakhouse in town, as soon as the bank cleared the cheque. It was the least I could do.

* * *

We were sitting at the steakhouse. The white tablecloth looked crisp and the serviettes were folded in a fancy way, like swans. The maître d' recommended sangria and the best Punta de Trasero (a traditional Venezuelan way of serving steak) for two. He told me in confidence that if we ordered for four we could not possibly eat it, because it would be too much. So we added avocado salad, Hallaquitas (similar to tamales) and Nata de leche (cream) to go with it. We had one of the most enjoyable meals of our lives.

Like Father said, "Someday you will remember me for this." I did!

I realized then: the only thing we have is our life, and what we should do is live it.

What does that mean?

Whatever you wish it to be.

If your idea of living is to have a 9-to-5 job for 30 years and raise a family, so be it. If, on the other hand, your ideal is adventure, pursue it. I have done both and never regretted them. One thing, though: success will happen and regret never hurts, if we do what we love. I have been very lucky to live my life that way, far from perfect, but following my call and not afraid to live. I am in love with my life and what came out of it. My life has been full of life.

* * *

I felt so good that I began to do stupid things again. Since we sold our car, because of my stubbornness to stay in Miami looking for a job that never came, I had to buy another one. But it so happened that now I had the money to buy it with cash.

I rushed to get something exotic and didn't consider any other factor. I located this new, imported, sharp, black-on-black, two-door Renault. One small detail was the car was located in San Cristobal, some 750 kilometres away. But I never gave up. I went there and stayed in one of Bella's brother's house, a brother who still lived there. Everything went 'smoothly,' like when one is about to make a major mistake.

When I came back, the whole family was delighted with the new car. Another 'small matter' was the car had a stick shift, and Bella didn't drive a manual transmission. I figured she could, but oops! She didn't, so we lived with it for a while.

The storm had passed, and now we were blessed with quiet times, on our way to stability again, but not quite. Bella went for her medical check-up, and the doctor found nodules around her thyroid gland, which had to be removed. Poor Bella, another operation! She had to stay three days in the hospital. Fortunately the nodules were benign, and she was only ordered to take antibiotics and rest for three weeks.

Once over this hurdle, I looked for more creative ways to spend Father's land money. Because I have a craving for status and was already in possession of a spanking new black Renault, I focused on another of my lifelong dreams: a gold Rolex. You may think it is silly, because it is, but to me it was important enough to have consumed many hours of my life wishing. You see, I was convinced a man who owned a gold Rolex had conquered success like the Time magazine ad said. I believed, by wearing one, I could sell my intellect at a higher price. Pitifully, I was confusing the symbols of success with success itself.

Let me explain. If you buy your gold Rolex with the money earned doing your trade, it is okay. If you buy your gold Rolex with your Father's land money, it is not okay. There were priorities, such as buying a house for the family.

I met this jeweller who showed me what was supposed to be his father's 'mint condition' watch that he never wore anymore because it was too heavy for his frail body. I paid half-price for it and must admit felt terrific when wearing it. Eager to share such a feeling, I also bought one for Bella.

Looking back, I think it was my way of 'getting even' with the catastrophic failure of our trip to Miami. Equipped with a new car and a gold watch, life looked brighter. But was it really?

Ready to move to a new place worthy of 'rich' us, we found a four-bedroom apartment, decorated in good taste by the landlord, who happened to be an architect. We still had our furniture, and after Bella and I were done with it, the apartment looked like a million dollars. And the girls, now fourteen and eleven, were able to go back to their dear Colegio Teresiano.

* * *

Before finding a decent job again I was forced to work very bizarre ones.

The sign read: Grupo Pontefino, the name of a well-known family. During the interview Mr. Pontefino and I agreed the job was perfect for me. I got the job. The company was as desperate as I was! Next day, I took charge of an office and a plant with three employees and a truck. The product was very innovative: one-layer micro-coating exterior sealant, which made unnecessary the usual two layers of stucco and paint finish. First, I managed to free the company from the clutches of one exclusive contractor, built a chain of new distributors, and initiated an aggressive marketing campaign. I did everything as if I owned the company, and the business thrived. It took me eight months to get the company into a growth cycle. But my luck hadn't changed yet. As soon as the Pontefino family learned how to run the business, they began to give me a rough time. I was fed up anyway with their 'small family' approach and moved on.

This time I was able to transition into my next job quickly. The next company was not 'crazy.' On the contrary, it was well respected in the field of electrical engineering design. I was chosen as a 'perfect fit' to be the General Manager and appointed by the senior partner, who trusted me completely, to the extreme of setting up the company's bank account with my signature only. Soon I found out the partners could not get along. The junior partner became incredibly jealous of me and waited for my first mistake, which didn't take long. One Friday, my secretary brought a total of 25 cheques for my signature and I signed them all. On Monday the bank called to notify us that our cheques had bounced as N.S.F. What happened?

Well, when my secretary retrieved my personal and the company's chequebooks, the bank had switched them, and a total of US $50,000 had been issued on my personal account, which of course did not have that amount. I notified the partners, who sent an auditor to assess the mix-up. This was enough for the jealous partner to make his case and justify my dismissal. I lasted five months.

* * *

My next chance came in the form of a financial consultancy firm. The owner of the consulting firm had valuable business connections that came attached to his well-known family name and translated into juicy service contracts. One of them had to do with Toyota buying the largest GM distributor in Venezuela. The price was agreed in advance as the result of our valuation. That, I must say, took a lot of courage from both parties. My team completed the job on time and the transaction was a success. Unfortunately, good things didn't last. From the beginning, I had a frisky relationship with the owner, who thought of me as 'unsociable.'

His son who was the vice-president, and the one who hired me, got along with me fine, but not the father, who actually owned the company. One day I told his son, "I could not work, not even for one day, directly with your dad. He is neurotic." I didn't know it, but I had just written my death sentence. The son was so loyal to his father that three days later I was asked to resign.

I ended up, as usual, sending resumes everywhere, literally everywhere. Eventually I was asked to interview for a company (a paper mill and printing operation owned by an Italian), coincidentally located around the corner from where we lived. Again, it looked like one of those catastrophic jobs I had been getting lately, but I was a man without a choice. I took it. He endowed me with the title of Vice-President of Operations, based more on my credentials than my responsibilities, because this owner controlled everything himself. My job became more of a concept. He saw the company as his kingdom and on my first day told me, "I want to make you a prince."

On a certain weekend, Mr. Sunday invited my family and me for brunch at his house. We rang the front door bell that morning and his wife received us with a loud, "Come in!" Bella and the girls were warned ahead of time.

The ritual began with a showing of the house, and by the time we went through the last corridor I was exhausted, like I finished the entire tour of the Louvre. At that point, we were ready for a Tuscan dinner and Chianti. Instead, Mr. Sunday invited us for a tour of the gardens of the mansion! He led his way pointing to the fountains, rose bushes, and the granite lions standing guard along the way. The visit, at this point, was unbearable.

We were about to faint when his wife appeared and announced that dinner was ready. That part made up for the previous ordeal; no one can go wrong with Italian fare and wine.

It took six months for Mr. Sunday to realize that his kingdom didn't need a prince and I was unemployed again.

* * *

Our set-up was expensive to maintain, and it only took us three months to go through my savings. I sent resumes right and left again, but the country shrank through my years of job hunting. At this point, I didn't mind and pawned our two gold Rolexes to import a ladies fashion collection and start a home business. We went to Miami and purchased a complete collection of ladies fashion samples.

Not having learned a lesson, we stayed at the same Dadeland Marriot of my disastrous job-hunting trip. Now that I think of it, this one was an comparable 'madness' with another theme.

Back home again, I transformed the study room into a store. Bella was against advertising in the newspaper, afraid we would attract crooks, so we limited our marketing strategy to family and friends. But you cannot maintain a business only with family and friends. The cost was high and we weren't selling as many dresses as we needed to make the trip worthwhile. To recuperate the investment, I had to mark up the merchandise too high. Of course it didn't work. About five dresses sold, out of an inventory of one hundred!

But I never give up, so I went out on the street and set up shop out of the trunk of our car, in front of a delicatessen. I was never ashamed to do whatever it took.

Thereafter, discounting the merchandise and dealing subtly with my lady customers, I managed to sell most of the dresses. We were able to survive a couple of more months that way, but we can't deny the business venture was a disaster.

In search of my next opportunity, I stumbled onto an ad in the *Universal*: Operations Manager - minimum five years experience. I had 25!

The company logo was a bright red sun bursting with iridescent spokes all around. It looked like a sign of good luck to me, so I mailed my resume. My qualifications were, as usual, beyond what they required, but I had no choice. I was once again in desperate need of a job, one to keep me away from tragedy. A week later I got a call requesting my presence for an interview. I was puzzled because the address they gave was in a residential subdivision.

I arrived at the designated house and recognised it, another large mansion that had called my attention many times before, because, among other things, a British cab was always parked in one of the driveways beside a burgundy Cadillac and a black Mercedes; and I had seen a heavyset man drive it from time to time. I rang the side entrance bell and a man who looked like a gardener answered, took me to the through-walkway, and asked me to sit on a bench near the end.

A few minutes later, a large and very amiable man appeared with a welcoming attitude. "And how is Mr. Márquez today?" he asked, leading me to an enormous meeting room. He was the same heavyset man I had seen driving the British cab before. He sat at the end of the table, pointed to a chair beside him and browsed through my resume, underlining that he also lived in England while attending university. I took it as a good sign.

He finished my interview and agreed to get in touch with me within a week. The sparkling sun did its trick. I was hired and excited, because I needed the job desperately and my heavyset new boss seemed to be amiable and polite.

The company's headquarters were in Puerto La Cruz, just across the channel from Margarita Island. In a way, unintentionally, I was killing two birds at a time: living and working in an international tourist resort. Puerto La Cruz itself was a world-class marina that attracted sailors from all over. The company lodged us in the best hotel, all-inclusive. I confess, it felt like an expensive vacation, and why not? We deserved it!

I tried to enrol the girls in the local Teresiano, but the nuns got too fussy about accepting them in mid-term. I ended up enrolling them in the local high school.

We took a small efficiency apartment in El Morro (a luxurious part of the international resort) that had its own marina and multimillion-dollar yachts tied to the moors for us to watch. The apartment was similar to the one we leased on Brickel Avenue; but this one, thank goodness, was furnished, and I had a job to pay the rent. Our weekends were spent floating on the clear blue waters of the swimming pool and barbecuing steaks, the ideal work-and-play combination. It was too perfect to be real, and soon I learned about a state of affairs that threatened our pleasant arrangement.

My boss' father (the senior shareholder) was on a medical leave in the U.S.A. In reality, he was taking time out from a tug-of-war between his partner and him for control of the company. He left his son (my boss) in charge, with instructions to annihilate the other partner, but soon the father disagreed with the way his son was managing the affair, including the hiring of an operations manager: me.

Trying my best to overcome the rift, I formulated a new operating plan, which apparently they liked very much, but inexplicably, as soon as the father arrived, he fired his son and me. When I confronted him, I tried to explain that I was only following orders from my superior, his son. To which he replied: "You should have known better."

* * *

Once again, we returned to Bella mother's house for shelter. Five months went by before I was offered another job. The Conglomerate family crossed my path once more. The 'apoderado' (agent or representative), called me for an interview in response to my resume. I discovered later that he hired me hoping to gain information about how the main office operated. He knew I worked directly for his boss before. This circumstance made me valuable to him for a while and entitled me to two titles: General Manager of the holding company, and Vice-President of Strategic Planning of the cement company in Valencia, all of which actually meant juggling massive numbers. This was the way I ended up again in the same group that sacked me a few years back.

The irony of it all was that, at a lower level, I had more status. "It is better to be the head of a mouse, than the tail of a lion," Father used to say.

My new boss, the 'Apoderado,' assigned me an office with a private in-suite washroom, a secretary, an assistant, and a new company car! In the beginning he was delighted that I made him look good in front of the board of directors every time they met.

We moved to Valencia and enrolled the girls in the local La Salle school, following the family tradition. Again, I was being as creative and resourceful as my genius allowed, but as conflictive as the situation required. Back in my perennial 'beginning,' both as exciting as spring and as frustrating as winter, it was a high price to pay for the sake of change: stagnation.

One day the CEO of The Conglomerate invited the 'Apoderado,' Robusto, and me to a meeting at Salomon Brothers, Wall Street, New York, about a development loan for the cement plant The Conglomerate owned. In the meeting, the due diligence lawyer, the bank representative and we were present. The CEO of The Conglomerate proposed hiring a new due diligence lawyer, who had been his college roommate, and when my turn to speak came up, I asked, "Wouldn't this delay the project?

Everyone looked at me in amazement. The present due diligence lawyer and the bank officials agreed. I had just achieved division of the meeting into two groups, placing me in the middle. The small detail was that my boss' boss, who owned The Conglomerate, and to whom I was due the utmost loyalty and respect, proposed the new lawyer. How dare I be so out of touch with reality!

The CEO of The Conglomerate complained to me later. I informed him I already apologised to the incumbent and promised to keep my mouth shut in the future. Actions like that came often from my most inner chambers, to devastate my stability and dig my own grave again.

Is there an animal that builds a trap for itself? No, there is not. It takes a human to do that. After three years of relative stability, I was fired again!

Chapter 16

One day having dinner at Bella's cousin's, "So, where are you working now, Luis Carlos?" Ramon asked.

"CANTV."

"Oh! The National Telephone Company! But how did you find this job? How did you?"

"Well, I sent a resume to a newspaper address, had two interviews, and they offered me the job."

"What position?" Ramon asked.

"Manager of Quality Control," I said.

"But that is a 7.2-billion dollar project!" Ramon said,

"Yes, it is a large project," I replied.

"But how did you?" Ramon asked again.

What Ramon wanted to know, was how I pulled it off, because I was 54 years old, with too many jobs in my resume, which gave away my instability, in a country where a man at 45 was finished.

Since Ramon knew I was not in the habit of sweet-talking anyone, he still could not understand how I managed to pull it off. He had been trying to do the same thing for some years without success. I continued to play dumb and repeated, "Yes, I just sent the resume."

I could see Ramon turning green with envy. At this point, he could not stand it anymore and changed the subject. "Do you want another drink?"

"Yes, thank you."

I was having a bit of good luck in 1995, and the family was happy to see me work again, especially in a position consistent with my experience. I was even assigned a company car again! The family remained in Valencia, for the time being, to avoid upsetting the girls' school year. My poor girls had more than their share of changes.

* * *

One Friday evening, to save some money while visiting the family, I decided to take the public bus to Valencia instead of the executive bus service. The trade-off was that I had to go to the public depot. Walking beside me, there was a tallish man in his mid-twenties, chanting a tune, which sounded like a coded message to somebody. "He is walking towards the passenger bus, the passenger bus, the passenger bus…"

I became suspicious, but nevertheless thought I could handle the situation, and continued to cross the parking lot, while the man kept following me, chanting his tune. Then, I cut between two buses to reach the sidewalk faster. When I was between the two buses, somebody grabbed me from behind in a headlock, choked me, and reached for my wallet, while another one, pulled on my briefcase and overnight bag. I lost consciousness. When I regained it and tried to talk, I couldn't; only a scratchy sound came out of my throat.

Later in Parque Sol (the family crash pad where I was temporarily staying), I called Bella and told her about my incredible incident. Before long, the phone rang and a detective from the police department told me they had found my wallet and briefcase, and I was welcome to pick them up. I went right away. Everything of value had disappeared, and it wasn't clear who had taken it.

When I was about to leave the station, a policeman approached me and said, "It's not safe to walk around this late at night. I advise you to take a taxi. If you want I could take you and will not charge you more than they do."

I realized I was being coerced and decided to take his offer. When we arrived at Parque Sol, I paid the policeman for the service, and thought to myself, "I wish I lived in a country where people didn't rob wallets and policeman didn't have to do taxi service to survive." I couldn't go home that weekend. The following Monday I was at my desk, wishing the week would go faster to get to see my family. I was bitter for a while and added the event to my long list of grievances, temporarily put away.

* * *

My new boss at the Telephone Company was a mild-mannered Italian-American who understood me very well. One bad day the area of Logistics was redefined, my American boss was sent home, and I ended up with a little man from the Spanish partners as boss. At first he was very appreciative of my work and even told me he would promote me to Director before his retirement. As time went on, I found how deceptive this little man was. He was anti-American and anybody appointed by them was considered his enemy.

First, he took away my company car, knowing very well I would rebel, then appointed as Director an ex-student of mine, knowing I would be humiliated. Then, when I issued a written complaint, he accused me of insubordination.

"Luis Carlos, I advise you to sign this letter of resignation, because if you don't, I will have to deliver this other one, stating that you used company proprietary information for your own private consultancy practice. I don't have to tell you what that means."

I signed.

There I was at 55, being blackmailed by a little Spanish man. I signed the resignation, unhooked my credentials from the wall, and went home. The job lasted three years. I didn't realize at the time how grave the situation would turn out to be, but at first I was relieved.

Back at the house, I said to Bella, "They tried to extort and destroy me, but they won't. We have enough to last a couple of months until I find another job." That night we had a good dinner, watched TV, and took it for granted that everything would be alright.

It didn't happen. After two miserable years out of work, we began to sell anything of value: my car, then our second car, the Cartier watches I bought for our anniversary, the television sets, books, old records, my life... Everything was sold except Bella's furniture and art that was considered sacred, because household items for most housewives are an extension of the heart. Red blood flows through those objects. If disposed of, it is the end.

* * *

By then Sis was a very successful lawyer, politician, and Vice-President of the Industrial Bank. One day, I could not take it anymore and asked her for a helping hand. She had done it before. I explained and Sis understood: I had to come back to Canada to save myself and what was left of my family. I was in desperate need of psychological and financial support. I had to get away from everything and had to use every bit of help I could.

Also, I still had one living son and decided to find out what that meant. I did not know his whereabouts, so I looked up his mother's name in the phonebook and called. As soon as she answered the phone I recognised her voice.

"I am looking for Ike. I would like to speak to him if I may," I said.

"Who is calling?" she asked.

"Luis Carlos Márquez, his father."

"Ike doesn't live here anymore, but if you wish I can give you his telephone number. I am the maid here."

I knew Chica was lying. She couldn't be straight. It was her way of feeling safe. I decided to play her game. "Yes, if you please," I said.

"This is his phone number. You may call him now, and he should be home."

"Thank you very much. You have been very kind."

I called Ike and arranged to see him that afternoon around five. We met at Centro Plaza Café, beside the escalators, at 5:00pm that day.

Five years before, we tried to integrate Ike into our family, but we found different blood ran through his veins, different values. There was no connection. Bella, the girls, and I tried, but it was hopeless. Sis always thought I placed too many conditions on him and didn't give him a chance. Maybe she was right; maybe I was predisposed.

This time, being for a specific purpose, I thought maybe we could concur. When I arrived, he was already sitting at a table, waiting for the man who, when Ike was eight years old, was his father. Now I was 57 and he was 32, a lawyer, married, and didn't act or look as if he was raised by me. His pants were too baggy, his hair too short, and he looked and acted like an old man. We did have something in common: he was insecure.

Standing up, "Hola," he said.

I embraced him and asked, "Cómo estás?"

We sat down and he ordered two beers. While the waiter brought the drinks, I started the conversation by saying, "I did not know what else to do. I am in terrible need. I can't stand it any longer. I have been out of work for two years, and this time can't find a solution. Nobody wants me anymore. The responsibilities are crushing me. If I don't go away fast I don't know what may happen. It's too bad I have to meet you in this way, but that's how it is. I need a little money to complete the trip. I must go back to Canada while I still have a chance."

After two beers and a couple of remembrances, we agreed to meet the next day at his office to see how he could help me. We embraced again and parted. I also visited the CEO of The Conglomerate (my old millionaire boss), about my intention to return to Canada. He gave me the air ticket to Toronto. In the end, I collected $3,800 from Sis and Ike, and the airline ticket from my CEO.

* * *

But how do you change your life? Do you change your attitude towards life? Do you change your activity in life? Do you change the place where you live? This time, I could not afford to make mistakes. I was 57 and forced into a new life. It broke my heart to leave my family behind on that September day of 1997.

When I was stepping out of the door, Bella cried, "Go ahead! Leave us and never come back!"

Bebé was sad, too sad to say anything. She always went mute when she was sad. She lost her companion. I was her companion. Carla eventually forgave me but at the time felt abandoned. Somehow, I could sense that things would never be the same again. All the same, I had to leave. I had no choice, but no one understood what I was doing or why I was doing it. No one understood how devastating it was to the spirit and self-esteem to have my career cut off at 57 and be out of work for two years, watching the anguish in my family. Reality had changed. I had to save my life and invent new dreams.

"Run soldier! You know very well at the end you will die regardless, and part from the war of wars: life! Run so you can live a little longer!"

* * *

"Taxi to the airport!" the driver shouted through the intercom.

I wanted to answer, "There is nobody home," and pretend this was not happening, that it was all a bad dream. But I had to answer, because it was happening. "Yes I will be down in a minute."

I was afraid my heart was going to stop. Everybody was in shock now. I kissed my two daughters goodbye and said to my Bella, "No matter what happens, I want you to know that I love you very much." Yes, I said those words. They came from the depth of my heart.

She wept.

"I will call you when I get to Toronto," I said and left with watery eyes and a lump in my throat. It was very clear to me, in spite of the pain we were all suffering, that I was doing the right thing for the best of the family.

I was silent on the way to the airport. My whole life passed through my mind, like I once read happens to people before they die, nature's way of giving us a last chance to rethink how things could have been, even though we cannot change anything, only understand better.

"Nice day," the driver said, trying to make conversation.

"Yes," I nodded, thinking to myself, *Can you not see that I am reviewing my life?*

Of course he didn't. No one can read someone else's mind, and if it were possible, it would not make the same sense anyway.

The trees along the side of the road as we passed looked like a watercolour painting, an indiscernible smudge of greens and browns, a semblance of my life. I wanted to freeze the motion to capture a glimpse of my land, my beloved country of the very dear South, my beautiful 'Little Venice.' Tears ran down my cheeks. For a moment I wished they were razors and would slice my throat, but nature does not cooperate without a reason. Instead, I shifted my thoughts to emptiness and kept looking out, all the way to the airport, not thinking.

* * *

"Good morning. This is your captain, John Gilligan, speaking. Welcome to Intercontinental flight 201 to New York City. We will be flying at an altitude of 12,000 feet, at a speed of 440 kilometres per hour. We should be arriving at La Guardia International Airport in four hours and fifteen minutes. The temperature in New York today is 32 degrees Celsius, with clear skies. Enjoy your flight."

There I was sitting in seat 22C, by the window, as I always preferred, but this time going to my destination with the most uncertain purpose. The coastline became smaller and smaller, until it disappeared when the plane turned into the deep blue waters of the Caribbean, heading north to New York and then to Toronto.

Going away always gives me mixed feelings: nostalgia for what is left behind and the joy of excitement, freedom, and expectation for things coming ahead. How would everything turn out this time? Would I be able to make it? Would it be for good? And in the back of my mind, *Will I ever come back?*

I picked out one of the magazines from the front compartment, a ritual I had performed many times before, every time I flew. I unfolded the small little table, placed the magazine on top, and browsed the flight boutique section, which I always thought was fantastic because of the innovative products pictured there: all kinds of bags, jewellery boxes, folding bikes, watches showing world times, and so many other wonderful things.

* * *

It was the fall of 1997. I was arriving at Toronto Pearson Airport on the Air Canada flight from Caracas. It was the third time I came to Canada. This time I intended to stay. The sign 'Immigration,' pointed the way to a few stairs and then a long passage that directed travelers to a gigantic lobby with many stalls.

I held my briefcase with my left hand. It was very heavy, because it contained all my credentials and my engineering manuals, which I took everywhere when looking for work. I held my passport in my right hand. I didn't have a powerful passport, only a modest South American one, but I had other attributes to serve me well. I learned when a was a Boy Scout in school how to do things either with my left or right hand, just in case. The queue advanced, and my turn came up.

"What brings you to Toronto, Sir?" the officer asked.

"Returning resident," I answered.

The immigration officer, after studying my file on his computer, concluded that I was still a Permanent Resident, subject to an inquiry to reinstate my Landed Immigrant status. Later, I was summoned and reinstated.

My first move was to secure a place to live. Once more, I followed my world-class method. But this time it was to be a cheap hostel, and then, as soon as possible, an inexpensive room. A wall poster at the airport advertised a $28-per night accommodation. Just what I needed!

"Is this the Marycielo hostel?"

"Yes. May I help you? I am the night clerk."

"Yes. I am calling about a room."

"Okay. These are shared rooms, with bathroom and kitchen facilities, at $28.00 plus tax a night."

"I'd like to reserve one bed for tonight. My name is Luis Carlos."

"Sure, Luis Carlos, as long as you occupy it before 10:00pm."

The man gave me directions and I hurried to get there before 10:00pm as he requested. I took the airport bus to Yorkdale subway station, then the University subway going south to King Street, and finally the streetcar along King Street West, right to the front door of the 'Marycielo.'

"My name is Luis Carlos."

'Hi, Luis Carlos. Come in. Please sign the registry, and I will show you to your room."

The hostel was an old Victorian guesthouse, similar in a way to the Spanish colonial ones I lived in when I was a kid. The difference was I didn't share my room with eight people before (except Riverside, where I knew my roommates)! At the hostel I didn't, and couldn't, figure out how to keep my luggage safe. For the time being, I placed my suitcase beside the night clerk's desk and asked him to watch it while I made a phone call. I only took my briefcase with me and went to the corner booth to make the phone call I promised Bella.

It was mid-September and the temperature was below the seasonal norm. A rainy breeze was blowing on my way to the red booth with folding doors. I was amazed the phone actually worked and I could use the coins I'd saved for the call. At home the receiver would have been missing and the coin slot jammed!

"Hello," Bella answered.

"I arrived a while ago and will spend two or three days at a hostel I found. Kiss the girls for me. I will call you again next week when I have more time and news."

On the way back to the hostel, I picked up a ham and cheese sandwich and a half pint of chocolate milk at the corner 7-Eleven store. That was dinner that night. Exhausted, I brushed my teeth and climbed up onto my bunk bed. Not knowing what else to do, I kept my clothes on, clutched the briefcase with my arms held tightly to my chest and my bag between my legs. I couldn't sleep for a while, trying to figure out how in the world I got to be where I was.

The next day another gentleman was at the desk. He presented himself as Kristian, the owner of the hostel. During our conversation, I let him know that I was looking for a permanent place, perhaps a room in a private house. As it was meant to be, he had a vacant room at his family home and I was more than welcome to have it. I asked how much the rent was and he said, "$280 a month." He was surprised I decided to take the room without even seeing it. He was not aware that anything was better than staying at his Marycielo. Neither of us wasted time. We went to his house, where I paid first and last months' rent, and he gave me the key that secured a roof over my head for at least two months.

Kristian's home was a sad grey stone house. I could tell there was no love there. Later, Kristian explained that he and his wife didn't live a common life. When I met her I understood why. She was a miserable-tempered, controlling woman. He told me he had thoughts about divorcing her but didn't want to lose the house, the Marycielo, or the children, so he was hanging onto a divided life. When I saw the way they lived, I had no doubts he could be better off without her, no matter what. But I had issues of my own to take care.

My room was not bright either. I had only an old bed, side table, reclining chair, a chest of drawers, and one dim yellow light bulb hanging in the middle of the room to keep me company. It reminded me of when Father sent me away to the La Salle monastery, so I had to make up for it with a little bit of my good humor. That night, lying flat on my bed while staring at the ceiling, I felt I had made a colossal mistake from which I would never recover. Loneliness does that to you. The window of the house next door was my only view and was always closed. I kept hoping one day it would open and somebody say, "Good morning!" It never happened.

The very next day I started job hunting, trying to replicate what I had done 25 years earlier. I bought *The Toronto Star* and went to the nearest office of Human Resources Canada. Many executive jobs advertised in the Careers section on Tuesdays, Thursdays, and Saturdays, and they all seemed feasible, considering the wealth of experience I had under my belt. But whoever was making the decisions did not agree with me. I was 57 years old and had no recent Canadian experience. *Sorry!*

Many years after, when already retired and having done all sorts of jobs, I found out I had spelled "résumé" wrong by not placing the accents. I thought, in English, one didn't have to place accents, but I was wrong for many years. This tribal detail cost me more opportunities than I care to admit.

* * *

Another curious situation happened the day I had an interview with the senior vice-president of an important consultancy firm. I was wearing progressive lenses that turn dark on sunny days. I entered the 31st floor, 100% glass-walled office, which that day was as brilliant as a supernova, and of course my glasses turned dark. When asked why I wore dark glasses, I answered, "They are not dark!"

Of course, I did not get the job.

* * *

During the following week of gorgeous bright days, I wore my red sweater every day to remind me that being alive and in pursuit of a dream was a blessing. I believe every man should own a bright red sweater to maintain a happy note, especially during the Christmas Season. I tried to keep a positive mood and promised myself that nights were to sleep, no matter how difficult the situation was and to avoid negative thoughts. This helped a lot.

Each day after a frugal breakfast I would go to the corner store, buy the paper, cross the street to the park, sit on a bench in peace, and select the jobs for which I would apply. Later on, I would make photocopies of my résumé, filling in the company's information by hand, and mail it. I thought this was as good as any other way, because I was being practical. What a stupid thing to do! How naive! Three weeks passed and still not even one call for an interview came. I was worried sick by this, because the money I had left the family would not cover the following month's expenses.

At that point, fed up with the waiting game, I put on a suit, grabbed a few copies of my résumé and went out to try my luck on the streets, to get a job, any job. I took the King streetcar going east, got off at Yonge, and walked north, looking at the shop windows for a "Help wanted" sign. No sign appeared.

When I hit the corner of Yonge and Bloor, I looked up at the building on the southwest corner: Number 1 Bloor Street West. The sign of the store 'England's' appeared, as I have seen it many times before, but this time a brilliant idea came to me. I paused to build enough courage and rehearsed a few words before going in.

When I entered, a tall, older, Irish gentleman, standing by the entrance, greeted me.

"How can I help you?" he asked.

"I am looking for a job. I have a copy of my résumé," I said.

"You may give it to me if you wish," he said.

I gave him a copy and he asked me to wait. When he came back, he told me Mr. Edward, the owner, wanted to speak with me. He directed me upstairs to the second floor, delivered me into a large meeting room, and placed me on the next-to-the-corner chair of an enormous meeting table.

As soon as I sat down, Mr. Edward, a late-sixties, well dressed gentleman, sporting a fine British worsted wool suit, came in and said in a very amiable way, "So, you are an engineer."

"Yes, Sir. I just arrived from Venezuela and I am in urgent need of a job. I happen to be, if I may say so, a very good salesman, and very fond of fashion too, and also I am willing to learn. I have lived in Canada before, in 1972, and just came back."

"When can you start?"

"Immediately," I said.

"Come tomorrow at ten," he said.

I was so happy! I thanked him several times, as I left the room. On my way out, I also thanked the tall, Irish gentleman standing at the door several times. He just smiled.

Unbelievable, I thought, that with all the specialized training and 30 years of experience, nobody was interested in me as an engineer. Even more startling, that without any experience in the field and only based on my personality and the way I looked, somebody was willing to give me this job. So I became a salesman, a fashion salesman. A very good men's fashion salesman!

I was so powerfully driven by need, that I broke all the sales records on the ground floor where they first deployed me. Mr. Edward had no choice than to upgrade me to the second floor, were the more expensive items were located.

Since I handled most of life's activities as a game anyway, I made believe selling suits was no different and after a while managed

254

to play it well. In the beginning, I was under the impression that I knew a lot about men's fashion. Soon I discovered the difference between an 'aficionado' and a 'professional making a living.' I had to learn how to fit shirts, suits, and shoes. My sales supervisor taught me the basics and I took off from there.

In the meantime, my three girls were going through tough times back home. Eventually, they were evicted from the apartment, because I was not sending enough money to survive and pay the rent. Some friends of Bella, who were very wealthy, came to the rescue and lent her a vacant apartment from their real estate portfolio.

We mended our souls, talked about what to do next, and agreed the best thing was for them to come to Canada with me. The problem was money. I was not being employed as an executive anymore and the job at England's was on commission. Even with my high performance, there was a ceiling as to what I could make, which barely cleared the poverty line. As soon as the family agreed to come, I started to look for a higher paying job within the same field, because no matter how hard I tried, no one wanted me as an engineer anymore.

Very much the same way I did with England's, one afternoon I walked west a little further on Bloor Street, and came to a much bigger luxury men's furnishings store: Jerry's. I walked into the store and asked for the manager. Soon this elegant, tanned Italian took my résumé and told me, "I see what I can do." A few days later, Gina from Jerry's called me for an interview with her and another guy named Rafael.

It ended up I got hired. Gina was to be my new manager and I had to start all over again on the ground floor, where everyone started. Rafael, who turned out to be the assistant manager, was assigned as my mentor. It was July 1998 and I was already 57. I could not believe, that after two graduate degrees and 30 years of technical experience, this was the best job I could get, but it was true. For a while I was assigned to the shirt department, reporting to Gina herself, a woman who knew how to give orders but did not know how to sell. The shirts were stacked by style from left to right and by size from top to bottom, starting with the smallest, size 14 ½, and ending with the biggest, 18, just like books on a shelf. The spare ones were kept in large drawers below the shelves, arranged by style and size from left to right, like office files.

Shirts sold very well, because it was a 'business executive' store and shirts were a relatively inexpensive way to enhance any suit, but we also made smaller pay cheques compared to other departments. Part of the day was spent tidying up the shirts and stacking up the new inventory, using innovated displays here and there, to make the merchandise more appealing. All and all, it was an ideal job for me, because I made believe I was playing 'store keeper,' like when I was a kid selling magazines out of the window in Father's office at the Sugar Cane Association. That way the days went by easier and masked my disappointment about not being able to get a proper engineering job. Greeting and engaging customers with a smile and a very welcoming "Hello," and, "How may I help you?" and, "How can I make you happy today?" became very personal greetings that customers found original and liked very much.

* * *

Eventually I was promoted to mezzanine, released from Gina's clutches, and turned over to Gus, a black guy who was even pickier because he was on his way up 'to be somebody.' But at least I had access to pricier items. His main activity was to congratulate me every time I made a good sale, "Nice sale, Luis Carlos!" and give me a 'sermon' behind the shoe shop every time another salesman complained about me grabbing customers they thought were theirs. In a nutshell, if I made more sales I was good, but if a jealous salesman complained I was not.

Every day was the same at Jerry's, like a play: exciting for the audience, but very boring after a while for the actors. Though, dressing well and showing off was fun. Every day we had a meeting in the morning, highlighting the achievements and mistakes of the previous day with a tour and presentation of the new arrivals. The doors opened for business at 9:00am sharp, and then we proceeded to check alterations, deliver ready garments, and begin selling to customers.

During the day, an army of managers scrutinized every movement. The salesmen were extremely zealous of their territory, like animals. Anybody trying 'too hard' was ostracized. I was earning a little more and eventually I was able to arrange for the family to join me, to try to build a new life like millions of others here in Canada.

To pay for the air tickets we sold the rest of the furniture--the Louis XV chair, the Persian rug, the Boole, the mahogany side table with the lion paws, never minding the loss, because we hoped it would be recuperated in no time. Anticipation was at its peak. Finally the Air Canada flight delivered my three girls at 10:00pm that night in 1998, after one year of separation.

They appeared at the gate at the same time, too much for me to bear. As if planned in a previous life, we all ran towards each other, clutched each other's arms around our shoulders and embraced in a circle like an ancient ritual, a circle of love. We have never been away from each other for so long, because even during the toughest times we stocked together. This time, I had to cross the valley first and tested the wolves before they could follow. Not like the time in Miami, when the wolves had a field day with us.

I would do anything to keep the family together. I had rented a small bachelor apartment in High Park, tiny but well decorated. In the end, the atmosphere was very much like a comfortable hotel suit. The girls enrolled in the ESL English course at Christie's and took a part-time position as 'merchandisers' at Jerry's. As it turned out, the set-up for a family starting fresh was not bad. Bella took care of the house and met us at closing time every Friday, to do some window-shopping and maybe eat out. I continued to look for the so-called executive job that never came. Life went on, and on, and on… At the end of two years the girls' English was fluent and they even had some savings.

But of course, life is not perfect, and my three girls found an excuse to leave in 1999. If you look closely, you can always find an excuse to justify a change in life. I have done it several times. In this case, the modest life I was giving them was not enough, not even similar to the life I had given them before. I went over and over my inability to find a better job and concluded it was because I was older.

I also found that life has hidden reasons for granting, or not, our wishes. Unavoidably, nature will lead us where we belong.

Anyway, they were not happy with the life I provided, which they considered 'mediocre,' and found a reason to change. When presented in this simple way, it was understandable. These are the 'twisters,' reasons life provides so people can find the courage to make decisions. My family watched me run from job to job, from town to town, from country to country, trying to mend my latest failure, for so many years. They got tired of it and this time ran back home. My three girls left me without much warning. Like my Grandma María and her seven children left Grandpa Juan in 1935, sadly, but nevertheless understood.

A taxi came to take them to the airport. The girls climbed in first, and then Bella. Before she closed the door I asked, "I guess this is what you wanted, no?" Then, silence, the most eloquent of words, followed. I guess, once in a while, one finds out what one wants out of life, and one must choose. They chose.

I stayed one additional month in the apartment, but every little detail reminded me of them, so I moved back to the rooming house in Isabella. My old room on the second floor was taken, so I ended up on the third floor, miles away from everything. The room itself was not bad; it even had a window that allowed me a nice view and a partial peek at the CN tower. But the rest of the floor I did not like at all. It was depressing. I felt like a tiny mouse trapped in a maze. Funny how my life had turned out to be. I traveled so many places and did so many things but ended up back where I started: nowhere. But isn't that what pigeons do? I tried to make some sense of all that but couldn't.

* * *

To amuse myself and save my soul from collapsing, I took temporary refuge in a woman. Calling it a 'casual encounter,' a trendy way of getting laid and justifying it's alright. I knew sex would not make it better, but at least it made me feel alive.

This woman had two sides: a sweet girl who needed attention and a chronic liar. So, I found myself on a merry-go-round of sweetness and bitter lies. We would prepare weekend dinners, crowned with red wine and love. She would send me flowers and, from time to time, leave sweet messages on my answering machine. On my birthday I walked into a room full of balloons. Many other little details made me expect too much from her.

One day, I found out everything about her was a lie. She was not who she said she was, and she was not where she claimed to be. Little by little, all her stories crumbled and proved to be false. This was devastating for someone with the kind of open wounds I had. I confronted her. I shouldn't have, because it destroyed our relationship, but I did. In reality I was reacting to my past. I couldn't accept a lie. Acceptance is a way to forgive, and at that point I still couldn't forgive.

Chapter 17

"I am Doctor Shapiro. Please have a seat. Doctor Kowalski, your family doctor, tells me you are not feeling well. What seems to be the matter?"

"I have been waiting for so many years for someone to ask me that question and be willing to listen. I have so much, so much to tell," I said.

* * *

The office was well appointed: a mahogany desk, two black leather chairs across from it, a black leather couch to the left on which a well-worn portfolio was resting. What called my attention the most was the way the accessories were placed. Every item was selected for a specific purpose, and placed correctly. Everything was useful: an appointment book, penholder, business cards, a magnifying glass, and a neat black leather pad. On the "L" of the desk there were: a telephone, a reading lamp, some framed family pictures, and a filling cabinet. A magnificent burgundy Persian rug partially covered the brown hardwood floor. I immediately began to love every detail.

If what you say has value, the way you say it makes it priceless. This man knew how to say it.

On the wall facing me were two framed photographs: one of a seven- or eight-year-old boy, dressed in an awesome, two-piece, white, silk lace suit and wearing a hat adorned with a fabulous white feather. The boy in the picture had expressive black eyes and a soft gentle smile. Under his image the word 'Austerlitz' stood out, and below it was a short legend I could not make out from where I was sitting. The framed picture was the centerpiece.

On the same wall, were a title, to the left, and a framed computer hard drive showing its naked inner workings, which I interpreted as a metaphor about the human brain. Still a little to the left, was a painting of a foggy temple, which I interpreted as the mysteries of the human soul. I have done that before, arranged objects in a way that I knew conveyed a message, and this is what I thought he was doing. I found some resemblance between the wall and my state of mind.

* * *

The doctor's voice brought me back from my imaginary trip, which I am sure only lasted two seconds. Oh, the wonderful wonders of the mind!

"Yes, I am not feeling well. In fact, I am feeling very bad. I have no desire to live. Never felt like this before. I mean I've not been able to sleep or eat for days now. I have lost twenty pounds. I do not understand it, but my life is crumbling, piece by piece. I am not able to control myself. I feel sad; everything hurts me. I attract miserable thoughts and purposely select those that make me suffer the most. I go over the same situations, over and over, back and forth, dwelling on the most unpleasant ones, again and again. I cannot stand it anymore. I feel like I am near the end."

"How long has this situation been going on?" the doctor asked.

"About six or seven months now, since the departure of my family. My wife and two daughters returned to Venezuela where we come from. I tried for two years to convince them to stay, but I failed."

"I wouldn't say you failed. People have choices and they just make them," Dr. Shapiro explained.

"I wish I could live in peace, but there are too many issues going on. My head feels like a tornado."

"You are right; there are too many things going on. The brain functions very much like a funnel. Let's say you pour liquid into the wider end. If you pour too much or too fast, the liquid will simply overflow. This is what is happening and what we must do is control the overflow. By draining a little at a time we will make that funnel work again. In the meantime you have to rest. You are not in a capacity to solve any problems now. I am going to prescribe some medication, which will help you block those recurrent thoughts, sleep better, and allow you to gain strength for the work ahead. This is my direct line, in case you need it. I shall see you in two weeks. Will 3:30 on Wednesday be okay?"

"Wednesday will be okay," I said.

"I will see you then and remember to call me if you need me. Bye."

Nothing had really changed, but as soon as I went out of the doctor's office I felt a little relieved, because I'd found someone to share what was happening to me. On the way home I picked up the prescription and felt lucky after all.

* * *

I continued to see Doctor Shapiro and, in time, he slowly confronted me with the fact that 'This Márquez Thing,' running in my family for generations was something called hypomania. The dilemma was unlocked, and the symptoms became as obvious as markings on a zebra and the catastrophic results as logical as ashes to fire. Sadly, they also explained what happened to Father and Grandpa. I never interpreted these symptoms this way before, which was a huge oversight on my part, considering how curious they were. On the one hand, they showed up as the abilities associated with high performance, creativity, and entrepreneurship. On the other hand, the results were dreadful and as dramatic as the sight of a shipwreck at the bottom of the sea.

The list of people who had fallen into the trap of hypomania was impressive. It almost made me want to belong! All *could* be well, except that our personality carries a high risk of depression in the midst of failure, loss, or anything blocking us from moving at our frantic pace. When this happens, we may feel something is not right. If depression doesn't stop us, we change direction and continue our quest, feeling invincible. Anything other than perfection is not acceptable, which is a tall order for fragile minds like ours.

Sometimes the consequences are disastrous. We may look back and find that our life has passed us by and we have ended up where we started, or we may find ourselves in front of a blind alley and decide to stop it right then and there.

Hypomania makes one undertake more tasks than one is able to mentally and physically achieve, constantly wooing the specter of depression in its various forms: psychological, spiritual, moral, intellectual, and physical.

* * *

Two gruelling years had passed, which I was able to survive only to keep the family afloat back home and help Bebé continue law school. But 30 years of struggling to build a family cannot be given up that easily. I arrived at the conclusion that Bella and my two girls were my life. Mother was old and Sis and Ike were done with me for the time being. I had been forced to choose family twice before when I had to move back to Venezuela in 1974 and 1986. Should I do it again? This time must be for good, I thought.

In April 2000, Bebé advised me to send my résumé to the University of Carabobo where she was attending law school. I did, and the president promised me a part-time teaching job on my arrival. This time, at 60, I figured there was nothing degrading about accepting less of everything. After all, people do it all the time. That's what people do in the later years of their life. As usual, I tried to idealize the situation and justify the circumstances, even imagining I could ride a bicycle to class, do exercise on campus, and keep a healthy salad diet for lunch.

In the interim, I moved to a pay-by-the-week suite to prepare for my departure and left my computer, TV, and bike in the care of a Toronto friend. When the time came, a few days past September 11, I took my flight back to Venezuela.

* * *

My three girls had been staying for about two years with Bella's mom and her sister in Valencia. During that length of time, we talked frequently on the phone and I was well aware of the limited conditions in which they were living. I arrived without pomp. The building was old, very much as I imagined it: surrounded by an improvised parking lot and a wrought iron fence. A red tile path crossed from a small gate to the five-step stairway leading to the front entrance. One master key opened all the entrance doors.

The room they occupied was almost filled to capacity by a double bed. Their suitcases consumed the rest of the space and left no room to move around. To shower and change clothes was a complicated task. It required opening the suitcases, selecting what to wear, and using the only available bathroom to wash and change. Four of us shared one double bed as we had done before in our moments of chaos, arranging ourselves across the width from left to right, alternating feet and heads like sardines in a can.

Bella was so ashamed of our situation that she insisted on keeping the door closed at all times, not allowing any fresh air inside, and shooting the temperature as high as 45 degrees C. Her mother and sister knew how crowded we were, but still she didn't want them to see it. We regarded the arrangement as temporary, and that's why we were able to stand it.

For a little while each of us continued to do what we were supposed to do. Carla worked as a marketing assistant at a mall, Bebé went to law school, Bella tended to our improvised house, and I looked for my next job. Three months went by and the university president didn't keep his promise. Just when I was about to give up, Bella's brother-in-law procured me a job through his political connections.

That is how I became 'Assistant to the President' of the National Hydroelectric Company, whatever that meant. In my new position I was assigned a company car, began to draw a half decent salary, and commuted daily from Valencia to Maracay, where the head office was. For a while things looked promising. It was only a matter of time until we could move to a place of our own and begin to live a normal life again, so I thought.

Soon my new boss, the president, a retired navy captain, was replaced. Another navy captain came. Immediately he began to look for excuses to replace everyone and bring his own team. It didn't take him long to arrive at my position. His first move was to take my company car away as a 'cost reduction,' knowing full well I couldn't possibly commute from Valencia without the car. I rebelled, well aware of the consequences. Of course I was fired, very much the same way it happened at the telephone company and very much for the same reasons.

* * *

When I arrived home that day, not knowing what else to do, I sat on the edge of the bed feeling sorry for myself and began to polish my shoes. With each stroke of the brush, a sad tear trickled down. I felt sorry for the way things turned out and frustrated for not having any solution. Soon I gave up, lay on the mattress, and sobbed my heart out.

Each soul has a breaking point. I'd reached mine. That moment became a turning point, the end of the road. The rails disappeared just short of a cliff, and I stopped the engine. Otherwise I could have gone over the edge like Grandpa and Father. I needed help and I wasn't getting it. I saw the end of my life approaching and turned around fast, because this was not a place where I could live.

I saw myself becoming less and less. I was dying before my very eyes, despite that I shouldn't allow history to repeat itself. At the time I thought I acted on free will, but I didn't. You see, most of our decisions in life are taken after seasoned reasoning and, even so, we are never sure if they were justified or even necessary. But a few times in life, this being one of those, we are placed in extreme, desperate situations when the subconscious takes over and reasoning is replaced by instinct. One just reacts to nature, relinquishing control to the great forces. Not to allow it would be more catastrophic.

The days before I left turned out to be the worst of my life. On the day I confirmed my departure, Carla burst into tears, saying, "Alright! Go ahead and leave us. We don't need you!" She and I knew that was far from true, but it was her way of expressing her pain. Bella hurt and her way through the pain was with resentment: "The thing I regret most is that you are the father of my children. I want you to go now!"

"But I have no place to go," I said.

"I don't care!" she responded.

Truthfully, she didn't care anymore. We had gone beyond each other's limits. We had tried too long and too hard to make our lives liveable, but it didn't work anymore. We just wanted different things out of life. The only sentiment we had left in common was that we both wanted a 'family,' but we didn't know how. Relentlessly, we pulled in opposite directions, without compromise or harmony.

Bebé kept silent, as always, and in an outburst of tenderness I said to her, "You are the pupils of my eyes; without you I cannot see." At the time, she and I knew it was true. She intervened and I was allowed to remain.

I had no clue how I was going to be able to get back, because my return ticket was expired and I had no money. I only knew I had to do it. For a week we went hungry, eating just a bun and a piece of cheese each day, because my severance pay was purposely held back.

At the end of that week I went to Maracay with Bebé to collect my severance cheque. We spent all day accomplishing that one task. Out of the total amount, I kept the minimum for my return and left the rest for my three girls to buy some furniture and move to a new apartment in Valencia. The following days were spent looking for the apartment and negotiating with the airline to accept my return ticket.

* * *

I didn't burn my last bridge, and as it developed I was technically able to return to Canada. This time I knew it was for good. I'd given the family everything I had, a final trial.

The day of my departure I was sad, but some things we must do no matter what. I discovered that 'never' and 'always' never happen. Bella would never know how sad I have always been to be forced to leave her. Every time I think about it this little song comes to my mind:

Patico, patico color de café

Porque estás tan triste quisiera saber

Tu pata yo vi muy lejos de aquí

Con otro patico color de café….

The problem about moving forward is that if you find a little happiness along the way, you feel guilty. Especially if the people you left behind didn't have similar luck. That is the price we pay for having a little good fortune. Some call it 'survivor's guilt' and it has no cure.

* * *

My taxi to the airport came, and I realized that during the past 30 years I ran away four times: in 1972, 1985, 1997, and now in 2001. What was I running from?

I'd circled this part of my life doing pigeon loops trying to return to Canada over and over. I could not think of anything I'd tried that hard. So clear was my destiny here that coming back became natural, despite the hardships I had to go through to get here.

This time arriving at the airport was easier, in spite of my chronic apprehension of airport authorities. The official who stamped my passport even said, "Welcome home."

I called Jazz, a young Indian friend I'd made in the pay-by-the-week rooming house where I was last housed, and asked him if I could stay at his place for two or three days until I could find my own place. He invited me to come over. That night we exchanged stories.

He told me about his decision to marry the girl his family chose back in India, instead of the one he met here in Canada, reasoning that "tradition" wins over "love" in his world. Within three days I moved to a small, furnished room on Metland Street, near

Kensington Market. On the go, I collected my computer, TV, and bike, the only possessions I had left.

My next move was to find a job, any job. I had to make some income quick, to send back home and continue to help Bebé with law school. For a while I felt guilty to look forward to a new life. But what is one to do? One cannot make the sadness of the world disappear by adding more sadness. In the end, I didn't expect anyone to understand. I went back to Dr. Shapiro and we established that I had as much right to live in peace and strive for happiness as anyone else. Truly everyone has the right and duty to live in peace.

* * *

It turned out to be a nice day and I went for a bike ride in Kensington Market. I stopped to have a Jamaican patty and coffee, sat on a small bench at the storefront, and soon a girl sat next to me to have one too.

"Nice patty," I said.

"Very much," she answered with her mouth half full, like we do when conversation comes unexpectedly. We struck up a conversation and, after clearing up the matters of accents and backgrounds, I made the comment that I was looking for a job, preferably within fashion retail, which was what I did last.

She pointed to a store across the street that belonged to a man she knew and for whom she worked part-time during his annual sale. Ron was his name. She would allow me to use her name, Alexandra, as a reference. I thanked her for her kindness and parted.

Sure enough, the next day I dressed like a salesman and went to deliver my résumé to Ron. He was delighted with my background. His colourful personality and the unconventional setting of the store also charmed me. Supposedly, it was a high-end merchandise store, within a fish-chicken-fruit market! He offered me 16 dollars an hour and no commissions. I took it.

Ron ran his store out of three adjoining Victorian houses. The gossip was that his father, a Polish immigrant, started some 50 years before selling used garments out of a modest little hole and putting in 16-hour work days, seven days a week, and he made it good.

Designer suits sold like pancakes at half price. Only the very snobbish didn't come to Ron's and continued to shop at Jerry's. During my time there, my body was at work, but my mind wandered back and forth to my past. Missing my three girls and faking my smiles to my customers became a habit. I felt sad knowing that for my sanity I could not join my family ever again. During those days, the only breath of fresh air became my visits to Doctor Shapiro. From him I got the guidance and support to carry on.

Ron had a peculiar way of showing his insecurities, terrorising us. To show he was the boss, at the opening hour he would stand by the entrance to make sure everyone had to pass by him and show up for work on time, and he made us feel miserable if we weren't. Often I was late and would whisk by him saying in a whisper, "Good morning," and avoiding any direct eye contact, but still he managed to make me feel guilty.

His back office was a cluttered mess and computer monitors gave him access to every corner of the store. This alone was enough to keep everyone doing all kinds of "tidying up" jobs to make him feel he was getting his money's worth. It was not uncommon for him to show up in the middle of a sale 'to help' and almost kill it. The merchandise was already priced but he insisted on bargaining with the customers like in a Turkish bazaar.

My life at that time was not happy, because I could not find the professional job I was trained to do. Nonetheless, I was grateful to have a job. I sold suits for three years and made enough to cover my expenses and put Bebé through law school.

* * *

One day, I felt abandoned, and in a stroke of genius raised my voice to the higher powers and sent out this message: *I am looking for a woman over thirty, with a soul as clear as spring water, to be each other's guardian angel. If you like the way I sound, please reply to box 2481.*

And I was heard.

The next day I had a message and I replied. I liked her voice. It was very sweet and sounded honest and sincere. Not for us to understand, things happen for a reason. When the time is right, if we think and do the right thing and have a lot of luck, things do happen in a magnificent way.

* * *

September 2009. I was riding the westbound train in Toronto on a beautiful cool day, looking out the window, enjoying the stunning autumn view, the red brick Victorian houses, the still-green lawns and the red maple leaves. I made this ride many times before. This time, I was thinking how good my life was. How lucky I was to be here and still have someone to love!

45 minutes passed and the train arrived at High Park. I took the escalator up and walked east on Bloor Street. A pleasant cool breeze blew west, I zipped up my jacket and stepped up my pace and decide to go for a stroll in the park. After all, it was an exquisite autumn day. I wandered down the main path, and sat on a green bench near the pond. The trees were swaying in harmony, giving the pleasant welcome one expects from nature. A few geese were gliding, and two beautiful swans followed each other, carving a rippled "V" on the blue water.

I heard that swans choose partners for life. I admired them for this unconditional commitment to each other. Likewise, I wanted to migrate north and spend the rest of my life here with the same woman. I tried hard, but didn't quite make it.

Now I was sitting on the very same bench where I was 38 years before. Life has this way of going round and around in circles, taking us to the same place we started. I wondered if there was any significance to that.

As I sat, I thought how fascinating the human mind is. How it can take us back to any time or place. What a marvellous freedom, that we are able to recreate moments whenever we want! I felt very sad about those who lose their mind. Losing one's mind must be the most terrible tragedy, aside from death itself. I was terrified to think I could lose mine someday.

Since I was an old man now, and I didn't have to make things happen anymore, one of my greatest pleasures was to relax and 'roll back' time. Sometimes, I found myself laughing, but often tears ran down my cheeks. It was like living again, again, and again…

I had seen my hands change through time, first small and chubby, then larger and lean, eventually slender and wrinkled, and now I saw bony tendons and veins. I had aged. I touched and felt them often, amazed how my hands served me so well for so many years. No wonder people say, "Your future is in your hands!"

The tranquility of this autumn day made me think about how I got to be here. If anybody told me I would be living in Toronto at the age of 68, I wouldn't have believed them. If I'd known about the perils I had to go through just to get here, I would have been terrified. On this day, it all seemed logical. I had been blessed to overcome most of the obstacles. Many, by the way, I created myself. It took enormous doses of poor judgement, impulsiveness and risk, but also confidence and vision; the same traits that drove me into trouble helped me get out of it!

I missed my father so very much, for so many years. He had touched every instant of my life, even if he was not present. I considered myself an extension of him and my life a continuation of his. My insecurities and weaknesses came from him. My bright moments and ascensions also came from him. His departure was early and senseless and marked my life forever. It hurt. I reviewed his absence over and over again numerous times, and it still made no sense. Sometimes I thought I made mistakes so as not to have a complete chance at happiness, because I felt guilty when I realized Father never did.

My story began long before I was born, with Mother and Father in the Andes Mountains. Often I envisioned them, when they were young and full of energy. This gave me the strength to go on. Everyone has an inner resource. They were mine. They reaffirmed my past, enlightened my present, and guided my future. Their memory gave me a sense of belonging and a deeper and more meaningful connection to life.

* * *

I walked to the edge of the pond, looked down, saw the reflection in the mirror of clear water, and realized I was now in the last stretch of my life. Again, I felt a great urge to review how it all happened, which I had done one hundred times before.

Many people I cared for disappeared from my life, or altogether, while I still remained here. Now I sat more often, walked less, and did not speak much. Everything had been said and forgiven. I preferred to think and write more, which was my way of getting even with the past.

I went to High Park in summer and some coffee shops in winter, where I sat, thought, and wrote. I wrote about things I didn't understand too well; but again, who understands anything too well? These silent moments of contemplation were probably the most important, because then is when the ideas that change us, and humanity, begin.

* * *

Dark, menacing rain clouds were casting from the West. I glanced at the pond and my two beautiful swans were not there anymore. I figured they already started their long trip south and wondered if they still flew together and if they still loved each other and if I would see them again... and if I would still be here in Spring.

Now I followed this ancestral caravan called Life in search of peace and understanding. Everything happened for a reason and life must continue, regardless. My super guardian angels continuously protected me, because I survived time and time again what others have not. I liked to think there was a reason and a purpose for me to still be here, even though I made bigger mistakes than most.

My childhood was the source of everything. It shaped what I'd done, where I'd been and who I'd become. It established the bipolar bearings through which I gravitated, back and forth, from my simple beginning, to my more or less complicated destiny.

On the way, I discovered that all I ever wanted was a country and a family. Was that asking too much? I managed to lose them both several times. Perseverance saved me, and of course I found them again in the most unlikely way. But the real key to survival was finding someone to love; this happened when least expected.

~

The only valid alternative in life is the pursuit of happiness.

~

ACKNOWLEDGMENTS

My friend and confidant Jacqueline gave me unconditional support. My two daughters Carla and Beatriz nourished my soul with much needed love. The Writer's Digest greatly facilitated my instruction process, which never ends. John Miller and The Toronto Writers Cooperative gifted me with invaluable critique. Dr. Serge Shapiro (may he rest in peace) took care of my psychological wounds for so many years. My editor Julie Saeger Nierenberg contributed precious advice.

Thanks! Without you all, this book never would have been written or published.

The author in 2008

Luis Carlos Márquez lives in Toronto, and is presently working on the Spanish version of this book.

www.ingramcontent.com/pod-product-compliance
Lightning Source LLC
Chambersburg PA
CBHW060239290526
45789CB00001B/108